LONDON RECORD SOCIETY
PUBLICATIONS

VOLUME L

A FREE-SPIRITED WOMAN

THE LONDON DIARIES OF GLADYS LANGFORD, 1936–1940

EDITED BY

PATRICIA and ROBERT MALCOLMSON

LONDON RECORD SOCIETY
THE BOYDELL PRESS
2014

First published 2014

A London Record Society publication
Published by The Boydell Press
an imprint of Boydell & Brewer Ltd
PO Box 9, Woodbridge, Suffolk IP12 3DF, UK
and of Boydell & Brewer Inc.
668 Mt Hope Avenue, Rochester, NY 14620–2731, USA
website: www.boydellandbrewer.com

ISBN 978–0–900952–55–5

A CIP catalogue record for this book is available
from the British Library

The publisher has no responsibility for the continued existence or
accuracy of URLs for external or third-party internet websites referred to
in this book, and does not guarantee that any content
on such websites is, or will remain, accurate or appropriate

This publication is printed on acid-free paper

'I've been re-reading my autobiographical novel and finding it good in parts though uneven in quality …
What joy it would be to get a book accepted.'

'I don't believe I disguise my feelings at all well.'

(Gladys Langford, 6 December 1939 and 3 April 1940)

CONTENTS

ILLUSTRATIONS

Plates are between pages 70 and 71

1. Islington High Street, c. 1934, looking north (Islington Local History Centre)
2. Islington High Street, c. 1934, looking south (Islington Local History Centre)
3. Map: Gladys Langford's Highbury (Islington Local History Centre)
4. Map: Hamond Square, Hoxton, and its neighbourhood (London Borough of Hackney Archives)
5. Hoxton Street, nos. 263–265, c. 1930 (London Borough of Hackney Archives)
6. Gladys Langford and her then husband, George, July 1914 (Islington Local History Centre)
7. Caledonian Market, 1935 (Islington Local History Centre)
8. Bacchus Walk, Hoxton, c. 1930 (London Borough of Hackney Archives)
9. Hackney Central Library, Mare Street, c. 1939 (London Borough of Hackney Archives)
10. A corner shop on Kingsnorth Place, Hoxton, 1934 (London Borough of Hackney Archives)
11. Astoria Cinema, Seven Sisters Road, Islington, 1936 (Islington Local History Centre)
12. Essex Street, Hoxton in the 1930s (London Borough of Hackney Archives)
13. 72–90 Highbury Park, by Northolme Road (London Metropolitan Archives)
14. 14–18 Northolme Road (London Metropolitan Archives)

ACKNOWLEDGEMENTS

The bulk of Gladys Langford's writings are held in the Islington Local History Centre at Finsbury Library, and we are very grateful for the assistance that we have been given by its librarians and archivists. Lorraine Lees was especially helpful during the early stages of our research, in 2007–2008, and Martin Banham, then the Local History Manager, kindly allowed us to purchase a microfilm of Gladys's diary for 1936–1940 and arranged for this work to be done. More recently, we have been much indebted to Mark Aston, the current Local History Manager, for his generosity in advising us on photographs, answering various questions by email, scanning a number of documents, and facilitating our several visits to the Islington Local History Centre in 2012 and 2013. His attentiveness and thoughtfulness are warmly appreciated.

We are also grateful for the help and advice of Ed Lyon at the Hackney Archives, and Jessica Scantlebury and her colleagues at the Mass Observation Archive, now housed in The Keep, near the University of Sussex. Our other debts are to Emma Hardy at the Geffrye Museum and Val Griggiths of the Skinners' School Old Girls' Association, and to the staff members of the London Metropolitan Archive, the Archive of the Institute of Education, University of London, the Archive of the London School of Economics, the Essex Record Office, the BBC Written Archives Centre, and the British Library, both at St Pancras and Colindale. Trevor Henderson sorted out a number of our word-processing and related problems. Living, as we do, at a considerable distance from London, we have been regularly dependent on the Interlibrary Loan services provided by the Nelson Municipal Library, and are particularly grateful to Heather Goldik for her attentive and efficient managing of this invaluable service.

There are several personal debts that we are happy to acknowledge. The most important of these is to Jerry White, our editor at the London Record Society. In the summer of 2013 he read a draft of this book with great care, discovered numerous errors and oversights, and offered several dozen suggestions for improvements and enhancements. The result is a much better publication than it would otherwise have been. Jerry also introduced us to Ann Stephenson, whose expertise in researching family history has been a major asset to parts of this book (and to several other projects that we have been working on). We are pleased to acknowledge her investigative assistance. Other important evidence concerning Gladys's family and friends has been generously provided (without our asking) by Caroline Barron, Chairman of the London Record Society, and her friend Paul Klein, and we thank them for their constructive contributions.

Nelson, British Columbia
January 2014

ABBREVIATIONS

ARP	Air Raid Precautions
BUF	British Union of Fascists
HSA	Health Savings Account
HP	hire purchase
IE/ISL	Institute of Education Archives, University of London, files for Islington
LCC	London County Council
M-O	Mass-Observation
MS	manuscript
TUC	Trades Union Congress

PRINCIPAL PEOPLE MENTIONED
IN THE DIARY[1]

FAMILY MEMBERS

Lil	Lillian Challis, older sister (b. 1874); lives in Camps Road, Helions Bumpstead, Essex
Challis	Husband (b. 1874) of Lil; his first name 'Herbert' is never given in the diary; had been a police constable
Bay	Alberta Lavinia, Gladys's niece (b. 1902); daughter and only child of Lil and Challis; lives in West London, initially in Acton, then (from 1939) in Hillingdon, Middlesex
Em	Emily Bennett, sister (b. 1880); lives in Ilford, Essex
Bee	William Bennett (b. 1882), husband of Em
Kennie	Kenneth Bennett, son (b. 1910) of Em and Bee
Margie	Marjorie Bennett (b. 1906), daughter of Em and Bee; lives with her parents (at least sometimes)
Denys	Denys Bennett (b. 1915), son of Em and Bee
Kathlyn	Kathlyn Bennett, child (b. about 1925), niece or great niece to Gladys; lives in Ilford

FELLOW TEACHERS IN HOXTON

Miss Hammond, Mr. Alec Kerr, Mr. Pickering (Headmaster)

---

1. While many of the women who appear in the diary are referred to by their first names, and often only by their first names, most of the men are identified only by their surnames, with or without an attached 'Mr'. Since Gladys provides only thin details on these people, if any at all, we know little about them. This may be because she had already identified them more fully in her diaries written before October 1936, which do not survive. Caroline Barron, Paul Klein, and Ann Stephenson kindly helped us in fully identifying some of these people.

FRIENDS AND ACQUAINTANCES (INTELLECTUAL AND SOCIAL)

Chambers sisters	Aged spinsters; live in Pyrland Road, Highbury
Charles Gaye	Employed in a bank
Clowser	Employed by *John Bull* magazine
Editha	Teacher, soon to retire
Kiernan	Husband of Editha; employed at a hospital
Leo Dunlop	In his twenties; wife German
Lottie	Teacher
Murray	Friend of Leo; said to be gay
Porter	Husband of Lottie
Stelle	Teacher
Wellings	Owner of commercial libraries (four of them in 1938); 'Arthur', his first name, is never given in the diary
Miss Wilshin	Mary Wilshin, close friend of Bay; probably lives in the same house as her for most of the 1930s

OTHER FRIENDS AND ACQUAINTANCES (JEWISH, AND MADE MOSTLY DURING HER COMMERCIAL EMPLOYMENT IN 1915–1920)

Clarrie Freeman	Lives in Brondesbury
Leonard[2]	Former and still occasional lover, now married with three children; born 1895
Leslie	Lives in Brondesbury
Marjorie Rosenberg	Lives in Brondesbury
Mrs. Rosenberg	Lives in Brondesbury

OTHER

Lallie was Gladys's cat
Mr. and Mrs. Lucas were Gladys's landlords for most of 1937–1940

---

2. A pseudonym; Gladys never discloses his surname.

INTRODUCTION

BIOGRAPHICAL BACKGROUND

Gladys Hilda Mears was born on 17 April 1890 in Bethnal Green. She was the last (by a decade) of the six children of Lavinia Baker and Albert Mears, who had married in 1869, when they were both in their late teens. The other five children were born between 1873 and 1880. Gladys's grandparents had all come from Essex. Her maternal grandfather had been a policeman and then the foreman of a labouring gang; her paternal grandfather was a sawyer in a timber firm. His son Albert, Gladys's father, became a timber merchant and seems to have been prospering in the early 1890s, when she was a young child. Then, in 1895, when she was five, Albert died, aged only forty-four, leaving his widow in straitened circumstances. Lavinia struggled to make ends meet, mainly by taking in sewing as a machinist. In the 1911 census she was identified as a 'machinist underclothing'.

In 1911 Gladys was still living with her mother and was described as a teacher. One of Lavinia's older daughters, Lilian (born 1874), had been married in 1898 to Herbert Challis, and in 1911 she too was living at 140 Dalston Lane in Hackney with her mother, along with her daughter, and only child, Alberta Lavinia, known as Bay, who had been born in 1902. Herbert, Lilian's husband, a police constable, was then listed, for whatever reason, as residing at 63 Senrab Street in Stepney. So Gladys, in her early twenties, was living in an entirely female household that included her mother, her much older sister, and a niece only twelve years younger than herself, who, we speculate, may have related to Gladys as a sort of older sister. We do not know whether this census captured only a brief moment in the lives of Lavinia's daughters and her granddaughter, or whether her household was composed in this multi-generational way for several years prior to around 1913, the year that Gladys married. A quarter of a century later, Lil and Bay remained close to Gladys, despite personal tensions and disagreements. Both her sister and niece appear frequently in Gladys's 1930s diary, and her mother, while dead by then, was often remembered in her writing.[1]

1. Most of the research that supports this paragraph was done by Paul Klein (who also supplied some later references to the Mears family), and we very much appreciate his work on our behalf. We are also indebted to Caroline Barron for acting to involve him in this project. While Gladys's mother was a long-time resident of Hackney, she had different addresses in

While Gladys grew up in Hackney in impoverished family circumstances, education was highly valued. After primary schooling, she won a scholarship to the high school for girls run by the Skinners' Company in the Stamford Hill area. These were not happy days for her, partly because she was so much poorer than most of the other students, and because she was intensely conscious of her poverty. We do not know exactly how long she remained at Skinners' School – probably until she was around fifteen. Subsequently, after a year or two at the Hackney Pupil Teacher Centre on Tottenham Road, Dalston, she studied for two years, 1908–1910, at the Islington Day Training College on Offord Road to become a teacher. Her practice teaching at Canonbury Road Girls' School received middling grades. According to one assessor in 1909, she 'has a very pleasant style but while she succeeds in interesting a small class, she is not so successful with a large one'.[2] No doubt like most novice teachers aged nineteen, Gladys still had a lot to learn (and improvement was noted in 1909–1910).

While at college Gladys met a fellow student, George William Langford – his teaching evaluations were poor in his first year, rather better in his second. They married on 28 July 1913. Both were then twenty-three, only a month apart in age. He was employed as a London County Council teacher, but we have no evidence concerning her paid employment beyond the reference in 1911 to her being a teacher. The marriage lasted only a little more than a year. Some fourteen months after their wedding, in September 1914, he – as she later put it – 'deserted' her, and in 1915 he petitioned to have the marriage annulled. His reason for so doing, as recorded in a document held in the National Archives, was 'That the said marriage has never been consummated owing to the incapacity of the said Gladys Hilda Langford ... to consummate the said marriage', an incapacity that she denied. An absolute annulment of the marriage was granted in November 1918.[3] Gladys, who retained her married name, did not remarry, though there is abundant evidence that she would have liked to.

From 1915 until 1920 Gladys held a position in the business world, with the Metwell Stone China Company in Kingsland Road, Dalston, a firm that manufactured stoneware china and was owned by Henry van Flyman, a Jew of Dutch descent. It was during these years that Gladys met and became friends with the various Jewish people who remained prominent in her life in the 1930s. Most if not all of them enjoyed much better financial circumstances than she ever did. In 1920 she began (or resumed) full-time work as a teacher, a career that was to

the borough: in 1913 she was living at 380 Mare Street and in August 1914 a postcard held in the Islington Local History Centre was addressed to her at 43 Spurstowe Road.
2. These records are held in the Institute of Education Archives, University of London, IE/ISL. We are grateful to Sarah Aitchison for supplying this information.
3. National Archives, J/17/1218/7060. For more on this marital breakdown and some of its aftermath, see below, pp. 80–1.

continue – with much discontent, even animus – until her retirement in 1950. In 1939 she identified herself to Mass-Observation, to which she was then contributing, as 'a London County Council schoolmistress in an East End Junior Boys' School'; the school was located in Hoxton, a part of Shoreditch. This was a teaching position she held during all the time she wrote the diaries that comprise this book (excepting a period of sick leave). Her three residences in 1936–1940 were well removed from Hoxton, all near each other in Highbury, North London.

GLADYS LANGFORD'S LONDON

The London in which Gladys Langford lived and worked and took her leisure was (at least for some people) a vibrant, exciting place. As one of the world's great cities and then the most populous, it was full of social and cultural amenities. Even in the 1930s, decidedly grim in other places, much of London enjoyed reasonable prosperity, some glitz, and many of the finer things of life. Gladys, a woman of slender means and often in debt, was nonetheless able to avail herself of the stimulating cultural attractions that London had to offer. Her pleasure-centred London was mainly in the West End, with its theatres, concert halls, cinemas, art galleries, museums, and eateries. When she was not at home or teaching, these were the places where she would often be found.[4]

The West End was, perhaps more than ever before, dripping in wealth and a showcase for consumerism. It boasted first-class shopping venues, including such famous department stores as William White-ley's of Westbourne Grove, Harrods of Knightsbridge, and Selfridges on revitalised Oxford Street, all of which targeted a fairly broad range of shoppers. The democratisation of consumption was widely evident, including in the substantially upper-class borough of Kensington, where (for example) a redesigned Kensington High Street tube station allowed shoppers direct access from its octagonal booking hall into two major department stores – Pontings on one side and Derry and Toms on the other (which in the late 1930s opened its soon-to-be popular roof garden).[5] Other redevelopments brought Art Deco flair to the High Street which helped to attract shoppers from across the metropolis and beyond, people with money in their purses and pockets, some of whom may also have visited one of the great museums on nearby Cromwell Road.

Other parts of the West End drew crowds as well. The famous quadrant of Regent Street curving from Oxford Circus to Piccadilly Circus

4. See, as well as the diary proper, Appendix B.
5. Gavin Weightman and Steve Humphries, *The Making of Modern London: A People's History of the Capital from 1815 to the Present* (London: Ebury Press, 2007), p. 111.

was another mecca for consumers. In the early twentieth century John Nash's original stucco facades had become shopworn, in poor repair and crumbling, but after the Great War the grand thoroughfare was rebuilt and officially reopened in 1927, marked by a visit from King George V and Queen Mary (perhaps no surprise since the Crown held and still holds title to the aptly named thoroughfare). The *Daily News* declared that the redevelopment typified 'the spirit of the age – in its vitality and audacity. It is more suited to the flashing bus and the rapid streams of polished motor-cars than to the old-fashioned coach and four.'[6] As owners of a good chunk of the real estate in the core of the nation's capital, the royal family had a vested interest in ensuring that the area remained a splendid centrepiece – for monarchical pomp and ceremony and for tourism. To emphasise the glories of the British Empire, magnificent settings were created for resplendent processions by its royal rulers. Buckingham Place was refaced, the Mall was widened, and a splendid memorial to Queen Victoria was erected at one end of the Mall and the impressive Admiralty Arch at the other. The Royal Parks – St. James's Park, Hyde Park, and Green Park – were popular recreational destinations for all sorts of Londoners.

London, of course, had its glamour, its fashionable clubs and jazz-age places of licence, and while these did not figure in Gladys's immediate experiences, the world of the arts certainly did. She was an habitual attender of concerts, plays, and films (where Hollywood reigned supreme), not to mention special cultural events, such as art exhibitions, that came to her notice. It was a rare week when she was not out at least twice for some cultural event, and her diaries include, pasted on intermittent pages, some of the programmes from these performances, usually those on stage, and clippings of newspaper reviews. While some of the theatres were longstanding, the cinemas, of course, were mostly new, some of them very new, and sleekly designed, such as the granite-clad Odeon in Leicester Square that in 1937 replaced the Alhambra theatre. Also new were many of the places where Gladys took refreshment, most of them modestly priced restaurants meant to cater to office workers at midday and theatre and cinema goers in the evening. Most famous of these was J. Lyons & Co.'s chain of tea shops and its slightly pricier Corner House that provided both decent food and a respectable meeting place. They were alternatives to bars and chop-houses that were not inclined to be welcoming to women on their own. (Gladys was almost never in a pub.) By the 1920s and 1930s the Corner House and a few of its rivals had become staple accompaniments to the traffic in London's neon-lit West End, and women, some with men, others without, were among their most important patrons.[7]

---

6.   Quoted in ibid, p. 110.
7.   Peter Bird, *The First Food Empire: A History of J. Lyons & Co.* (Chichester: Phillimore, 2000), chap. 9.

There are two other districts of London that figured prominently in Gladys's life: Highbury, where she lived, and Hoxton, where she taught. Highbury, in the borough of Islington, was an area with, in some parts, Italianate villas built up to the 1870s, and in its northerly parts more densely packed terraced housing, most of it dating from roughly the thirty-five years prior to the Great War. Thereafter there were few changes in the residential stock until the 1940s and beyond. Gladys lived in rented flats and rooming houses, all located within a few blocks of each other. In 1934, shortly before her surviving diary begins, her residence was at 8 Highbury Crescent. By 1936 she was living a little to the north-east, at 50 Highbury Park (which no longer exists); in 1937 she moved the short distance to 4 Northolme Road; and in early 1940 she moved again to a residential hotel two blocks to the south, on Highbury Grange. All were London N5 addresses and situated in pleasant neighbourhoods not far from Highbury Fields (her 1934 address overlooks them), the largest open space in the borough. Her home for most of the time she was writing in 1937 through early 1940 was on Northolme Road. The red-bricked houses on this nicely treed street were originally built for successful middle-class families and later, in some cases, divided into flats. Matters relating to accommodation come up repeatedly in Gladys's diary – one of the perennial preoccupations of Londoners of all eras.

Hoxton, where Gladys taught, was very different. Then in Shoreditch, now part of Hackney, Hoxton was notorious for its poverty, squalor, and unruliness. It was a rough part of London – as is made clear in the memoir of Bryan Magee, who was born there in 1930 and spent almost all of his first decade living at 276–278 Hoxton Street, very near where Gladys was teaching (though he did not attend the school where she worked). Hoxton Street, running mostly north–south, was the main artery, along with Pitfield Street to the west; and as well as this core there were, as Magee recalls, 'all the lesser streets that ran across and between them – and all the slits and walks that ran off *them*, a rabbit-warren of cut-throughs and alleyways, wood-yards and cobbled courts, teeming with humanity'.[8] It was one of the most densely packed and probably most unhealthy districts of the metropolis. Detailed maps of Hoxton – including the map on overcrowding in the *New Survey of London*[9] – testify to this urban congestion. Hamond Square, where Gladys's school was located, did not even make it into London's *A to Z Atlas* from 1938/1939, apparently because there was insufficient space on the relevant map for the name to be printed. Another map from

8. Bryan Magee, *Clouds of Glory: A Hoxton Childhood* (London: Jonathan Cape, 2003), p. 37; also p. 77. Further testimony to Hoxton's roughness is found in A. S. Jasper, *A Hoxton Childhood* (London: Centreprise Publications, 1969).
9. 'Map of Overcrowding in the London Survey Area (1931)', Map no. 7 in vol. IV of *The New Survey of London Life and Labour* (9 vols.; London: P. S. King, 1930–1935); see also vol. III (1932), p. 350.

the *New Survey of London* shows three significant pockets of extreme poverty and marked criminality within 300 yards of this school.[10] Trees were few and parks virtually non-existent in Hoxton. Warehouses and workshops, many employing no more than half a dozen men, especially those related to furniture-making, were mixed in with houses; Gladys's school adjoined a cabinet works. The former stern-looking workhouse on nearby Hoxton Street had become St. Leonard's Hospital.

Such an inner-city settlement was not likely to be kind to the education of children. Problems were obvious in the 1930s – and remained so in 1951, when an inspector's report was issued on Gladys's school, now renamed Burbage Primary School. 'The neighbourhood of the school is a district in which housing and industry are at present inextricably entangled with one another,' it was said. 'Slum-clearance, started before the war, has not yet advanced very far, and mean streets still alternate with new blocks of flats and bombed sites. The main thoroughfare [Hoxton Street], dangerously narrow at the entrance to the school playground, is a busy street market, and the main artery of a succession of narrow streets in which housing conditions are, to say the least, indifferent.'[11] Kingsland Road, slightly to the east, was not much different. According to one knowledgeable observer, it 'is by no means an inviting thoroughfare, and the streets running into it are narrow and sordid to a depressing degree'.[12] The school inspector's 1951 report portrayed Hoxton much as Bryan Magee would later remember it. 'Socially, Hoxton has not a good reputation. While the staple industry of the furnishing trades demands and secures a good level of workmanship, and supports a sound artisan population, there are many less skilled and less reputable occupations, and a considerable shifting population.' Unskilled and little skilled workers predominated, and they were poorly paid.

This 1951 report presented a sympathetic assessment of some of the facts of local life. 'Except for a small recreation ground, there are no open spaces within reach that would afford a safe and pleasant playground for the children when school is over. In a word, the district is not one in which children can live the active carefree life which one would wish for them.' Then there were the children's homes to consider. Overcrowding was the norm, and 'there is an unusually large number of children in the schools who have a home background that contributes very little to any aspect of their education'. This is a verdict that, at least implicitly, also runs through much of Gladys's writing

10. London School of Economics and Political Science Archives, NSOL/3/1, Map no. 1 (1929–1930) of the Inner North East.
11. London Metropolitan Archives, EO/PS/12/H75/7. All but one of the following quotations concerning Hoxton are also from this confidential document.
12. Molly Harrison, *Museum Adventure: The Geffrye Museum and its Educational Activities* (London: University of London Press, 1950), p. 26. The museum is on Kingsland Road. See also Gladys's diary for 20 January 1937.

from the 1930s. Hoxton was not fertile ground for formal learning. 'The children themselves', it was said, 'have all the lively friendliness of the London slum-dweller and a courage in the face of adversity that compels admiration. Conditions, however, make them more restless and less able to concentrate than children for whom life flows more smoothly.... A number of children are obviously affected physically by their indifferent home conditions. Delinquency and truancy occur, but the number of cases is happily on the decline.'[13]

The dramatic contrasts between rich London and poor London are, of course, well known; aspects of modernity that were taken for granted in some districts were completely absent in others. In his 1934 book *London in My Time*, for instance, Thomas Burke remarked (p. 218) that while gas and electricity were then widespread, 'Yet in inner London whole streets may be found where electricity is unknown.' Gladys Langford was one of those people who routinely (though not as a rule from free choice) crossed these boundaries between affluence and poverty, privilege and deprivation, respectability and roughness.

GLADYS LANGFORD AND HER DIARIES

We were first alerted to the existence of Gladys Langford's diary from reading David Kynaston's *Austerity Britain 1945–1951* (London: Bloomsbury, 2007), which often draws on it. In late 2007 we began reading what she had written during the Second World War, hoping to find interesting accounts of wartime London. However, we discovered that, with the exception of later 1939, her pre-war writing was much richer and more engaging than what she wrote in the 1940s. Diaries from these decades are often like this: during some periods an author writes fully and vibrantly, at other times much less so.

The thirty-seven handwritten notebooks and workbooks that comprise Gladys's diary for 25 October 1936 through 11 November 1969 are held in the Islington Local History Centre at Finsbury Library. The first four of these volumes, each a hardback notebook, are the foundation for this edition. Our editorial principles are discussed below. While we cannot be certain about the provenance of the collection, a file card in the Islington Local History Centre suggests that the diaries were prob-ably deposited there in 1971, a year before Gladys's death, perhaps by Alfred Friend, one of her two heirs, who was named on this card as an

---

13. The author also remarked on the disruptiveness of the recent war. 'The social and educational upheaval of the war was exceptionally severe in an area so heavily bombed, and with parents who found evacuation so distasteful that they were seldom willing to leave their children in the safety of the reception area for long.' It was thought that gradually, with post-war reconstruction, 'conditions of life are improving', albeit modestly. (We have no testimony from Gladys concerning the London Blitz in 1940–1941 since at that time she was – unusually – doing no diary-writing.)

informant concerning the diary material. We think it likely that Gladys, in her declining days, had asked him to make this deposit. For several months in 1939, Gladys also wrote for the social research organisation Mass-Observation. Details concerning this writing and its inclusion in our edition are presented in Chapter 5 and parts of Chapters 6 and 7.

Like many personal writings, Gladys's diaries can be read and appreciated on several levels. First, they are clearly an outlet for feelings and opinions that (for the most part) could not or should not be conveyed to others – certainly not to their faces. This is the confiding side of her diaries, much of which is harsh and acerbic. Many entries also highlight her gnawing unhappiness and lack of fulfilment. Indeed, aspects of her diary are akin to themes in the best-selling 1938 novel by Winifred Watson, *Miss Pettigrew Lives for a Day*, in which a down-on-her-luck middle-aged single woman briefly escapes into a dashing world of luxury, sophistication, and excitement. She, like Gladys, was often lonely, disliked her work (as a governess), and as the book opens feels that life has passed her by.

Second, Gladys saw herself as in some sense a writer, as a person with thoughts to express and interesting views to convey, and diary-writing allowed her to cultivate an art that she admired. There are many entries in which she seems to be self-consciously writing up incidents or descriptions of people as a novelist or journalist might.[14] We know that she tried her hand at writing fiction, but found no publisher.

Third, her diaries are also records of observation – observations, from her own perspective of course, and usually with evaluative commentary, of diverse aspects of London life in the later 1930s. Some of these observations were of the public realm; others were of private conversations and intimate human relations out of the public gaze. There are also passages in which she reminisces, usually about experiences prior to the Great War. Gladys had a good eye for certain kinds of detail. And her likes and dislikes, which were not always consistent, were routinely expressed with verve.

While Gladys's diaries are in many respects personal, she was also an observer of society – often an astute one: she had something of a sociologist's sensibility – and was an active consumer of the cultural products of her day. Among these, books were prominent; she read some eighty to ninety books a year. Few were classics. Many were new publications, and almost all had been written since the Great War. Gladys's tastes were modernist, centred mainly on patterns of living in the contemporary world, and the fiction she read had a strong bias towards social realism. Most of these novels were rooted in the material facts and circumstances of her own society, especially that of London. Fantasy held no appeal for her, and she was indifferent to religion.

---

14. See Appendix A for an example of this disposition.

This interest in writing and images with a documentary tilt is often evident in her diaries. Here, to illustrate the point, is a passage from a novel she was reading on 4 November 1936. Jeffery Marston's *The Rocket* (1936) was embedded in a world of money-making and relations between the sexes and set partly in London. Early in the book (p. 15) the author sets the stage for an incident in his story, just as a playwright composing for a London audience might.

> Travelling by the Central London Railway from the City, Jerry got out at Bond Street and walked briskly northwards to his lodgings in Marylebone. He occupied a furnished bed-sitting-room on the first floor of an 'apartment' house in a quiet side turning off Baker Street. The two pounds a week which he paid included breakfast, service and the use of the bathroom. His evening meal, if he chose to have it at home, cost him half a crown. But tonight he did not so choose. He had a dinner appointment. By the time he had glanced through the evening paper – noting with satisfaction reports of slight activity in certain industrial shares (Good man, Frank! He's got busy already, he thought) – and had changed from his business clothes into a light grey suit and hosiery in keeping, it was past seven. Ten minutes later he was seated at a corner table for two at Ballino's Restaurant in Baker Street. He ordered Martinis, a sweet and a dry, but waved away the waiter who flourished a menu before him. 'I'm expecting a lady,' he said. He had not long to wait.

This fictional description was very much in accord with Gladys's actual world. This was a world of lodgings, addresses, place names, street life, eating out, prices, transportation, and other material realities.[15] Hers was also a world in which, as in so many contemporary novels, there was a lot of dialogue. Dialogue of one sort or another is a central feature of her diaries. Some of this dialogue is internal – discussions between parts of her self, ruminations, confessions and regrets, expressions of ambivalence, perhaps imagined conversations with

---

15. A book Gladys mentioned on 4 April 1938, *To Beg I am Ashamed* (see below, Chapter 2, note 29), which purported to be written by a prostitute but was transparently the work of a professional writer (and almost certainly a man), took pains to connect with its targeted London readership by scattering familiar place names throughout the text: Battersea, Streatham Common, Clapham, Wandsworth, Brixton, Lavender Hill, Vauxhall Bridge, Canvey Island, Maida Vale, Regent Street, Victoria, Oxford Street, Richmond Park, Bond Street, Marylebone, Harley Street, Baker Street, Selfridge's, Hampstead, Golders Green, the Cenotaph, Kensington, Bayswater, Chelsea, Knightsbridge, Wood Green stadium, Lyons' Corner House, Houndsditch, Hoxton, Regent Palace, Shaftesbury Avenue, Soho, Mayfair, Canonbury, Box Hill, Holloway Road, Paddington, the Ritz, St. Martin's Lane, Wimbledon Common, Finsbury Park, the Criterion, Hatton Garden, Piccadilly, Lisle Street, Henrietta Street, Hornsey, St. Pancras, Camden Town, Wanstead, Seven Dials, Hendon, Queen's Gate, Half Moon Street, Wardour Street, Euston Road, the Elephant, and Sackville Street are all mentioned at least once.

others. Other dialogues are reportages of external episodes, commonly of conversations and connections with others. They testify to social relations as they were experienced (normally) face-to-face. From them we learn of friendships, rivalries, dislikes, worries, disappointments, and the like, usually as recently experienced.

Then there are the dialogues between self and society. These are the passages that reveal the diarist's perspective on the society that he or she inhabits. They are also the passages that tend to determine the publishability – or lack of publishability – of modern diaries by otherwise unknown persons. When well composed, thoughtful, varied in content, and full of detail, they are sources that allow us to enter into, as no other source is likely to do, one individual's everyday life, both the predictable routines and the unexpected events, both life's pleasures and pains, its accomplishments and failures. And almost always they are marked by the merit of immediacy and unvarnished by knowledge of what the future would bring.

EDITING THE DIARY

While there are arguments for reproducing a diary in full, this approach involves problems. Gladys's diary, like many other relatively modern diaries, is often repetitious, and there is little to be gained from reading the same sentiments – in her case often glumness and displeasure – or even the same words, again and again.[16] As for the question as to what is or is not 'interesting' and worth putting into print, editorial subjectivity is bound to play a role. But most people, we think, would regard some diary entries as unremarkable – perhaps the report of a dull day in the diarist's life, perhaps an entry that is brief and unrevealing, perhaps a revisiting of an outlook or grievance that has been already well documented. Our selections, which represent around half of Gladys's diary-writing from 1936–1940, give prominence to her writing that conveys detailed descriptions and/or thoughtful reflections. We reproduce all of her writing for some weeks, for other weeks nothing (or almost nothing) at all.[17] Many editions of twentieth-century diaries present 'the best' of the diarist's efforts, and this is what we have tried to do

16. Reproducing a diary in full, or largely in full, seems to work best when the diary is relatively short and the writing succinct and unrepetitious, or when only a portion of a diary can readily be selected for publication, leaving the rest of the diary unpublished. An example of the former is Patricia and Robert Malcolmson, eds., *Dorset in Wartime: The Diary of Phyllis Walther, 1941–1942* (Dorset Record Society, 2009); an example of the latter is Robert Malcolmson and Peter Searby, eds., *Wartime Norfolk: The Diary of Rachel Dhonau, 1941–1942* (Norfolk Record Society, 2004).

17. Perhaps our most frequent substantive omissions concern her critiques of some of the many films and plays she saw (other critiques we have selected for inclusion). A reader with a special interest in these matters is advised to consult the original MS diary. Appendix B itemises most of the cultural content of her life in 1937.

with Gladys Langford. Whenever at least one day's diary entry has been omitted, we insert a line of asterisks or summarise in our own words some of the omitted writing. Whenever material is reproduced in full, as is often the case for 1939 in particular, we make this clear.

Since Gladys knew how to write, little of her text requires correction. We have silently corrected misspellings, usually of proper names, and have sometimes altered punctuation for the sake of clarity. When a word seems to be missing, we have supplied one in square brackets.

Our annotations to Gladys's writing are designed: (1) mainly to identify matters that she mentions and often to offer additional information concerning them; and (2) sometimes to enlarge upon an issue that she raises by citing or quoting other evidence, whether from primary or secondary sources. In this way we hope that as one reads through the diary an increasingly rich portrait will emerge of her life and circumstances, as well as the lives and circumstances of people she knew and observed, during a period of a little over three years.

PART ONE: 1936–1939

1

October 1936–July 1937

Up Close

Sunday, 25 October 1936. Plenty of my own company nowadays. Hardly see a soul in the house, though Mrs. Robinson gave me some trifle, evidently because I gave *her* pastries yesterday.[1] In pursuance of my plan to do something with my Sundays went to the Tate Gallery this afternoon to see the [Henry] Tonks exhibits. Cannot say I found them appealing. Nos. 13, 73, portraits I thought good; also two children seated in a green field and a small child lying on its back playing with its toes. Quite a few people there, probably inspired by Jan Gordon's article in today's *Observer* ['Art and Artists: The New English, and Professor Tonks', p. 18]. Intended attending South Place Concert this evening but a heavy hail-storm and a thunderstorm made home appeal very strong. Then too I'm reading a new novel (I don't read many since Wellings' gibe), *Cathedral Close* [1936], and finding it very interesting. It is by Susan Goodyear [Margaret Bryan Matthews], a new writer I presume.[2] I do love my home; I wish I had more time to enjoy it. An ex-Servicemen's meeting protesting against Fascism was in progress in Trafalgar Square. A company of policemen 'stood at ease' and great numbers stood about but no trouble appeared to be threatening.

Monday, 26 October. My half-term holiday but I did not get the rest I need. 9 a.m. Em phoned. Then I phoned Bay at her office for

---

1. Gladys was at this time living in a house at 50 Highbury Park, N5, which she shared with eight other people. (The house no longer exists.) Elsie and Robin Reginald Robinson appear to have been the landlords. In 1934 she had been living nearby at 8 Highbury Crescent, overlooking Highbury Fields. All four of her residences between the mid-1930s and early 1940s were close to each other in Highbury (see Map, Plate 3).
2. One character in this novel, Muriel Raven, 'had read D. H. Lawrence, Aldous Huxley, and some of the new psychology and so was familiar with the idea that sexual experience holds a key to life which must be used if one is to become a whole person. But she did not need them to tell her that it was a key which rusts if it is held too long in the hand – and she was thirty-eight' (pp. 48–49). The modernist concerns of Gladys and some of her friends, including an eye for 'hidden motives', are often revealed in the diary. Wellings' 'gibe' may have been reported in a previous entry, but none of her diaries from before this date has survived.

Mr. Morlert's address as I knew Lil was going to that dentist's. Met her at Hackney Station and went to Dadd's the oculist's [Mare Street, Hackney] for my glasses. I can't see small print with these. Obtained rebate of 4s 6d for HSA [Health Savings Account] contribution. Had luncheon at the Peacock in Islington. Went on to Piccadilly to shop-gaze. Saw a delightful jumper for £1 1s 0d [a guinea] but I couldn't afford it. To library at Hackney tonight.

Tuesday, 27 October. Second and last day of my half-term holiday and little pleasure in it. The 'char' came, talked a bit and 'scamped' her work. I don't like 'chars'. Went to the Tivoli to see *Dodsworth* – enjoyed the film. Ruth Chatterton and Walter Huston *can* act and Mary Astor pleases the eye and ear.[3] Walked from the Strand to Tottenham Court Road by a circuitous path but wind so high I gladly returned home – only to find all my lights had failed AND it's not a fuse. Another expense! Phoned Sylvia Cohen for news of Eric Riebold. Had a long talk with her and accepted an invitation for Sunday week. I have a bad eye. I hope it isn't conjunctivitis. There have been several cases at school. Am reading C. Delius's book, *Frederick Delius*. It's typical of biographies written by women of successful members of their families, full of tiny uninteresting family anecdotes.[4] Read at a sitting *Saturday Night at the Greyhound* by John Hampson, a queer book. The death, or rather killing, of the Greyhound, Pertinax, a grim happening.[5]

Wednesday, 28 October. To school. A new class and the children know nothing despite the marvels (alleged) of Miss Hammond's teaching. She's NEVER in her room. She is the slackest woman I ever met. Went to Dadd's for my new spectacles and to Lottie's. She has resigned herself to Vernon's adventures with women and says he's at least hers legally and he comes back at night. She gave an amusing account of their visit to Lionel Britton who lives with, and is apparently supported by, a middle-aged woman in the Civil Service. This woman has bought a tiny boat and she, Britton and a young man spent their holiday on the Thames. Sanitation was non-existent and when Lottie and the others had eaten a meal, hosts and guests retired one by

---

3. This film, directed by William Wyler, was adapted from a 1929 novel by Sinclair Lewis.
4. Clare Delius's 1935 book, subtitled *Memories of My Brother*, is indeed (in its first half) mainly an exercise in reminiscing, and is full of the details of family life. The Bradford-born composer lived from 1862 to 1934.
5. Hampson's novel, which takes place over the course of a single day in a public house (named 'The Greyhound') in rural Derbyshire, was published in February 1931 to wide and immediate acclaim, which propelled it through two reprints in ten days. The brief, stark, and chilling tale draws heavily on the author's own experiences of poverty, degradation, and low life. It is enriched by an understanding of the many ways in which social background and flawed temperament work together to determine people's fates. The dog, Pertinax, is subjected to a brutal, premeditated execution by hanging and stabbing.

one to a tiny cabin and used a *6d* Woolworth's saucepan as a chamber pot!!

Thursday, 29 October. Reply from Borough Councillor. I *may* run wireless set from lighting circuit. Paid first instalment of furniture to Chippendale. Visited Leonard. He was bursting with an account of his doings as Vice President of the Musical Manufacturers' Association and his recent visit to Italy in connection therewith. He read over his speeches. He told his retorts. He explained his attitude and thoroughly enjoyed himself in the telling thereof. He has aged even more than I. He's going bald and his face is lined as a turtle's back. He is going to get me some baize or felt for my table.[6] Lil wrote.

Friday, 30 October. Home at tea-time to find electrician had been – had worked for about four hours, searching for a loose connection, but had left no bill so I'm still on tenterhooks about it. To Brondesbury. Marjorie's ailments persist – and will while they make her the centre of interest. The Samuels came up. Mrs. S. *is* a rowdy and common woman. How well I realise what a tragedy it would have been had Leonard and I married. His associates are moneyed but mannerless and his family is always at his heels. Went down with Mr. Samuels to his flat to admire the re-decorations.

Saturday, 31 October. Lil came this morning. She brought me jelly, wine, apples, took me to Pritchard's to luncheon and bought me a half pound of chocolates. I *am* getting fat. It *does* grieve me. Sometimes I feel inclined to commit suicide when I see my enormous hulk. I weigh 10 stone 9lbs. Came home to spend the evening in peace and quiet. The Jarrow marchers held up our bus this morning.[7]

---

6. Leonard (a pseudonym), Gladys's lover in the 1920s – and still occasional lover (see below) – almost certainly made frequent appearances in her pre-1936 diaries, which are now lost. He was almost five years younger than her, Jewish, and by the 1930s married with children. She never disclosed his surname.
7. The famous marchers from the shipyard town of Jarrow, protesting the miseries of their lives, massive unemployment, and lack of government concern for their plight, arrived in London over several days. Though well publicised and enjoying widespread support, the march got little sympathy from the government and its impact on policy was negligible. Some of the protesters were publicly welcomed in Islington, as they had been elsewhere on their journey south (*Islington and Holloway Press*, 7 November 1936, p. 4 and 14 November, p. 3); and 'extensive activities' were undertaken 'to gain popular support for the Hunger Marchers' by Islington's Labour Party and Trades Council. A public meeting was to be held at the Islington Central Library, and the *Islington Reporter*, 30 October 1936, p. 7, carried a long and detailed account of these plans. 'Every effort is to be made ... to show the solidarity of Islington workers with the cause of the marchers', including their demands for improved terms for unemployment assistance. The local Communist Party was intending to hold its own meeting in the Town Hall 'to prepare the ground for a large gathering of Islington workers going out to meet the women marchers before they arrive in Islington'; the meeting was to be addressed by William Gallacher, the Communist MP for West Fife.

Sunday, 1 November. Spoke to Em on phone. Pritchards played special music and gave wedding-cakes to each woman guest. Wellings phoned last night inviting me for supper tonight. Bay phoned. She is going to lend me £3 until November 21st. Wrote several letters, one to Mr. Gaye.

Monday, 2 November. To Wellings' last night. Clowser there. He's gone 'Anti-Semitic' since his visit to Germany. Very dull weather and school consequently wearisome. Phoned Editha for those scholarship papers I lent her. As usual, she's full of 'school-shop'.

* * * * * *

Friday, 13 November. An angry mother at school today because I had rapped the boy's fingers with a stick of pencil yet no one comes to complain of Mr. Kerr who hits boys' heads with a screw-driver! To Rosenbergs tonight. Margie, although declared fit by specialist, has eye trouble still and wears dark glasses. She has bought two new gowns – *most* unsuitable for one so fat and dumpy. One is of bright green satin, the other of beige but having *huge* epaulettes of brown fur making her look like a haystack in motion. Mrs. R, weighing 18 stone and with one huge breast having a growth in it, wearing gowns suitable for 50 at 70, then gave me a lecturette on dressing badly. She said I ought to have one really good outfit instead of a lot of rubbish. I felt rather sore as I usually pay a good price for my clothes which are nearly always dark now I am stout. Leslie pressed me to attend his Ladies' Night but I know I don't shine socially and persistently refused. Samuels came in. I like Mr. S. but his wife is 'low'. I never knew such a dirty-mouthed woman outside a 'four ale bar' in the long ago.

* * * * * *

Saturday, 21 November. Phoned Em. Margie is changing her job again. Shopping this morning, to Library this afternoon. Paid upholsterer 10s. He says trade is terrible; he hasn't had a customer this week! To the Empire to see *Libelled Lady*. Story of film [a comedy] negligible but players and dialogue excellent. Jean Harlow's breasts are a little too full. Spencer Tracy is very like Clowser. William Powell scores every point possible. Also an excellent film of Rotha's, *Roof-tops of London*. Particularly liked the shots of workmen cleaning and repairing roofs.[8]

---

8. Paul Rotha (1907–1984) was an innovative maker of documentary films. This 1936 film is described by the British Film Institute as: 'Views of London from overhead and the ingenious uses to which roofs of a crowded city can be put.' A year later Gladys again lauded Rotha's work, after an evening at the Tatler. 'An excellent Paul Rotha film – *Today We Live* – showing the derelict areas and the efforts towards social life made there. The women members of the Village Institute were excellent – as good as any crowd in the much belauded French films' (17 November 1937). Rotha's 1936 book, *Documentary Film*, was in a later edition (1939) given the subtitle *The use of the film medium to interpret creatively*

Sunday, 22 November. Went today to Queen Mary's Hall, Bloomsbury to hear British Symphony Orchestra, a body of unemployed musi-
cians conducted by Charles Hambourg. He is a stocky little man with
a bulging bottom much accentuated by a very short lounge jacket. The
news of the evacuation of Madrid makes me so sad.[9] What a terrible
lot of unnecessary suffering there is in the world.

* * * * * *

Tuesday, 1 December. A bad night, a bad headache and a bad temper
in consequence. Feel bilious too – very unusual for me. Crystal Palace
burnt down last night.[10] Duke of Kent among the onlookers – trying
on helmets of firemen and getting drenched by hose-pipes. What a
nuisance he must have been to the firemen, or did he think he was a

and in social terms the life of the people as it exists in reality. As he put it in the book's
Foreword, dated October 1935, the documentary strives 'to bring alive the modern world.
It asks understanding of human values and knowledge of the issues governing our society
today as well as in the past. It asks for the mind of the trained sociologist as well as the
abilities of the professional film technician.' Here was robust testimony to the sociological
sensibilities of 'thinking' people in the 1930s, who clearly included film-going Gladys
Langford. Rotha's later book, *Documentary Diary: An Informal History of the British
Documentary Film, 1928–1939* (London: Secker & Warburg, 1973), chap. 7, recalls 1935–
1937.

9. She is presumably referring to the withdrawal of Franco's forces from their assault against
   Republican-controlled Madrid, which had withstood (though barely) several weeks of
   ferocious attack.

10. The famous Crystal Palace, a large cast-iron and plate-glass building, was constructed for
    the Great Exhibition of 1851 and sited in Hyde Park. Afterwards, the structure was rebuilt
    in an enlarged and redesigned form at Penge, South London, where it stood as something
    of a landmark, covering 25 acres. The fire that broke out on the night of 30 November
    could not be contained and destroyed all but two water towers. Crowds were reported to
    have gathered to view the spectacle from distant places, such as Harrow and the Guildford
    area, and dramatic photographs reached a wide audience. 'Some 500 firemen were engaged,
    with over ninety fire-fighting appliances – a record for a London fire' (*Illustrated London
    News*, 5 December 1936, pp. 1000 and 1016–17). One Member of Parliament, on his way
    that evening to the House of Commons, found 'the dark sky was ablaze with light, and it
    looked like a Venetian sunset. It was the Crystal Palace that was burning.' There was 'only
    one tower left [he said] – a reminder of the Victorian Age' (Robert Rhodes James, ed.,
    Chips: The Diaries of Sir Henry Channon [London: Phoenix, 1996; 1st publ. 1967], pp.
    87–8). 'Even as far away as us in Hoxton, families went out into the streets to look at the
    redness in the sky' – and people talked 'about it for days afterwards' (Magee, *Clouds of
    Glory*, p. 308). The demise of this famous structure had a big impact at the time and was
    long remembered by some people, among them Winston Churchill's then fourteen-year-old
    daughter Mary, who was living at her home in Chartwell, Kent. 'I remember being woken
    up and going downstairs to join the rest of the family and household who were gathered on
    the lawn, gazing in disbelief at the great glow in the sky to the north. I think perhaps this
    event had the same effect on me as the sinking of the *Titanic* had on an earlier generation:
    the unthinkable could happen' (Mary Soames, *A Daughter's Tale: The Memoir of Winston
    Churchill's Youngest Child* [New York: Random House, 2011], p. 107). As Juliet Gardiner
    has remarked, 'The fire gripped the imagination of the British public' and 'photographs and
    stories filled the newspapers for days afterwards' (soon to be superceded by news of the
    King's abdication). Some observers, she thinks, saw 'in the Crystal Palace fire much the
    same sort of augury as the sinking of the *Titanic* in 1912, which had become in retrospect a
    portent of the end of an era, if approaching Armageddon' (Juliet Gardiner, *The Thirties: An
    Intimate History* [London: Harper Press, 2010], p. 476). The loss of the *Titanic* has proven
    to be much more memorable to later generations than the loss of the Crystal Palace.

reincarnation of Charles II at the Great Fire [in 1666]? After being in telephonic communication with Chippendale's last night, this morning I had a communication from the Bankers saying they had had no payment from Chippendale's and would I please pay *them* in future. I phoned C's tonight and in return they assured me they were making it right with the Bankers. Funny behaviour! No more Hire Purchase dealings with this firm for me. Em sent me a bathroom cabinet for my Xmas present.

Wednesday, 2 December. Parcel arrived from Lil. School wearisome as ever. Wellings phoned late last night, quoted new additions to his library; said Clowser thought I only thought I liked Lottie better than Mr. Porter. Said his eyes were troubling him again. Said he would let me have parts of his new book to read.

Thursday, 3 December. Nation-wide excitement. The King wants to marry Mrs. Simpson, the twice divorced American woman of 40. The Cabinet do not approve. Lots of people have spoken of the affair. American papers have openly referred to it but discreet silence has been maintained in England. The Bishop of Bradford seems to have brought affairs to a head by rebuking the King indirectly for irreligiosity among other things.[11] All sorts of possibilities are mooted, the King's abdication, the passing of a Barrier Act making the Duke of York and his heirs succeed, not the possible children of Mrs. Simpson. *I* think the King is to be congratulated on having the courage to break free from hypocrisy and precedent. I envy Mrs. Simpson who is loved by a man who is prepared to let a kingdom totter for her sake. My views are not common though. Women are furious. They keep exclaiming 'She's already had two husbands'. Men seem to think he might have continued 'an affair' and not imperilled 'Big Business'. Affairs are still

---

11. The Bishop of Bradford's speech stressed that the coronation ceremony 'is a sacramental rite closely tied to the Anglican service of Holy Communion', and was less than enthusiastic about the King's qualifications for taking part in this sacrament. The Bishop commended Edward 'to God's grace, which he will so abundantly need … if he is to do his duty faithfully. We hope that he is aware of his need. Some of us wish that he gave more positive signs of his awareness.' He argued that through the coronation, as properly carried out, the people as well as the King 'consecrate' themselves 'to the service of God and the welfare of mankind'. 'Whatever it may mean, much or little, to the individual who is crowned, to the people as a whole it means their dedication of the English monarchy to the care of God in whose rule and governance are the hearts of Kings.' He objected to any watering down of the sacrament of the coronation to accommodate Edward and his intended wife. A listener or reader might well have come to wonder, along with the Bishop (implicitly), if God would look kindly upon a king with Edward's religious credentials. And yet 'there never was a clearer need than there is at present', he concluded, 'for a great rally to religion', citing the turmoil and violence in European civilisation (*The Times*, 2 December 1936, p. 11a). Another diarist, the Secretary of State for War, read of the Bishop's speech on a train back to London from Leeds: 'I suppose it was the first time in the century that the sovereign of Great Britain had been openly rebuked' (John Julius Norwich, ed., *The Duff Cooper Diaries 1915–1951* [London: Phoenix, pb, 2006; 1st publ. 2005], pp. 234–5).

in the melting pot. Some folks say Queen Mary [widow of George V] approves. Perhaps she had enough of an arranged marriage herself.

Friday, 4 December. Men teachers, or some of them, are filthy. Mr. Conway spits into the wastepaper basket. Poor cleaners! There seems more likelihood of the King's marriage being carried through and less likelihood of an abdication. Fierce arguments everywhere – in bus, shop, at stall too. I have contributed my share at school and at Rosenbergs. Leslie, [up] in arms, says 'Fancy wanting her at third hand'. He continues that all men will feel free to indulge in wife-stealing with the King as example. I haven't noticed their refraining while they had the very proper old King at the head of affairs. Leslie says 'Why should subjects have been expected to give up their all when the King isn't prepared to give up his mistress?' Mrs. Rosenberg is enjoying ill health again – heart trouble this time. She was lying in bed with a brimming chamber pot in the forefront of the picture. Marjorie quite happy, having persuaded the specialist to say hers is a unique case needing a physician's attentions as well as an oculist's. She has bi-weekly colonic irrigation and anticipates a 36 hour stay in a nursing home for eye exam. She also goes out with her rambling club but has to have someone 'hold her hand after dark' – a man of course. Poor Marjorie! She's more sex-hungry than I am myself. Leslie, by request, is giving me a bedroom rug for Christmas.

Saturday, 5 December. To Hackney Library this morning. Met Vera Mannering. She *is* a hideosity. Why do middle-aged women omit to wash corners of their eyes? Leo phoned. He has removed to Cleveland Square, Lancaster Gate. Rushed through torrential rain to Westminster Theatre and *much* enjoyed *Waste* [by Harley Granville-Barker], although I thought the last act unnecessary and Nicholas Hannen miscast. The consultation scene with the Prime Minister (Felix Aylmer) is superb. Imagine my astonishment to come out of the theatre and walk into Darling Charles, who was standing at the kerb, obviously waiting for someone. It proved to be ME. I had said in my last letter I was going and he decided to see me afterwards. He carried me off to tea and left me at 7.40 p.m. when he had an engagement. (How like Sedwell he is, in looks.) We talked about the play, the Royal Scandal, the rising generation, God in man, esoteric religions, the gift of faith, mutual friends and other matters. We laughed a lot, teased each other a little and confided beliefs to one another. When he left me he said 'Well you do encourage me to talk'. I showed great interest (and felt it) in a lecture he is to give.

Sunday, 6 December. Don't like the sound of the newspapers. It seems possible that the King may abdicate. I *am* sorry for him. Mrs. Simpson's suicide or departure from the world's and the King's ken would help. No woman could hope to make up to him for the loss of a nation. Em phoned. She seems little interested in the Royal dilemma. Bay phoned. To my surprise, she agrees with me. Wrote to Lil and to Mr. Gaye. Sent him two articles from the *Observer*, one relating to Voltaire, the other to a book on Victorian England.

Monday, 7 December. Leo arrived at tea-time with a bunch of chrysanthemums. He is full of a scheme by means of which he and Murray will run a boarding house in Bayswater – on a capital of £20!! The house has 16 rooms and they will let some furnished and some unfurnished, using HP [Hire Purchase] terms. To Queen's Hall. Bitterly cold. Malcolm Sargent conducting, Egon Petri at the piano – a Mozart concerto, second Liszt concerto, and finally Berlioz's *Symphonie Fantastique*. My first hearing of the last named and I much enjoyed it. Booked 1s seat for next Beecham concert.[12]

Tuesday, 8 December. Brought Miss Hammond home to meet Bay and Miss Wilshin. Both the latter very indignant because Lil has cancelled her holiday plans for Folkestone. *I'm* going to [Helions] Bumpstead [in Essex] for Xmas. Mrs. Robinson is going to mind Lallie and I'm going to lend my bedroom for her parents. Very glad to see the back of my guests.

Wednesday, 9 December. No decision about the Royal wedding. Wild rumours about Mrs. Simpson's being with child by the King. It's like living in Charles II's reign. Mr. Gaye very much in my mind. I wonder if anything will come of the friendship. Reading [Mark] Benney's book *Low Company* [1936]. I like his style [written in the third person], his taste in odd and unusual words, but I don't think he's a 'desirable'.[13]

---

12. Queen's Hall, Langham Place, which had opened in 1893, accommodated an audience of 2,500. At this time it was the base for both the BBC Symphony Orchestra and the London Philharmonic Orchestra. It was largely destroyed by German bombing on the night of 10–11 May 1941 and was never rebuilt.

13. Mark Benney (b. 1910) was a pseudonym for Henry Ernest Degras, a burglar, who described in this book, in colourful language, his life of crime and his associations from youth with the 'Wide people', including his mother, who 'live gaily, love promiscuously, drink vastly, sing loudly, lie brazenly, swagger outrageously and hate dangerously. Above all they never work. Work is the province of Mugs' (p. 25). The word 'wide' in this context referred to people who were dishonestly cunning, skilled in sharp practices, engaged in shady dealings, and the like; a 'wide boy' was a sort of 'spiv' (*OED*). The word was used in another novel of the time that Gladys was reading on 12 October 1937, *Wide Boys Never Work* (1937) by Robert Westerby, in which the main character (she declared) 'is too much like our young Hoxtonians' (12 October 1937). A general message of the novel was that in very poor urban areas most people are beaten down and hence passive and unimaginative; only the young have any fight – and often turn to criminal activities as a means of escape from slum life.

Gladys's assessment of Hoxton was widely shared. According to vol. III (1932) of the *New Survey of London*, the district 'has long been recognised as one of the worst parts of London, and it still deserves that distinction. Poverty and overcrowding are characteristic of practically the whole district, crime and degradation of certain parts of it. The worst streets

Thursday, 10 December. Weather *so* dull. King Edward VIII abdicated today and his brother, the Duke of York, becomes Albert I with the 'smiling Duchess' as Queen Elizabeth – silly Smug-face. King Edward VIII will probably leave England tomorrow. Why couldn't the country be allowed to choose whether it would favour a morganatic marriage or not? Wellings invited me for Sunday. He phoned late last night. Cinemas lose no time; at the Tatler [on Charing Cross Road], films of the new King and Queen were shown. I wonder if he will be crowned next May instead of his brother?[14]

Friday, 11 December. The new King is assuming the title of George VI after all. I went to Queen's Hall tonight to hear [Guila] Bustabo [violinist] and the interval was reduced to five minutes so that the late King, or rather ex-King's speech, might be broadcast. It was like waiting beside a death-bed in the space between the concert's end and the beginning of the speech. People avoided each other's eyes and wriggled self-consciously. I thought it a very moving speech with its reference to 'the woman I love' and I still believe there's something behind the whole affair. Maybe we shall never know what it is but why Mr. Baldwin [the Prime Minister] took so much upon himself, I don't know.

Saturday, 12 December. Despite a dismal drizzle, I decided to go to hear the Proclamation of the new King at Charing Cross. There were crowds but very subdued crowds in and around Trafalgar Square. I managed to get close to the 'movie' camera man and by the broadcasting apparatus. I couldn't see more than the bobbing heads and scarlet cloaks of the soldiery and the coachmen and tops of the gilded coaches but I could hear every word. Dozens of women used bag-mirrors as periscopes. Hawkers sold programmes and also souvenirs of the ex-King. I never can understand people's buying all that rubbish. The cheering was very perfunctory, I thought, and I smiled grimly at *God Save the King*'s being sung on one night for Edward – God duly saved him as per request – and *God Save the King*'s being sung the next night for George VI. Nevertheless, I think the idea of monarchy has had a nasty shaking. Sample box from Emma has come via Lil. Em phoned.

---

are a little group of seven running north from Nile Street, Kingsland Road, and a third group round Wilmer Gardens', though Wilmer Gardens, just to the north of the school where Gladys taught, was then being rebuilt and some of the houses off Nile Street demolished (p. 349). Three of these streets were coloured black, signifying criminality, on the *New Survey*'s map of this area.

14. According to one of the main local papers, the *Islington Gazette*, writing about 'The King's Abdication' (11 December 1936, p. 7), 'It is scarcely believable that Edward's services to his people are no longer available as King ... A wonderful association with his people seems as a golden and severed cord. But there it is.'

Sunday, 13 December. Bay phoned. To Covent Garden Beecham Concert but did not stay for Brahms *Requiem*. Saw Leo, Murray and Mrs. O. in the distance. Talked with a stodgy man on my right, sallow and rather smelly. Garvin's article in the *Observer* ['Sorrow and Strength', p. 16] nearly made me vomit with its slush and the reference to our new King who fought at Jutland. I bet he was well out of the firing range?

Monday, 14 December. Lil wrote. She is still suffering gastric trouble. I do hope it isn't cancer. Gale blowing all day. Wireless and newspapers still all mush about the new King and Queen.

Tuesday, 15 December. Lil wrote, also Lily Monkhouse. The latter has been for two months with Wackers who had a motor accident. Mrs. W. has been in bed that time. I'll never begrudge them Pollie Monkhouse's legacy after their enduring two months of Lily! Met Mrs. Morton for tea. She let me pay as always. Impudence! It's not the money – it's the encroachment. Met Nina and Denys in Hackney but they did not see me. Had they done so and had Denys spoken, I should have copied St. Peter and denied him. I don't want to identify myself with that crew again. Suffered a frightful outburst of temper today at a boy's dullardry.

Wednesday, 16 December. Somewhat more amiable today. Lil wrote. Shopping tonight. Crowds out and travelling a consequent trial of strength. Bought a cheap hat. Phoned Editha about my Xmas purchases. She carefully evades inviting me to a meal. She will leave the goods here when she goes to Aubert Park [in Highbury] tomorrow.

Thursday, 17 December. Marjorie Rose wrote. She has been to yet another eye specialist. This one said 'Throw away your dark spectacles and forget yourself in work and play'. Miss Hammond and I 'in collision' again. She says I 'soft soap' people and she can't endure it. She also alleges that I 'soft soap' all men regardless of their age and show women I don't care for them. If that were true I shouldn't have so many boring women hanging round me. Maybe I do show what I think of *her* – Miss Hammond. Not much.

Friday, 18 December. Sent a note in to Miss Hammond suggesting perhaps she'd rather not walk tram-wards with me at night. Alas! She sent in to say she often felt very fond of me; I only annoyed her sometimes. I had hoped to lose her company. The school-keeper's wife had an accident – fell in a faint and cut the back of her head. To Rosenbergs. Rug from Leslie. Silk stockings from Mrs. Rosenberg. Table-mats from Clarrie and table-cloth and napkins from Marjorie. Marjorie has seen yet another specialist. The latest verdict is NO eye-trouble but stomach-trouble.

Saturday, 19 December. Winnie Riebold phoned. She sounded hopelessly incoherent and insanely voluble. Evie left £200. Winnie accuses her mother of treachery and apparently her mother accuses her and Dollie similarly. I think there is little doubt Mrs. Robinson [Gladys's landlady] is pregnant.

* * * * * *

Tuesday, 22 December. Bout of hysteria and no wonder. Xmas party at school. Bedlam let loose! Home, prepared to entertain Em and found *no* goods delivered from Lyons, parcels and oddments galore scattered around by 'char' who had also put cat's pan at such an angle as to force him to be dirty on the floor. Letter from Leonard announcing his probable arrival tonight. Consternation reigned supreme. I knew he wouldn't want to meet Em. Then he phoned. He'd try to see me during next week – very likely will come here. Em and Kathlyn [aged about eleven] not very attractive guests. K. has scratched my mahogany table *very* badly with a book I lent her.

Wednesday, 23 December. Somewhat calmer at school. Mr. Pickering *is* a mean man. He never sends his staff so much as a card at Christmas. He is so negligent he never even troubled to see there were bags of goodies for my boys when they were being distributed to the whole school – but I'd paid the same amount as the others. Finally we retrieved enough bags for all except the boy Thomas, whose mother has given clothes and done so much for the school. I thought Pickering would surely have produced 6d but no, he merely said 'Hard luck, Thomas, old boy, you're left out'. Then they say men are better and more understanding as teachers of boys than women are! Imagine the disappointment of the lad. Fortunately I had bought a special present for the boy as he'd given me one. I also gave him the six oranges Mr. Hewson had given me. Rushed 'up west'; changed the gaudy gloves Leonard had bought at Weiss's for a 10s 11d pair of black and white kid ones. Home to find card from Griffiths and Miss Short. Despatched scarf to Lily Monkhouse and engagement pad to Leo. Reading queer book by Geoffrey Gorer, who wrote *Africa Dances* [1935]. It is called *Bali and Angkor* [*or, Looking at Life and Death*, 1936] and dwells on mysticism and the supernatural – most interesting.[15]

Thursday, 24 December, Xmas Eve. So quiet. Few letters and cards. Present from Mrs. Bowden last night, stationery from Stelle, but

---

15. The social anthropologist Geoffrey Gorer (1905–1985) was the sort of writer who would have appealed to Gladys's taste for social observation, which she was to make full use of in 1939 as a Mass-Observer (below, Part Two). She does not indicate whether she had read Gorer's 1936 book, *Nobody Talks Politics: A Satire with an Appendix on our Political Intelligentsia*.

no letter. Little desultory shopping. To Library. Phoned Editha. Leo phoned me. Many *young* women the worse for drink.

Monday, 28 December. Returned from Bumpstead last night. Lil and Challis did everything to pleasure me but, oh, how bored I was! They care for nought that interests me. Challis, at 64, plays for hours with two penny trick toys, card games and such childlike diversions. He knows everything – according to himself – his oracle being Lady Houston, whom he quotes for politics, psychical research and cough cures![16] He's usually wrong on matters of common knowledge. How Lil endures him, I don't know. He offends the eye, the ear and the brain. To make matters worse, I had to travel to and from with Annie Challis who is as inane and nearly as dogmatic as her brother.

At midday Bay phoned, then my beloved Leonard saying he would meet me this afternoon. He came at 3 p.m. and we indulged in a wild orgy of love-making. No one would realise that the almost cruelly fond bed-mate is the sober, satirical middle-aged man of office-hours. After all these years, his lightest touch sets all my pulses a'throb, yet I'm glad now we never married. He is too much engulfed by his family. Yet it gratifies me to know that I, at 46⅔, can still rouse him to a demonstration of mad passion. Went to Editha's to supper, a very light supper it was, too, but I enjoyed myself. Kiernan has a good pawky humour.

Tuesday, 29 December. Bought two new blouses. My party. The Porters came; she brought me a fine cut-glass powder-bowl. Wellings brought my atlas, a Xmas box. Clowser promised a book which I don't particularly want. Gaye – Darling Charles – looked radiant and was very pleased at his having achieved publication – in his Bank magazine! Only that! He told us of the ill-treatment his sister had received at the hands of Mary Flynn and her paramour (the couple convicted for the murder of the Shepherd's Bush widow). Mary Flynn worked as a servant for Gayes for three months and then stayed out all night, returning when his sister was alone, with the man who beat Miss Gaye to her knees twice. She had to escape via two back-gardens and when neighbours phoned for the police, they found the couple had gone and taken £5, all the available cash, with them.[17] Leslie phoned. He seemed

16. Dame Fanny Lucy Houston (b. 1857), who claimed prophetic powers, was a strident and wealthy right-wing chauvinist and seen by many as deranged. She was also a passionate supporter of Edward VIII and, in reaction to his abdication, had stopped eating. She would die the next day.
17. Mary Flynn was convicted with Alfred Stratford for the murder of Elizabeth Ada Fortescue (alias Fortschunk) at Roseford Gardens, Shepherds Bush, on 11 August 1936. On 19 November 1936 Stratford was sentenced to death (which, with a jury recommendation for mercy, was soon commuted to life imprisonment) while Mary Flynn was to serve eight years for manslaughter. The felons were Bethnal Green neighbours who decided to exchange their grim lives for ones of adventure and hoped-for riches. He was a 41-year-old decorated former soldier with an arm withered by war wounds while she was an attractive, shapely

to think me negligent for not having written about the rug he sent me, but I had already thanked him once.

* * * * * *

Thursday, 31 December. Returned magazine with a letter to Charles. Offered my services as volunteer librarian to Red Cross Library. Wrote to Bay and an affectionate letter to Wellings. Went to Leo's last night. Murray's face had been burned by flying fat. It's a grand house in Clevedon Square where they live but of course all let out in rooms and the bathroom a welter of squashed dentifrice tubes and shabby tooth-brushes. They are furnishing their Colville Square house piecemeal. Leo *is* a dangerous person. He is always writing threatening letters to people who offend him. I make no New Year's resolutions as I once did but I feel calmer and more serene this year than I have ever done before.

* * * * * *

Monday, 4 January 1937. Joan Sutton wrote. To Wellings' last night but needless to say Editha did not phone invitation as she had promised to do. She *never* keeps her word. Clowser brought my Xmas box, a book I didn't particularly want. He also lent me [Henry Fielding's] *Tom Jones*, at my request. He still talks of buying a house and my sharing it. Miss Newton, Head Mistress of Skinners School in my time, is much in my thoughts nowadays. For years I have hated her and wished her ill for the humiliation to which I was subjected when I was a 'Scholar-ship' girl at her school. At long last that hatred has gone. I realise now that she could have known nothing of the agony of spirit to which she subjected a very poor adolescent girl. She thought only of the prestige of her school.[18] I am glad that there is no one against whom I am embittered. I even understand my ex-mother-in-law's spitefulness for I spoiled her boy's life even as he spoiled mine. Poor George!

Tuesday, 5 January. To Caledonian Market. Bought a fine brown pottery jug (very like a bel-ami jug without the usual face on it) for 6d.

20-year-old domestic servant with a spritely walk. A hazy photo of them used by police for identification purposes reveals a cheerful 'Bonnie and Clyde'-like duo with more optimism than good sense. At trial they admitted to robbing and tying up the victim but did not think they had killed her. Police evidence seemed to verify that death by suffocation was accidental. The two admitted having earlier attacked and robbed Mary Flynn's previous employer, who was able to escape. It is possible that this mistress was a member of Gaye's family; we cannot be certain. Flynn and Stratford's convictions owed much to new technology as well as police persistence. The photo mentioned above was purchased by police from a news agency and, with the help of the Kodak Company's projection equipment, shown on screens over 7,300 times to possible witnesses before the suspects were identified and apprehended. A full account of this case is available in the National Archives, MEPO 3/1716.

18. Emily Newton was headmistress at the Skinners' Company high school for girls in Hackney between 1900 and 1927.

Excellent value.[19] Bay came. Cooked her a hot dinner and gave her my grey costume.

Wednesday, 6 January. Leonard sent a £5 note – a loan. Delay due to his having been in bed with a cold. I expect he caught it here. My bedroom *was* chilly and he is delicate. *Dear* Leonard! Shopping at the sales but bought little. I wish the German–Spanish feud would die out. I do so dread war!

Thursday, 7 January. To Sadler's Wells last night for *Figaro*. In the pit queue a young man started a conversation with me and inside he seated himself beside me. He came originally from Oxford but had lived in the North too, also for longish periods in Portugal. His father was in Wireless & Cables and now the boy is in their Home Staff. He is living at the Tottenham Court Road YMCA and goes to quite a few films, theatres, etc. We were talking gaily about Studio One when a middle-aged couple in front joined in and we had quite a jolly evening together. Opera company was *very* good. Letter from Lil. Walked around Islington this afternoon, Colebrooke Row, Duncan Terrace [just east of the Angel station] and Cross Street [near Canonbury station] – 'Fallen glory'. To the Academy Cinema. Saw *Confetti* – quite amusing – and *The Secret Agent* with John Gielgud looking brave but bilious, Peter Lorre like a black boy servant in a Rossetti picture, and Madeline Carroll very pretty and completely brainless. A silly film.

Friday, 8 January. To Chapel Street market this afternoon; fruit very cheap, peaches 2d each. Called at Wellings' Library for *Manhattan Side Street*, very like *Street Scene*.[20] To Brondesbury. Mrs. Rosenberg at loggerheads with Sophie Samuel who failed to make herself agreeable at a party Clarrie gave. Later we went down to Samuels' flat and played 'Monopoly', a most idiotic game that went on and on so long

19. The Caledonian Market, about a mile north of King's Cross Station, was described in 1936 as 'the largest and most popular of all the London street markets' (Mary Benedetta, *The Street Markets of London* [London; 1936; reprinted New York: Benjamin Blom, 1972], p. 155). On some days of the week it was a cattle market, but on Tuesday and Friday it became the lively venue for the sale of all sorts of goods, such as radio sets, car parts, locks and files, antiques, and fine bits of silver (many with tell-tale coats of arms burnished off). The hundreds of stall-holders were supplemented by other sellers and pedlars of junk who simply laid their wares out on the pavement. For many Londoners, the market was as much a source of entertainment as a place to shop. Some memories of the market from the between the two world wars are recorded in Marjorie Edwards, *Up the Cally: The History and Recollections of London's Old Caledonian Market* (London: Marketprompt, 1989). 'To spend a day at the Cally was like spending a day in another world – a friendly, warm, intimate world of fun and laughter and jostling crowds. The Cally was all things to all people' (pp. 33–4). With the outbreak of the Second World War it ceased to exist and the space was taken over by the military.

20. Jay J. Dratler was the author of the 1936 novel *Manhattan Side Street*; *Street Scene* was a three-act play of 1929 by the American playwright Elmer Rice.

I nearly lost the last train home. I can't understand reasonable adults sitting for hours over such rubbishy amusements.

* * * * * *

Monday, 18 January. Dirty day and I'm on playground duty! Lil wrote. Enjoyed my visit to Wellings' very much last night. Much talk of books and I didn't have to appear too great an ignoramus as I do when art or music are the topics under consideration. I read Lecky's *History of European Morals* and Gibbon's *Decline and Fall* years before I met either Wellings *or* Clowser – in fact, in the days when I read to please Leonard. Mr. Kerr had at school an extract from an American paper referring to our Royal family in most insulting terms – sneering at George VI's having served at Jutland and describing Edward VIII as one who was a notorious drunkard and brawler at rowdy parties, alleging he had fouled at least four men's beds as an adulterer, and as for 'odd nights' he was a 'tramp' where beds were concerned. It pointed out [the husband] Simpson's helplessness since he could hardly punch his King's nose! It added Simpson would be amply revenged when 'Davy' (Edward VIII) was tied to a woman soon to become a withered hag, however much her hair was dyed and her face lifted and who would when they quarrelled, as they inevitably would, say 'Well, Davy, you weren't much "spec" yourself'.

* * * * * *

Wednesday, 20 January. Mr. Pickering suddenly asked this afternoon if I would accompany him to the Geffrye Museum where Mrs. [Marjorie] Quennell is now Curator and she was going to lecture to teachers. Nine of us turned up.[21] Mrs. Quennell proved to be very attrac-

---

21. The Geffrye Museum on Kingsland Road, not far from Hamond Square School where Gladys was teaching, was housed in almshouses built around 1715 at the bequest of a former Mayor of London and Master of the Ironmongers' Company, Sir Robert Geffrye. The museum featured (as it still does) displays of English domestic interiors; it aimed to provide 'a picture of family life, as lived through the centuries before our own, as well as being a collection of wood and ironwork for the use of students' (LCC pamphlet on the museum from 1938) – this neighbourhood of Shoreditch was a centre of furniture and cabinet making.

   In the later 1930s the Geffrye was being reorganised and one of its new priorities (documented by press clippings from 1938–1948 in a book also held in the museum's archive) was educational outreach; it was to offer tours to school children and their teachers. In his *Clouds of Glory*, p. 307, Hoxtonian Bryan Magee (b. 1930) recalls how much he valued the museum as a child in the later 1930s. 'Because it was City-oriented, yet in a positive way ungrand, it showed me the past of a London I recognised, and I could see its continuity with the present. I found it compellingly interesting. I identified with it personally, and thought of it as showing me my own history. And because the museum was free I dropped in many times', often with a friend, sometimes on his own, thereby reinforcing his attachment to this part of London. See also Molly Harrison, *Museum Adventure: The Geffrye Museum and its Educational Activities* (London: University of London Press, 1950), pp. 40–2. (While there were twenty-three primary schools in Shoreditch, there was no secondary school: *New Survey of London*, III, 350.) The curator's husband was the social historian Peter Quennell and together they produced a number of popular works of social history, which was

tive – *I* thought. She is fortyish, florid, fattish, well-groomed, and with a lovely sheen in her yellow-brown hair. I can't say she struck me as being particularly well suited for her job. She was too fond of dilating on personal matters, too repetitive and too hazy about details, while she made continual reference to her childhood days, her nursery, the cook and so on. She wants to find out where she can obtain book backs to fill the book-shelves in the Alfred Stevens room. I said I'd enquire from Wellings [owner of four private libraries] and let her know. I was the only woman present who spoke, and *I* looked drab and ugly. To the Tatler tonight. Disappointing programme – *The Immortal Swan* I'd seen and disliked before, the Disney cartoon, *Mickey's Circus*, I'd seen twice before. Gave Mrs. Bowden a bunch of tulips for her 94th birthday!

Thursday, 21 January. Pay-day – £24.2.6. Met Daisy Fulford – Mrs. Gray – also Editha. The latter was taking a party of girls to the Cinema. Editha told me of a man who recently went to 'Barts' [hospital] for treatment for V.D. When he was uncovered in readiness for the injection to be made the surgeon and students were confronted with his tattooed bottom on which appeared a woman's face and the words 'A Merry Christmas. Come again soon!'

Friday, 22 January. To Brondesbury. Leslie and I indulged in some amateurish psychoanalysis and thereby annoyed Mrs. Rosenberg who likes talk to be 'small'.

Saturday, 23 January. Went to Em's new house in Eastern Avenue in a deluge. House is good enough but district is depressing. It's neither town nor country. Hoardings start up like mushrooms. Railed in spaces raise weeds and derelict petrol cans. Bought a tweed coat for 59s 11d. To Hackney Library. Hackney Town Hall is either under repair or removal – couldn't see which in the dark.[22]

* * * * * *

Monday, 25 January. School again! Conway absent. Letters from Porters and Lil. The former cannot come on the 4th. I expect I shall cancel the party. To the Tatler tonight. My neighbour, a middle-aged foreigner, pinched my legs and held my hand in a vice-like grip so I kindly said 'You know I'm not young', not wanting to give him a

then relatively new and clearly compatible with Gladys's interest in things social, whether current or past. We are grateful to Emma Hardy for her advice on sources relating to the museum.

22. 'Hackney alters out of all recognition', she wrote a few days later, on 4 February. 'The Town Hall is being pulled down. A new road leading to blocks of modern flats is at the top of Well Street and a new cinema, the Regal, is there. Parnells have closed down. Marks & Spencer have superseded Matthew Rose.'

shock when the lights went up. Soon after this revelation he left. These men are queer, almost like dogs poking about the female form.

* * * * * *

Thursday, 4 March. Polling day for London County Council. Still cold. Better tempered at school. Bay phoned. To Queen's Hall to hear [violinist Jascha] Heifetz play, Nicolai Malko conducting. He was accorded a tremendous ovation and was recalled again and again but would not give an encore. While waiting at Tottenham Court Road for a bus was astonished by an apparently respectable but very lame middle-aged man who lifted up his sticks and clashed them in mid-air again and again, calling down meanwhile curses upon Christ and God, shouting menaces at the heaven and obscene derision to the stars. Bitterly cold.

* * * * * *

Wednesday, 17 March. Porters, Clowser and Wellings came. Lottie's unsatisfactory sex-life makes for fearsome behaviour *and* conversation. I wonder if I am similarly affected? She told me [she] recently went to a chiropodist's and while in the waiting room had an unconquerable desire to make water. She therefore took a large vase from the mantelpiece, went behind a piano and used it as a chamber pot. She tried to empty the vase out of a window but was prevented from so doing by a wedged window-frame so had to leave the vase full of urine. Finally, after two days of anxiously wondering what developments had occurred, she phoned to make another engagement. She returned, this time taking a large empty pickle-jar with her. The room was empty as before and the vase was unemptied but now had innumerable cigarette ends added to its liquid contents. She emptied the whole into the pickle jar, screwed on its top, saw the chiropodist and finally returned home emptying the jar by the way.

Looked at a flat in Northolme Road tonight – 22s 6d for three rooms and bathroom and lavatory. The usual very ordinary middle-aged woman as landlady but quite pleasant and the rooms and staircase are a marked improvement on these [at 50 Highbury Park].[23] Lil wrote. We have to give 5s each to Topley's present. There are terrible floods in the Fenland and a landslide at Folkestone.

23. Gladys's search for a new place to live had thus far not gone well. On 17 January she had inspected a flat on Chetwynd Road, NW5. 'People have impudence to offer you such accommodation at a guinea a week! Two dark slip-like rooms under the eaves, not even newly decorated, one without a fireplace. The third was a small landing rigged up with gas-stove and a miniature sink! All very dark and nowhere near Hampstead Heath, as advertised – nearer tram-lines.' She again went flat-hunting on 5 February 'but the one in Highbury Hill I viewed had no bathroom of its own'.

Thursday, 18 March. School very aggravating as Pickering's word cannot be relied on for five minutes. I have to take my own handwork *and* drill next term. Perhaps it has advantages for I'm not fond of changing classes. To look once again at flat and the good landlady, Mrs. Lucas, undertakes to clean stairs for 6d extra each week. She also promises to re-paper room within at least a year. I think Robinsons will take over this flat and maybe buy my coal. Phoned Editha and removal contractor.

* * * * * *

Thursday, 25 March. Removed today to 4 Northolme Road, N.5, a three-roomed flat with my own bathroom and lavatory – at last. This is the first time I have undertaken a removal without even the aid of a 'char' and I *am* weary. Went first to the Sun Insurance Company to get policy altered. Then went back to find gas-fitters in operation. To new flat where landlord helped me to lay carpet and hang curtains. Then Mrs. Robinson gave me a hot luncheon and Mr. R. made me a cup of tea. Removal men experienced great difficulty in getting chair upstairs here. Lil sent a letter of welcome, Bay a Greetings telegram. Slaved at getting place straight, much hindered by the fact that electric light is not on yet.

Good Friday, 26 March. Snow and sleet and a high wind. Bad night because cat is so unhappy in new abode. Wrote to Lil and Mr. Gaye and Postmaster of district. All straight now except stair-carpet which is not yet laid. Wireless set in flat beneath brays aplenty.

Saturday, 27 March. Leo and Murray came last night but the promised installation of wireless is hardly a success. Leo has only done one room. I gave him a picture and some curtains for his new house. I am to visit it on the day after I go back to school. Mr. Freeman wrote, also Lily Monkhouse. She's still staying on with the Wackers. To the Gaumont Theatre this afternoon and saw the *Three Smart Girls*, a film that has been highly praised but which I found foolish in the extreme. Did not go into the Tatler as it's an all-Disney programme and I've seen most of the films being shown, more than once. Begin to feel lonely here.

Easter Sunday, 28 March. Bright but cold and I've no spare cash so I stayed at home, getting progressively gloomier as I always do when I stay within doors for hours on end. The houses all seem in a dead faint. I suppose their occupants are away for the holiday. Wrote several letters.

Easter Monday, 29 March. My landlord laid the stair-carpet. He would not let me pay him so I bought a pound of biscuits for 1s 6d at

Lyons' for his wife. Went westwards this afternoon and saw *Road to Rome* [by Robert E. Sherwood, 1927] at the Savoy. I saw it on its first production in London and liked it immensely then but either my taste has changed or my first judgment was unduly favourable for I found it very ordinary this time, just facetious in the main and only occasionally witty.

Tuesday, 30 March. Saw the film *Good Earth* [about Chinese farmers struggling to survive] at the Palace, paying 2s 6d for a deplorable seat, high as Olympus. The photography was exquisite, Luise Rainer superb, conveying so much expression, so little by speech. She alone of the adult characters appeared to age. I thought Paul Muni miscast. He was too 'busy', more like a Simon Tappertit than a Wai Lun. Besides I never knew Chinese labourers continually guffawed. I thought they hardly smiled. The woman's character is grim, frightening. Whenever I see films of other lands, I rejoice I live in England where weather may be aggravating but is not appalling (in the true sense) and where famine does not threaten. I thought the Uncle's character just cheaply funny. What crowds of Hindus there are in England!

Wednesday, 31 March. Since the sun shone for once I went to Hampstead Heath and sat in the Spaniards Road but the cold wind soon drove me home. In the evening I went to Sadler's Wells where I heard [Mozart's] *The Magic Flute.* I enjoyed it but I was so aching for conversation – I've had so much of my own company this holiday – I entered into conversation unasked with a pleasant youth on my right.

Thursday, 1 April. Met Lil and Challis at King's Cross and I felt at first elated. I thought we should recapture some of the days of pleasurable excitement I used to know as a child when Lil took me out. Alas, we have all changed. I demand more real companionship, she no longer takes any interest in anything save acquiring more and more oddments. Challis, whose intellect was never remarkable, is now an arrant fool. He stands for hours gaping at 'novelties' and trick toys. He runs about thrusting information, usually wrong, upon other visitors. He tells Exhibition salesmen how to run their own jobs and he looks like an old countryman whose acquaintance with cleanliness is only of the nodding variety. His handkerchief was filthy, his hands grimed, his table manners disgusting. Lil and he had a system for viewing the Ideal Homes Exhibition.[24] They kept parting and meeting and wasting valuable time showing one another where to meet next time. We had to leave at 5 p.m. as they wanted to catch a coach. I was relieved to see

---

24. This 21st *Daily Mail* Ideal Home Exhibition at Olympia was opened by the Duke and Duchess of Gloucester and much celebrated by the newspaper (30 March 1937, pp. 3 and 4).

them go, particularly as there had been 'an incident' during the day. I said I wanted to go alone to see the vacuum cleaners. I did, and the demonstration by the Goblin salesman took so long Lil grew anxious and thought I was lost. Why, goodness knows, as I had said where I was going and they had only to walk along the vacuum cleaners' display section to have seen me. I paid 10s deposit on a cleaner and have to pay the balance of £10.10.0 in 21 payments. Finally I bought a few trifles before we had to come away and then I rushed home and off again to the Queen's Hall. Duke and Duchess of Kent were there. I liked the Arnold Bax item and even found Delius' *Florida* attractive but I loathed the brassy violence of Vaughan Williams' *Flourish for a Coronation*.

* * * * * *

Sunday, 4 April. Editha came to tea yesterday. She admired the flat. She makes me smile because, according to her, no one manages her own life properly. She is always inveighing against mothers who are too possessive, wives who cling like ivy and husbands who treat their wives as play-things. But be her idiosyncrasies what they may, I'm very fond of Editha. Then I went on to sup at Lottie's. The Duttons were there. Mr. D. shows signs of wear and tear but his wife, thanks to hairdresser, dentist and corsetiere, shows little sign of aging. There was another couple there, an Australian woman married to a man who had been in that Colony over ten years but who is now farming in Hertfordshire. The farmer would have been interesting but Lottie allows no one to monopolise the conversation except herself and she always gives it a lewd tone. She surpassed herself last night, telling us all how she and Vernon bathed together, not in the sea but in the bathroom, and how they didn't know which part of which anatomy was washed by which! I feel sorry for her since, apparently, her unsatisfactory married life makes her get her sex gratification in this unfortunate way. Porter looked absolutely murderous – and small wonder! Phoned Leo this morning. He wants to come on Tuesday and finish wiring the rooms so my tea-party assumes a yet more unwieldy size.

Monday, 5 April. Lil wrote. Em phoned. To Wellings' last night; Clowser there. He hates to be proved wrong and hedges at once as he did when we discussed the correct usage of the word 'rostrum'. He also decries concerts, plays, players that he hasn't recommended. Housework today. Now going off to last of the Courtauld [Malcolm] Sargent concerts.

Tuesday, 6 April. School re-opened. Ugh! Met a pleasant young female at the Concert and told her I would invite her here. I fancy she has designs on Leo. Did a foolish thing. Invited a crowd when I might have known I would be weary from a first day back at school.

22

Em and the loathsome Margaret, Bay and Miss Wilshin and Leo. The latter turned the place upside down and then departed – after 11 p.m. – leaving the set useless as before.

Wednesday, 7 April. Rushed home, bathed, then to Leo's. He and Murray have worked miracles, furnishing that 16-roomed house out of oddments bought at street-markets. These have been re-upholstered, re-painted and what not. I was introduced to Fraulein Schubert, a guest staying with them on a non-profit basis. She was fortyish, fair and faded; agreeable and obviously middle class. Her English was idiomatic but queerly accented. Later Miss Greaves, another 'non-profit' guest, arrived. She was 69 and a crank religionist, very anxious to be noticed. I find school *very* wearisome; such young children madden me and there are constant interruptions in these days. Goblin cleaner delivered but I had no time to try it.

Thursday, 8 April. What a day! I was nearly distraught. School unbearable and my foot is bad again. Home to housework and to find cleaner difficult to manipulate, wireless, despite all Leo's tinkering AND purchases, useless. Then Mr. Lucas came up. Bought sundry oddments for wireless from *him*; then his daughter came up to demonstrate correct use of cleaner. Then Mrs. Cora Gordon phoned!!! I was so bewildered at first I muddled her with Mrs. Quennell. Then I remembered I had written to Mrs. G. about a character in one of her books. We talked about a half hour and she says if ever I go to hear her lecture I must introduce myself. I will![25] Then I discovered Lallie was missing. Mrs. Lucas, Mr. Lucas and I scoured the streets and gardens. Finally I went round to 50 Highbury Park. Here to my utter amazement Miss Bowden accused me of having taken away electric light fitments. She lit a candle and took me up to demonstrate her loss only to find the fitments were there!! She's hopelessly incapable. Back I came and further street-hunt produced my darling cat. He had gone about 100 yards down the road.

Friday, 9 April. Just as irritable at school. I wish I could curb my ill-humour but I *do* hate my work and I feel so lonely, no Leonard, no Darling Charles. Used my cleaner tonight. Mr. Lucas has put my wireless into action, thank goodness. Did much laundering.

Saturday, 10 April. Em phoned. I'm borrowing more money of her and visiting her on Tuesday. After shopping went to see the film *Elephant Boy* at Leicester Square Theatre. No sex interest but an enthralling film and the little Hindu boy was a delight to eye and ear, slim little body, mellow voice. Tea at an Express Dairy Depot, then to

---

25. Cora Gordon was the author, with Jan Gordon (mentioned above, 25 October), of numerous books, including *The London Roundabout* (1933), which was illustrated by the authors.

the Phoenix to see *Climbing*, surely the most idiotic farce yet produced. Here and there is a clever satirical touch but mostly faulty farce. No wonder the theatre was practically empty! Saw a perfectly strange man volunteer to take a piece of grit out of a lady's eye at the bus-stop at the corner. He apparently succeeded too.

*The next several weeks, while not uneventful, produced little in the way of noteworthy diary-writing. For a few days Gladys was in ill humour, especially at school. 17 April was, 'Alas, my 47th birthday!! And I'm not wearing well though I'm getting much slimmer again.' The next day, a Sunday, she 'Hoped – but in vain – that Leonard might come. It seems that the break is here at last.' 'Temper not very angelic', she wrote on 22 April. 'I wish I could cure it. I know I'm mentally tired and physically unsatisfied.' As usual, her weeks were full of outings to concerts, the cinema, and the theatre. On Saturday, 24 April she went to the National Gallery 'to see new French pictures on loan there'. Preparations for the upcoming Coronation (on 12 May) were much in evidence, as she noted on 8 May. 'Streets are packed with people, largely provincials, all agape to see the decorations, which are very similar to those up at the Jubilee and the Royal Weddings. I'm weary of the Royal pictures in cinema programmes, Coronation items in daily papers and weekly magazines. In an animal dealer's, I actually saw tortoises with Union Jacks painted on their backs!' The King and Queen paid a flying visit to Islington and there were of course local coronation festivities (*Islington and Holloway Press, 15 May 1937, p. 1 and 22 May, pp. 6 and 7*). During the holidays for the Coronation Gladys visited her sister Lil in Helions Bumpstead, did some sightseeing in nearby Suffolk, and had a row with her brother-in-law, Challis.*

Monday, 24 May. Decidedly warm and still no buses [they were on strike]. Very hot journey to Wellings' last night. Clowser came late. Coming home saw a very unpleasant incident. A young couple, enthralled by each other, gazed fondly into each other's eyes while seated on a tram-seat. Another young couple seated behind had a young child which they plied with bananas and chocolate. As they jogged the child up and down it suddenly vomited all over the young lovers in front. The young woman looked as though she had been in a snow-storm – spectacles, face and rose-pink costume were all drenched.

Mr. Gaye wrote – a charming letter but complaining I was too Martha-like [domestically attentive] in entertaining. Kitty O'Brien is not coming tomorrow [to her party]. Leo phoned. He has no boarders and talks of giving up the [rooming] house. He says he, Murray and Fraulein Schubert (!!!) will take an unfurnished flat and live together. He was very annoyed when I said, 'Well, you *have* a mother-fixation. You do like old women.' 'She's not old,' he said angrily. Now she's quite 40 and he's 26 or 27.

On Saturday, 29 May Gladys went to Richmond and sat by the Thames. 'Spoke to no one, saw no one I knew and came back feeling sick horror of returning to Hoxton on Monday. Sometimes I wish I could get my breakdown pension.'Occasionally she took note of public sights. 'What a lot of street walkers have pet dogs with them nowadays!' (2 June).[26] *When queuing for the ballet that evening she was entertained by a 'very clever performer' – 'a queer little Cockney, ugly, unwashed'; 'his tricks were based in simple scientific facts but his "patter" was superb'. The next day she had a meal with Bay at Flemings. 'Talked to the waitress who looked so tired. She said her hours were 10 a.m.to 11 p.m.' On Saturday, 5 June she 'Saw girls in scanty costume advertising Health and Beauty Display in Hyde Park by parading as sandwich women in Piccadilly'.*

Monday, 14 June. For once I was anxious to return to school to allay my fears. On Friday, because a boy deliberately lied to me, I rapped his finger tips with a stick of pencil and one finger bled. It had obviously been bitten to the quick and had bled before but he declared I had wrought the mischief although he didn't seem to bear me any [ill] will. As a matter of fact I like the boy and he knows it and had I not been over-hot and with frayed nerves, I doubt if I should have spanked him. I fully expected his mother this morning, probably armed with a summons. Nothing however materialised and I have tried to be more amiable today.[27] To Wellings' last night. Clowser there 'all het up' with the marvels of Maiden Castle [an Iron Age hill fort near Dorchester]. I thought his enthusiasm a little exaggerated but then I've not seen the earthworks. Wrote ten closely covered pages to Gaye tonight.

* * * * * *

Wednesday, 16 June. Bay wrote and I replied. My temper remains highly inflammable. Miss Hammond had an unpleasant experience today. She caned a boy and he fainted in her arms. She found out he had a splinter in his hand. It had been there a week and was very painful. I'm glad it wasn't *my* bad luck. Housework tonight – after consuming a pound of strawberries too, 8d per pound in Hoxton, 10d and 1s locally. Mr. Pickering had to go to Mandeville Street LCC School today. He found the Head Mistress in a fume. The Basque refugee children adopted by the Salvation Army [as a consequence of the Spanish Civil War] climb over the wall at the Congress Hall [on

---

26. Later this year she again remarked on these women: 'Gerrard Street is full of prostitutes. One, very fashionably attired, came teetering along on high heels and a second called across to a third, also waiting for custom, "She makes me want to piss to look at her!"' (1 October 1937).
27. Bryan Magee (b. 1930), who attended the nearby Gopsall Street School in Hoxton in the 1930s, recalled that teachers routinely smacked their students (*Clouds of Glory*, pp. 47–9; also p. 178).

Linscott Road, Clapton, where they were being accommodated] and raid the district. They steal the school children's balls and invade the playground in hosts so the police had to be called.[28]

* * * * * *

Friday, 18 June. Not quite so bad-tempered at school. The senior school – the Whitmore – to which we send our older scholars, had a holiday today and several of the boys called. The first few stayed awhile and finally asked permission to return for my General Knowledge questions and Literature story after 'play-time'. I gave permission and they duly returned bringing others till I had about 20 and some were from other schools. My pride was much gratified. After the questions I told the story of *Macbeth*. Lil wrote.

Saturday, 19 June. To the Hippodrome to see the Philadelphia Ballet but did not go in as I refused to pay 2s 6d for standing-room. Sat in St. James's Park instead. Put down 6d campstool in New Theatre queue for *The Great Romancer* [by Jules Eckert Goodman]. Enjoyed the play immensely. Robert Morley, the newly 'arrived' young actor, was splendid. He reminded me of a much kindlier Charles Laughton. Not a very crowded 'house'. Man in fantastic dress brought a monkey in a red jacket as a queue performer. He said *he* wasn't going to plead poverty or whine for coppers for a bed. He continued he was a genuine artist and had broadcast and was going to be televised. At the junction of St. John's Road and Theobald's Road saw the horse of a London Midland and Scotland van fall and smash its left shaft while the driver was flung through space, landing on his feet with a terrible jar on the pavement. People screamed, men flew to the rescue but the bus in which I rode passed on.

---

28. The *Hackney Gazette and North Islington Advertiser*, 28 May 1937, p. 5, reported enthusiastically on the arrival of these child refugees, some 400 of them. 'Clutching dolls, toys and Coronation flags, they might have been mistaken for school children on an outing, except for an occasional strained and weary little face and the distinguishing mark of the refugee – pathetic little bundles and parcels of clothes, anxiously gripped. Each child wore a label marked "Expedicion a Ingleterra," and bearing his or her name and that of the town or village from which the child came.' They were greeted by a crowd of about 2,000, 'mainly mothers and their children', and as the Basque children walked from their coaches 'Men and women patted them on the heads, and other children shouted gaily to them. Presents were thrust into their hands, a poorly-dressed woman emptying her purse to buy bars of chocolate which she distributed among a batch of the children. Perched on top of the stone pillars at the side of the Congress Hall gates a number of boys started to sing "The Cururacea," and the Basque children shouted happily back to them.' *The Times*, 27 May 1937, p. 13d, noted how well the refugees were to be cared for: 'The children will sleep in the top floor dormitories at the Congress Hall and will receive educational instruction in class rooms in another part of the building. A daily timetable has been worked out, including periods for physical drill in the gymnasium. The children will also be taken to play in the open air on Hackney Downs. Food will be provided from the large service kitchen, and care has been taken to see that the children get food they are accustomed to.' The Basque Children's Committee was appealing for further support over a year later (*Islington Gazette*, 5 October 1938, p. 1).

* * * * * *

Tuesday, 22 June. Postcard from Leo. He has married Fraulein [Lena] Schubert and she is now on honeymoon with him and Murray!!! I think it's pretty evident she's out to get English nationality. He hasn't even decent clothing. She can't advertise for lessons while she has German nationality. I wonder if they sleep together? Editha is certain she's a spy! Editha insists on coming to *Victoria Regina* with Bay and me tomorrow. Jewish 'supply' teacher at school, male; he says point-blank he's not going to teach the children. He comes late and goes early, even at the dinner interval. He says he has no maid and his child is ill so he has to go home and cook the dinner! I wish the ratepayers would 'jib' at paying for such poor material. Sent 10s to London Teachers' Association and 4s to Lil.

Wednesday, 23 June. Wrote to tell Clowser of Leo's marriage. Met Norah Fisher (now Mrs. Something Else) in the bus. I wonder if I look such a wreck as she does – a whiskery face, battered hat, shiny nose, grey, untidy hair and grievances galore. Her second marriage doesn't appear too happy. He's apparently not prosperous and the child they hoped for proved a miscarriage. She talks about adopting a child. Met Editha and Bay and had a most enjoyable although a suffocatingly hot evening at the Lyric where we saw *Victoria Regina* [by Laurence Housman]. It was very well produced and Pamela Stanley proved a more convincing old woman than a young one. Carl Esmond as the Prince Consort appealed to the feminine eye. Ernest Milton is too mannered an actor nowadays. I thought it strange that none of Victoria's children appeared in the play nor was any reference made to them. I have a violent cold and a high temperature.

Thursday, 24 June. Day of incident at school. Boy in my class fainted in prayer-time. Fire-drill, and while boys drank their milk Norman Tillson sucked up a piece of glass from his bottle. I notified Mr. Pickering who seemed little concerned when I sent the message by the child so I went to him myself and dilated on possibly horrible results. Eventually he sent a note to the mother and the father came up this afternoon to say the child was in hospital under observation.[29] Then I had another boy with running sores to deal with. Meanwhile I've a bad cold, pain in my chest and sore throat and a diabolical temper. I wish I could restrain the latter. It runs away with me and I feel murderous. Not so many people as usual appeared to be Alexandra roses yesterday.[30] Clowser replied.

---

29. This mishap was one of the few recorded by the headteacher in the school's log book for the 1930s (London Metropolitan Archive, EO/DIV4/HAM/LB/2, p. 252).
30. Alexandra Rose Day, named in honour of Queen Alexandra (d. 1925), the wife of Edward VII, was intended to raise money for various charities through the sale of artificial roses.

Friday, 25 June. Kept a more even temper this morning, thank goodness. Lil wrote. To Tatler tonight. Saw a good film of Germany with German commentator, *Overland Express*. For the first time for months, a man in the Tatler pinched my arms and legs and I was grateful for this poor semblance of youth that remains to me. I am so sexually hungry. A woman teacher obtained 20 guineas cost from a landlord who kissed her twice. I should have thought any landlord who kissed a school marm deserved 20 guineas reward!

* * * * * *

Sunday, 27 June. Felt so sure Leonard would come today but he didn't. Bay phoned. Went tonight to St. James's Park. Crowds of ex-servicemen and their womenfolk there after the Royal Review in Hyde Park.[31] One very funny man, tremendously fat and with a Henry VIII face, wore a tiny bowler on top of his huge face. I seem to be putting on weight again. Am reading Gide's book on his recent visit to the USSR explaining his disappointment at the deterioration of the Revolutionary movement.[32]

Monday, 28 June. Card from Wellings who is at Tenby. Phoned Leonard at dinner-time and arranged to meet him at Dawson's at 6 p.m. At first, after this six months' break, I hardly knew what to say to him. He looks old and tired and has no more claim to beauty than I have now. However, we soon got into our stride and by the time we were having ices at King's Cross we were well away on political and historical topics. He lent me £6 for holiday expenses, said he would come to the flat when he could and that perhaps we could have a day's drive together in the summer holidays. He says maybe I should find married life much more trying than single life now. He says I have got into a groove and am too old to change now. He says I want everything from life and want to give nothing. I want to tie someone else but not be tied. He also says I have deliberately ignored social contacts that might have led to wider friendships. Remembering this, I went to call on Wilmots tonight but can't say I had a warm welcome. Mrs. W. showed me the garden but did not offer to introduce me to Ruth and her husband who are living in the upper part of the house. When Mr. W. came in he just spoke and then went upstairs. I stopped talking to Mrs. W. Then though I accepted the proffered cigarette, I wouldn't have coffee, port or sherry. Their place *is* dirty. A litter of oddments covers

---

The *Daily Mail*, 24 June 1937, p. 13, printed a photo of the Duchess of Kent, President of Alexandra Day, acquiring a bouquet of roses before setting out to visit some of the rose depots in London.

31. Some 80,000 veterans from all parts of the country attended this review by the King (*Daily Mail*, 28 June 1937, p. 11).

32. André Gide (b. 1869), a former communist sympathiser, had published *Back from the U.S.S.R.* (translated from the French) earlier that year.

chairs, tables etc. The ornaments are thick with dust and the cigarette box had rouge and lip-stick jammed in it. Ruth may have made a good match but to live in a half-house doesn't strike me as being impressive. Leonard tells me Teddy Rosen floated the Ultra Wireless Co. for £250,000 and is chairman of the company. Mrs. Rosenberg is back.

* * * * * *

Saturday, 3 July. Phoned Em. Denys now seems bent on quarrelling with his brother Kennie. Kennie and his wife, Hylda, have given hospitality and friendship to Denys and Nina and now, because Hylda wrote a letter to Denys, he has answered her very rudely and told her she ought not to address him personally but write joint letters to Mr. and Mrs. Bennett![33] Bought new brown shoes 27s 9d this morning at Barratts in Oxford Street.

This afternoon went by boat from Westminster to Greenwich. An ugly old American woman with a grubby neck and a bewhiskered chin took a good deal of shaking off. Snatched a snack on the quayside, then returned and spent the early evening in St. James's Park. Too hot, alas, for theatre. Miss Hardwick wrote. Interesting to see the great boats going downstream, hauled by tiny tugs. The skipper pointed out those ships of neutral colours likely to be in Spanish waters and bearing their national colours painted on their sides. St. James's Park seems to enshrine the spirit of Charles II. I always feel his presence there. The ducks and waterfowl are very alluring. People's clothing grows ever scantier. A girl in the Park wore a sun-bathing costume and I've seen two youths in the streets today naked save for khaki shorts.

Sunday, 4 July. Bay phoned. I read all day.

Monday, 5 July. To Brondesbury tonight and I enjoyed the visit. Clarrie and Mrs. Freeman, Leslie and 'Tree' there. Leslie in good form, plays and films discussed and I and the two men argued on 'What *is* morality?' Leslie and I argued geography and period decided, Mr. Freeman was all for reducing morality to the confines of chastity. Leslie invited me to join him on his trip north in August. I told him he'd better decide if he really wanted an old woman in tow and tell me next time he saw me.

Tuesday, 6 July. Saw a boy run over in New North Road last night. Bay came. Spoke to Wellings on the phone last night. Miss [Amelia]

---

33. On 15 June Gladys had written that her sister Em was 'terribly upset about Denys's wedding. Apparently the bride's people gave a beer-fight. Kennie and his wife and Denys's best friend, Ralph Butcher, left in disgust but not before they heard Denys pleading with his bride to go home, while she replied "You can go if you like. I'm staying here." They were going to go on drinking all night.'

Earhart is not yet saved [she and her airplane had been lost at sea].
Appeal for Basque children sent round the schools.

Wednesday, 7 July. Went tonight to Covent Garden but the queue was
so long went across instead to the Gaiety to see Uday Shan-Kar and
his Hindu dancers. Talked with a man in the queue and sat with him
inside. He was quite entertaining – had enlisted in 1914 for the Great
War at 16, served in India and been stationed at Benares. He spoke of
the burning ghâts, the fakirs and the bazaars. He had then gone on to
France, been taken prisoner and had endured two years of horror in a
German prison camp at Minden. He showed me a scar over his eye,
the result of a blow with a hammer from a German guard. He also said
that when, from impoverishment of blood and overwork, he developed
an underarm abscess while working in a coal-mine, the German doctor,
who had no antiseptics to spare for enemy prisoners, simply took a
scalpel knife and carved out the growth. He could say no good word
for the German nation. He is now a spiritualist and tried to persuade
me to go to a seance.

The dancers were most alluring though so different from the ordinary
ballet dancers. Their bare feet showed such pliancy, one might almost
fancy they expressed emotion. The hand movements were exquisite
too. The instruments were most peculiar. One man played on a series of
about a dozen drums of varied size, none being larger than an ordinary
market-basket. The fluttering fingers and elastic wrists were amazingly
deft. Another man squatted over a series of porcelain bowls, not unlike
those in which eels are sold on East-end market-stalls. These too varied
in size and as he struck them with a tiny rod, they gave out a most
mellifluous note. Lil wrote.

Thursday, 8 July. Communication from Telephone Service about
dialing 999 for emergency calls. To Hardwicks tonight. Those old
dames are like dried rose-buds, pleasing but somewhat pitiful. Much
amused on return journey in bus by the invasion of a party of mourners
just emerged from the Havelock Arms. Says the woman 'I'm glad I
came now. I *'ave* enjoyed myself.' 'I told yer, yer would', replied the
elder man. 'We 'ad a grand time when ole' Alf "passed out".' Em
phoned.

Friday, 9 July. Prize distribution at school. Mrs. Girling, OBE,
presided, accompanied by her fellow school-manager and toady, a pop-
eyed woman in spectacles with thick lenses and wearing stockings that
concertinaed round her ankles. Deaf old Mr. Cohen supported them
and a pig-faced man with a bland smile. Mrs. Girling has a mouth
like a hard-driven horse and a skin like a nutmeg-grater. Mr. Pickering
showed her decoration – in its case – up the rows of boys. He then
spoke of her efforts and success of the Labour Party as though they had

been her personal rewards. Everybody patted everybody else's back metaphorically and talked themselves into a state of semi-intoxication. Celebrated half-holiday by visiting Free and Boots Library and then cleaning two rooms and the bathroom. Then I went to Editha's and had a scant meal but a pleasant evening. She is coming with me to see Uday Shan-Kar and his dancers on Thursday. Paid telephone bill.

* * * * * *

Thursday, 15 July. Violent storm at 4 p.m. Never saw such forked lightning before. Editha here to tea. She looks ghastly – like a living corpse. Went to the Gaiety again – a different programme for the Hindu ballet this time. A Harvest Dance was very good and so was the long ceremonial one at the end. We met Leo there. He is much fatter. He has left his wife in Berlin. She is arranging for some of her furniture to be brought out of Germany with Anthony Walbrook's (the film actor). He isn't exiled but he *is* suspected of anti-Nazi sympathies Leo says. Leo and his wife are going to Italy later in the year. Clowser and Wellings came to speak to me in the queue. Clowser lent me opera glasses.

Friday, 16 July. Ivor Meadows brought me a Southend rock (confectionery). He said his grandmother sent it to me. I don't know his grandmother but he says his grandmother knows me. I presume she's one of the women in Hoxton who speak to me as I come to and fro. To Brondesbury tonight. Mrs. Rosenberg enjoying another spate of bad health and Leslie with a sore throat and stomach trouble. After dinner he took us out for a drive. Marjorie wouldn't come so the Samuels were invited. Mrs. S. sat at the back and nearly flattened me. I could hardly breathe. It would have been a delightful drive – through Buckinghamshire, Beaconsfield, Chalfont St. Giles, Penn – only the conversation of my companions was constant and contemptible. The new car had 'to speed' – 75 miles per hour on uncontrolled roads – and the wireless played jazz music unceasingly.

Mrs. Rosenberg gave me yet another hat – not a bad one this time but I'll have to have it cleaned it's so greasy. Fancy such rich people wearing such dirty things![34] Needless to say Leslie never referred to the trip together northwards. I expect he's quite forgotten it. His firm is being robbed of stock. The receiver is caught but not the thief.

Wednesday, 21 July was pay day – 'Double month, £49.3.8'. School had ended. 'Holiday begun and I've made no plans.'

---

34. Gladys's reactions to Mrs. Rosenberg were variable and sometimes sympathetic. 'To Rosenbergs' tonight,' she had written on 12 March 1937. 'Mrs. R. looks ghastly. She is fast breaking up and I dread her dying. For 20 years her home has been a second home to me and there is nothing and no one to take her place.' Some of her later portrayals of Mrs. Rosenberg were noticeably acid. Gladys was rarely consistent in her views of others: a person who was damned or praised one day might later be portrayed in very different colours.

2

July 1937–July 1938

Moments in Time

Gladys now had a break of some five weeks from teaching. She took a few trips – day trips to Buckinghamshire (twice), Dorchester, and Hertford, a weekend in Deal – and she continued to see films, to visit and be visited, and to render judgments. Editha visited on 23 July. 'I was surprised to see, when she was trying on one of my blouses, that she lets the hair under her arms grow thick and brown! Unpleasant!' Three days later there was a small public incident that attracted her notice. 'Saw a girl, and a very plain one too, at a bus stop in Marylebone Road, making up her face, eyebrows, lips, just as though she were in the privacy of her bedroom.' On 28 July she recorded an anniversary: '24 years ago today I went through the form of marriage with George Langford, whose name I continue to use. I had quite forgotten it until this moment. Queer how tragedy dies down like everything else. Once I should have thought it impossible to have forgotten the date.'

A week later, 4 August, was another significant date: '23rd anniversary of outbreak of War. Shall I ever forget that ghastly holiday with George – our only one together. Queer that I jangled with him so much. I've never jangled with anyone else![1] *School resumed – 'Ugh!' – on 24 August.*

Friday, 27 August. A little more amiable! Editha phoned to tell me [about] a mouth-wash. Bay phoned. She's back at the office. To Brondesbury. Mrs. Rosenberg alone with me for the meal. Later we drove in her car to Clarrie's where I saw Leonard – only not the Leonard I have idolised for over 21 years. This one is going bald, chews a cigar, talks staccato out of one side of his mouth and tells cheap Yiddish jokes or recounts smart (?) sayings of his children. At first he hardly addressed me. Later he and I broke away from the general conversation and argued on revolution v. evolution, the place of the firebrand

---

1. By using 'jangle', she may have meant either that she squabbled with him or that she talked a lot, perhaps in a babbling fashion. For more on her failed marriage see below, pp. 36 and 53–55.

in society. Mrs. Rosenberg talks of giving me another (!) hat. I almost wish she would die. Why should I wear a septuagenarian's hat! Met Mrs. Robinson.

Saturday, 28 August. Em phoned. Had a terrible night dreaming of Leonard and awoke crying. He is dead to me in every sense now. He'll never come. He is common and non-literary in tastes now. If only someone would marry me – someone presentable – so I might flaunt my conquest in his face. Was at Duchess Theatre by 4 p.m. but all seats for tonight's performance were then sold. Walked around, had a meal at Fleming's and then sat in St. James's Park. Lil wrote.

* * * * * *

Tuesday, 31 August. Very close. Children half-asleep through having been up half the night listening to broadcast of Tommy Farr's fight.[2] Met Bay at Piccadilly. Gave her a fair meal and then we went to the Comedy Theatre queue.[3] Talked with a pleasant woman clerk standing in front of us and she joined us in the theatre. Alas, on my right, three cackling girls, clerks, talked steadily and laughed loudly throughout the first act. I said fairly loudly to Bay, 'I shall have to move at the end of this act. I can't hear a thing.' They merely made derisive remarks and talked more loudly than before. I then said angrily, as the curtain fell, 'I can't endure nitwits like these', and marched out. Bay sat and suffered their further rude remarks but I was so infuriated I complained to the commissionaire, who said I ought to have kept my seat and he would have quietened them. I gave him a tip – which he didn't want to accept – and he stood immediately behind them throughout the next act so they *had* to be quiet. Bay and I left at the end of the second act. I *never* saw so poor a play [*Busman's Holiday*, a Peter Wimsey detective comedy] and one acted so amateurishly. Mrs. Robinson wrote saying she was going to invite me when she came back from Canvey Island.

Wednesday, 1 September. Bought coach ticket for Friday. Replied to Mrs. Robinson. Mrs. Dunn very concerned about Mr. Topley's poor health. He is too uxorious, perhaps, she thinks. She says, 'I wouldn't

---

2. The previous night, 10 p.m. in New York, 3 a.m. in London, the British heavyweight boxing champion, Tommy Farr, had fought the reigning world champion, Joe Louis. This was a huge event; the *Evening Standard* on 31 August devoted five pages to covering it – and also published a 'Farr Fight Edition'. There was a major spike in the demand for electricity while the fight was on. Although Farr lost, he fought well and won (it was said) the respect of the crowd and his opponent. A few days later a 'complete film of the great fight' was available for viewing at the Angel Islington cinema (*Islington and Holloway Press*, 4 September 1937, p. 8).

3. Queuing for performances was normal, and required patience and stamina. Some weeks later, on Friday, 1 October 1937, Gladys intended to see the Russian Ballet, but 'when I went to put down a stool, I found 403 people were in front of me. Stool-renter says people are often waiting for him when he comes on duty at 7.30 a.m. I then put down stool at the Comedy for *The Last Straw*, a thriller that thrilled with a vengeance.'

discuss things before a young, single girl like Miss Hammond'. I laughed and said, 'Theoretically if not practically, I should think it likely Miss H. could give information to you and me'.

Thursday, 2 September. An eventful day! Letter from Stelle to announce John Morris's death. Left a little late only to find Highbury tram delayed by workmen who were setting up poles for the trolley-buses that are to supersede the trams so I was late to school – for the first time in the 6½ years I've been to Hamond Square [School],[4] for the second time in my teaching career of 17½ years. (The last time was during the Great Strike [in 1926].) At school I found I had no purse and supposed I had lost it so notified the Police Station in Upper Street. However, tonight I discovered I had left it on the bedroom mantel shelf.

Friday, 3 September. To Lil's straight from school. Reached Bumpstead in tears, being quite overwrought. A small boy, bound for a Church Army Farm Colony, had been placed in my charge by a soapy-smiling young man, all mouth and thick-lensed spectacles. Then a baby aboard yelled steadily from London to Bumpstead. My head seemed to be suffering anvil strokes.

* * * * * *

Wednesday, 8 September. I *have* stormed at the poor brats today. They *are* so lazy. One boy, Harry Freed, I baited so unmercifully, with tongue and rod, his mouth grew dry and he could hardly speak and I was ashamed at my own harshness. But what can one do? It's not that the children are silly so much as they are idle and *won't* concentrate. Am reading and enjoying immensely James Agate's *Ego 2* [1936].[5] To the Tatler tonight; a good Disney film, *Woodland Café*, a delightful African one, *Rivers of Natal*, an interesting *March of Time* dealing with women's employment and the Dustbowl Area as two items, and one of the so-many Keep Fit films, this time from Poland.

Thursday, 9 September. Letter from Norman Ginsbury. His play is running now at Bournemouth.[6] He says Laughton 'let him down' with regard to *Prince Regent* but he's writing a third play – Tchekovian

---

4. It still exists as the Burbage Primary School. When Gladys was teaching there the school accommodated around 600 students. Almost none of the residential stock in the neighbourhood from the 1930s survives.
5. James Agate (1877–1947), a prominent drama critic, wrote about the theatre for the *Sunday Times*, 1923–1947, and had been critic for the BBC between 1925 and 1932. From 1935 he published nine volumes of diaries, each titled *Ego*, which talked mainly of the London cultural scene to which Gladys was much attached.
6. Norman Ginsbury (1902–1991) was a Hackney-educated playwright with whom Gladys enjoyed a sort of friendship. The play that had just opened at the Pavilion in Bournemouth was *Viceroy Sarah*, with Irene Vanbrugh. See also below, pp. 60, 79, 84, 107, 119 and 141.

in type. Headache and acute ill-humour at school. Miss Hammond is such a nuisance and the children are so dull. Rushed home and determined not to suffer Mrs. Lucas's conversation so sped off to the New Theatre to see Dodie Smith's new play, *Bonnet over the Windmill* [a light comedy]. The authoress has no literary talent but is a *very* clever craftswoman. She caters for all tastes – modernism in sex matters, sentimentality for the middle-aged, a glimpse of high and also of low life. Every woman in the audience can identify herself with one or other of the attractive women, be she fat, fortyish or only fantastical-introspective. The character of Janet enraged me and I disliked Anne Firth, all gaunt, seraphically smiling and remote. There was nothing to suggest she had the makings of a great actress in *her*. Such a lot of men in the audience. Unusual! They clung to the wall in the intervals like flies on a warm winter's day. Lil wrote. Talked with my neighbour, a Scottish woman who declared she had only once before been in a theatre gallery.

Friday, 10 September. Miss Hammond away. Her substitute a man like a bewildered cherub in a cycling suit apparently purchased in the nineties. To Rosenbergs. Wellings phoned late. I've to go to help in his Edgware Road shop tomorrow. I don't want to but he's hard pushed for assistance. I'll have to sleep all Sunday.

Saturday, 11 September. I haven't worked so hard since I was at Metwell Company 20 years ago. Reached Red Library, Edgware Road [one of Wellings four private libraries] by 11 a.m. Began work at once and never left off save for a 20 minutes' snack in the ABC till 9 p.m. The shop was full. Customers tethered dogs to the table-legs, 'parked' children under the counter and consulted us for choice of books, queries as to authors, possibilities of reserving books. Sour-tempered folk openly resented absence of books they wanted; contentious customers argued about paying 'overdue fines', self-righteous folk who could not prove place of residence jibbed at paying 2s deposit and asserted their honesty with ferocity. Chinese, Japanese and Australian visitors came in. People mumbled their names or else remembered at long last they'd had books issued on a relative's or neighbour's ticket – all complicating issue of books, of course. I was perturbed to find lavatory accommodation was only to be reached by going out into main road, then down a side-turning and finally into the basement of the row of buildings and shops! Wellings phoned last thing. Was so tired I swallowed a half pint of beer, a half pint of hot milk and fell into bed in a heap.

* * * * * *

Tuesday, 14 September. I keep thinking of Wellings who spoke on Sunday of Clowser's horror of marital infidelity and he added 'I myself thought of adultery as terrible until I had committed it'. Now I have always thought the blonde manageress of his Islington shop was his mistress – I wonder. To Leo's straight from school on Tuesday. How different is the atmosphere there *now*! He and Murray both very quiet. Mrs. Dunlop pranced about in a semi-evening gown – in a fireless room too. Later she put on a woolly coat. I felt or fancied I could feel marked antagonism towards me. Murray came to the bus with me. He said 'Madam wants continual service. She is not willing to take Leo about with her. He is not well enough dressed. She says she is a Society girl and I say "Girls' Friendly"?' She was determined I shouldn't see the bedroom scenery. I had to disrobe in the hall.

* * * * * *

Sunday, 19 September. Twenty-three years ago since George deserted me. Life seemed done for me then. It *is* done for me now. I'm 47 and I make no new friends. I go pleasuring but I'm *never* happy, merely free from anxiety. I talked with Wellings by phone last night. His girl at Edgware Road apparently made a mistake in her ledger entries last week and she told him it was due to *my* including deposits with takings. I never handled a deposit at all. What a thankless job it is doing anything for anyone. It's the very girl who caused deposits in the bank to be lost through letting her German sweetheart handle the money. I went to Pyrland Road this morning. It was a very depressing visit. Miss Chambers anticipates eventual blindness. She won't make any effort to prepare for it by learning Braille or going out and about and memorising local landmarks.

Monday, 20 September. Miss Hammond makes me sick. Every day she has a new complaint. Today it's weakness at the knees. A fairly amiable day at school but I rapped Saunders' fingers with a stick of pencil without noticing that he already had a sore finger which promptly bled. I nearly always look before I smack but he is such a saucy boy. Funny incidents – a soft-footed waitress creeping behind my chair and hissing into my ears in blood-curdling tones 'No-o-o-w do you want trifle?' as though she were offering me a death-blow rather than a sweet. Later when visiting Lottie, her old father, who says never a word nowadays, suddenly looked across at me and announced malevolently 'You're an old crock now'. Lastly in the Library, Miss Tedbury said venomously in passing 'The day I leave I'm going to throw books at all the people who breathe down my neck as I put books on the shelves'. Lil wrote.

* * * * * *

Monday, 4 October. Wrote yesterday, on the spur of the moment, to Leonard saying though he might change into a Charlie Peace [burglar and murderer] or a Clarence Hatry [embezzler] yet would I not dethrone my god, the boy who once introduced me to Epstein's work and Ibsen's plays, among other things. He has answered – by return of post – telling me to remember the Law of Change, and to tell me to visit him and that he has a photograph of himself for me. Dear Leonard! Even yet, though I no longer love him as I once did, the sight of his hand-writing makes my heart beat faster. Many arrests in yesterday's Fascists' march.[7]

* * * * * *

Wednesday, 6 October. Bay wrote – too, too flatteringly about the blouse and costume I let her have cheaply. The gift of a sable coat could hardly have evoked greater gratitude!! Met Leonard at his office. No ill-feeling. He showed me his new catalogue, each one of which cost 10s to produce. He spoke of the annoyance Margie occasions him. I asked for news of Charlie's latest investments in O.K. Bazaar shares. They are going down so he's dropped money and I'm glad though I horrified Leonard by saying so. These Lucases must explore my place in my absence. Mr. L. told me today he didn't like my floor-polish. I said 'How do you know what it's like?' 'Oh, I opened your wardrobe and took it out', he said. Leonard let me choose a photograph of him. I have one with the little half-smile and parted lips he had when love-making. That will never come again, I fear. He is lame with rheumatism and only says 'Come and see me again. You can't come too often.' I hate acknowledging the end, yet end it is. It *is* hard to grow old and have still the unsatisfied appetites of youth.

During the next five weeks Gladys reported on various public activities, including watching the opening of Parliament – 'Wedged myself into a swaying mass of people by the Horse Guards Parade. The smell of bloaters and brilliantine came from left and right' (26 October) – and on 1 November she 'Voted for Municipal Reform candidates'.[8] 'I wish the papers weren't perpetually referring to the horrors of war', she wrote on 7 October. On Saturday, 16 October she and Bay took a Green Line bus to Hertford, took a long walk, and visited the market. 'The cheapjacks [hawkers] were very amusing. They carefully gave one another a chance to "hold the floor".' On 20 October she 'Saw a girl stand writing a letter under a lamp-post in the fog while she

---

7. According the *Evening Standard*, 4 October 1937, p. 4, the demonstration was outside the Tower Bridge police court. Some 100 people had been charged with such offences as carrying an offensive weapon and throwing missiles during a Fascist march in South London the previous weekend.

8. Municipal Reform candidates presented themselves as 'anti-socialist' (*Islington Gazette*, 29 October 1937, p. 4). Labour at this election gained at least seven seats on Islington Borough Council, and the following week it was reported that 'Islington's first woman Mayor [a mother of six] makes a promise to the backstreet woman. "I will not let the women down, and I will certainly not forget the women in the backstreets"' (*Islington and Holloway Press*, 6 November, 1937, p. 2 and 13 November 1937, p. 1).

waited for a bus at 11.15 p.m.' Although Gladys had numerous Jewish friends, including her occasional lover, Leonard, anti-Semitic remarks peppered her diary. She thought Igor Stravinsky, whom she saw conduct part of a concert on 18 October, 'looked like a servile little Jew selling lace-curtains by Dutch auction in a street market'. Weeks before, while attending a play on 21 August, she was 'Much annoyed by the fat and noisy Jewesses in the audience'.

Wednesday, 11 November. The usual feeble dissertation for Armistice Day at school. All a farce! Great War, Boer War or Crimean War are all alike to these children. Many of their fathers are even too young to have fought in it [the Great War]. 'An incident' at the Cenotaph. An alleged lunatic burst through police and military guards and shouted 'All this hypocrisy! You are arming for a new War!' Wireless listeners heard the scuffle as ten or so policemen lay on him and stifled him. The newspapers say he was picked up unconscious. Poor wretch! Apparently he was the only sane one there! A woman cried out 'Lynch him' – of the gentle sex!

Met Wellings. Had food in a horrid semi-Bohemian place he favours and I loathe. *Then* I learned the tickets Clowser had obtained for us were for the STALLS at the Ambassadors. I was utterly wretched. All around me were bare-bosomed beauties and men in boiled shirts while Wellings and I were obviously in 'paper' seats. I thought of Xmas 1905 when through the prize-giving rehearsal at Skinners' School I and Laura Callaghan had to squat on the floor in the middle of the hall while all the girls practised bowing and curtseying for the Great Event. We two were not allowed to go because we couldn't afford to get white party frocks, and everyone knew why we sat there so conspicuously and why we were not going![9]

The play *Yes and No* [by Kenneth Horne] was well enough acted but was gossamer [flimsy] in quality. It made no strain on the intelligence but great demands on one's credulity. I cannot believe so absent-minded a vicar ever existed. I was so miserable, felt so old and ugly. I refused Wellings' invitation for Sunday. Anyway it's a bad thing to form a habit. When a break comes one is so crushed. Not that Wellings appeals to me sexually!

Friday, 12 November. Mr. Pickering tells me Mrs. McKenzie came to school and was most flattering about my effect upon her boy. She said his progress was remarkable and his character was equally improved.

9.　Several years later she wrote of 'the humiliation I endured in my well-nigh sole-less shoes at Skinners' School' for girls in Hackney (1 July 1943). For more about her impoverished girlhood, see Chapter 5. In July 1906 she passed the Oxford and Cambridge Lower Certificate, with a First in Arithmetic and English and a Second in French, English History, and Additional Mathematics. (Certificate in the final box of her diaries in the Islington Local History Centre.)

To Editha's tonight. Not enough fire and not enough food – as usual. She had a nasty fall passing from one room to another. Frankie and Ivy Yale were there, F. more smug than ever and quite certain he knows everything – scientific, diplomatic and politic. Thank God I never married him. Ivy and he exchange no remark. Aren't married people peculiar? Wasn't sorry to come home.

Saturday, 13 November. Window cleaner says Nancy McMillan has gone into a home. Mr. McMillan is home again but incapable of working. Still very cold. To Tatler this afternoon. A good *Happy Harmony* cartoon, *Little Cheese,* owing its inspiration to Disney's *Pluto's Guardian Angel.* There was a pleasing Swedish film, *Igloo,* but it had too much skiing and too little Arctic life for my taste. Bay phoned. Bought myself a half bottle [of] Invalid port I feel so depressed.

Sunday, 14 November. Wellings phoned last night and again invited me for tonight but I refused. Em on the wire this morning but no news there. To National Gallery this afternoon. Was admiring the 15th century painting lent by the Governor of Malta, also some of the Dutch paintings. I can like Cézanne no more than I have ever liked Turner. I liked 'Flatford Mill' and 'Malvern Hall' of Constable's. Very many visitors there.

Later. I'm gradually climbing out of the morass of gloom that has threatened to swamp me. Reading *Georgian England* by [A.E.] Richardson has made me decide that there is much of interest, much to please still left for me if sex must be cut out, but, oh, Leonard, while you were in evidence, life was a glowing dream.[10]

* * * * * *

Saturday, 20 November. Editha phoned and I talked with Em. To Sadler's Wells this afternoon but only achieved a back seat. Seventy-three children there from a school and they went separately and collectively to the lavatory, treading over my feet at each journey to and from their seats. Went to Victoria and booked a seat for next Thursday at the Westminster to see *Mourning becomes Electra.*[11] Then journeyed to the Palladium to get seats for November 28th and December 5th. Moiseiwitch and Szigeti.[12] Find I am dribbling a lot of money away.

---

10. This book is subtitled *A Survey of Social Life, Trades, Industries and Art from 1700–1820.* Gladys seems to be saying that she was engaged by this book, and that intellectual pursuits compensated to some degree for her deprived sex life.
11. She found Eugene O'Neill's play 'a weird mixture of classic myth and half-digested psycho-analysis' (25 November).
12. On Sunday, 5 December she 'enjoyed the Mendelssohn Violin Concerto but found the Corelli item too much for me. The height of the gallery there makes me feel too dizzy for complete enjoyment.' The previous Thursday she had gone to a concert at Queen's Hall: 'A Sibelius concert with Beecham conducting – walking on the platform as though he were God in the Garden of Eden.'

I don't live well yet I live expensively. Keep paying odd amounts to Lucases but they do so much for me I can't help myself. Most remarkable looking street-singer in Regent Street. He wore a kind of Zouave jacket,[13] wore his hair in long, greasy strands to his shoulders, his brow being high and bald. His voice was mighty in volume and crowds watched him.

Gladys's diary during the following five weeks recorded the usual full slate of films, plays, and concerts, while at her place of work the main event was the temporary relocation of her school at Hamond Square, which was scheduled for renovation, to nearby Hoxton House School.[14] *On 6 December she wrote that 'Leonard sent me a very nice umbrella for Xmas box but, alas, brown! Fancy his having known a woman* intimately *for 22 years and never having noticed she* never *wore brown!!!' On 9 December she went to hear 'W. H. Auden lecture on "The Teaching of English". He's a tall, slackly-built, sensual-mouthed fellow, mainly inaudible and with painful mannerisms. The word Democracy occurs in every other sentence and he knows about as much about The People as I do about The Aristocracy.' On 18 December she 'Saw in Shepherd's Market a queer little eating-house bearing a card with the words "Customers are requested not to bring their own food between the hours of 12 and 2 p.m." I recalled Charles Lamb's account of patronising an inn for drink and producing his own eatables – so he was accordingly looked at askance.' Later in the month came the Christmas holidays.*

Saturday, 25 December, Xmas Day. Surely the quietest I have ever spent. A heavy fog, like that described by Dickens in *Bleak House*, closes in like a pall and I feel stifled. My latest complaint is a violent attack of diarrhoea and an awful feeling of sickness. I ate some of the mighty meal Mrs. Lucas provided but have had little else. Kelsy phoned good wishes before 9 a.m., a few cards arrived and I chatted downstairs awhile this morning, talking to 'Syd' and the Lucas family and drinking two glasses of port. Sat reading *Tunbridge Wells*, a most entertaining book [of 1937 by Margaret Barton], through the day and wrote letters tonight. Listened to the King's speech – very slow in delivery and even more slight in substance. There was one painful pause due to his stammer. Phoned good wishes to [fellow teacher] Alec Kerr.

---

13. A Zouave jacket was short, open-fronted and with long sleeves.
14. The reconditioning of Hamond Square School, estimated to cost around £6,500, is documented in a file in the National Archives, ED 21/57272. Some facilities were upgraded and enlarged. The boys' department, where Gladys taught, was on the first floor. Shoreditch's population was declining, and since student numbers at the school had fallen by some 25 per cent to 30 per cent since 1930, by August 1938, when it reopened, overcrowding was presumably less of a problem.

Sunday, 26 December, Boxing Day. Feel slightly better and *much* improved in spirits after a violent fit of love-making, more befitting Cleopatra than me. Leonard came this afternoon and we made the very most of our hour and half together. *He* was quite exhausted when he left but I was merely gleeful. I am 47⅔ and still able to rouse him to frenzy. Leo phoned just as we were getting ready to leave and I asked him to phone later. He did and talked for about half an hour. He has quite deserted poor Mrs. Osborne it seems. He speaks slightingly of Murray. Says he doesn't want him dependent on him any longer. Couldn't settle down to reading after this afternoon's excitement. Leonard begs me to forget him – but how can I?

Monday, 27 December. Lil wrote. Mrs. Lucas sent up a huge and most tasty dinner. Walked this afternoon around Stoke Newington, Kingsland, Dalston and Highbury. *How* the district alters! The blocks of flats have replaced the houses in Church Street facing the park and the houses I admired so much at the top of Albion Road have given place to a new Town Hall – very modern in aspect. Am decidedly better. Beginning to enjoy my food again. Bay phoned.

Tuesday, 28 December. Em phoned late last night, Editha this morning. Ginsbury wrote – such a humorous letter I laughed aloud again and again. Housework! Ugh, how I hate it! To Library this afternoon. Intended going westwards but it's misty and drizzly so I stay at home to read and 'listen in'. Urinals *are* getting modern in style. Twice I have mistaken new ones for kiosks.

Wednesday, 29 December. Replied to Ginsbury. Received cards from Griffiths! And Kathlyn Morton, sent on from Highbury Park. To Hackney this morning and westwards this afternoon. Bought sheets and overall at Stagg's sale. Saw Florrie Woods (Mrs. Denny), her husband and a woman friend there. Florrie looked old but pretty – quite 60. Denny looked as though shrunken by too much washing. Saw two other teachers I knew. Needing a hat I went into Bourne and Hollingsworth's. An assistant produced quite a score but none of them suited me. They were all so weird and ultra-modern. I'm not going to add to the number of elderly scarecrows dressed like street-walkers. Finally I insisted on the girl's taking 2s for herself to compensate her for any commission she might have earned from serving another customer while she had been serving me and I walked out without making a purchase. Made an appointment with the dentist for tomorrow, 10.30 a.m. I hate the thought of artificial teeth [she had only fifteen of her own teeth left] but I hate toothache even more.

Thursday, 30 December. To the dentist's. Tooth extracted by gas and new ones to be put in lower jaw – four guineas. Have decided to apply

41

for cash for six certificates tomorrow. Applied for HSA [health insurance] grant. Bay, Joan Sutton, Em and Editha here tonight. Em looked hideously ugly. Joan Sutton told a good tale. Her aunt, who is very patronising to children, stopped and patted the head of a three-year old sitting on a doorstep in South London playing with what she thought was a toy mouse. 'Let me look at your pretty mouse, dear!' says she. 'Git away you silly bugger, can't yer see it's a fish!' the mite bawled, to her confusion.

Friday, 31 December. Bought a hat with an eye-veil but it's too stylish for me to enjoy wearing it. To Leo's tonight and really enjoyed myself. Murray had cooked an elaborate meal and after it we adjourned to Mrs. Dunlop's room – she *has* impressed her personality on it. Pictures in oils, a queer pewter stove for heating rum-punch, a good substantial rocking-chair and quaintly embroidered table-cloths and a gay Xmas tree all ablaze with candles. She told tales of film stars she had known in Germany and she tells tales well. I do envy a woman like that, travelled and cultured and a pleasant companion though she's certainly no beauty. I always feel so 'common' in her company. She gave me one of her many photographs of Anton Walbrook.[15] It is evident how much she loves him – evident too how much she misses her German home and friends. Home by Tube because I couldn't get a bus.

Saturday, 1 January, 1938. Lil sent a tea-cosy, Mrs. Eldridge a card. Barbers [fellow tenants at 4 Northolme Road; see also Appendix A] came home at 3 a.m. and made a most unearthly noise but I didn't mind as they wakened me from a nightmare – born of indigestion I suspect. Had my hair trimmed at a new shop in Blackstock Road [Islington and Hackney] – a tiny place run by a fat and bald Jew whose few remaining hairs were dyed a mahogany tinge. His fat wife operated on another customer in the next chair – no division between customers – and a balloon-faced baby was being 'cosseted' in a corner of the shop, the proprietor's own brat. The man breathed fast and damply down my neck as he clipped and snipped. He gave me his life and origins in tabloid form and was so voluble he cheated me out of 6d change before I had a chance to notice it.

During the following weeks Gladys endured a lot of dental work – she got two plates – and resumed teaching. 'Temper like fireworks today,' she wrote on 20 January. 'I get to hate these children.'

Thursday, 27 January. Miss Hammond's absurd accounts of her men victims bore me. She sends me in notes to tell me her dentist

---

15. Anton Walbrook (b. 1896) was an Austrian actor who, from 1936, settled in England and enjoyed a successful career.

wants to rape her, the men on the Staff kiss her and tell her they'll give her babies! Great gawk! And she is a mass of blackheads! She and Mr. Topley allege my face is a study in disapproval during the singing lessons. No wonder! It's a crime against culture to let children bellow community songs of the silliest when they might be learning to appreciate real music. To Tatler tonight. I longed for a man to sit beside me. I'm as sex-hungry as Miss Hammond only I don't talk about it or say men love me or that they ever did though I too 'could a tale unfold'. I only noticed myself when I collided with the school milkman, a rather virile man of middle age. We caught one another to prevent falling and I noticed how greedily I held him. Saw in *Telegraph* an account of a 21 year old cat's agility. I only hope my boy [Lallie] lives that long.

* * * * * *

Sunday, 30 January. So gloomy last night. I phoned Editha and she suggested we should all go to the pictures together. We did and saw *Gribouille* at the Curzon [a 1937 French comedy]. The story was improbable but the acting excellent including the minor parts. One woman who had to give a few sentences as evidence in the character of a prostitute was superb. There were two cartoons, *Donald and Pluto* which I'd seen before, and *Mickey's Elephant* which was less funny than Disney cartoons usually are. Then there was the news item and a 'short', *Tell me if it hurts*, a skit on dentistry which hardly pleased me – with *two* new dental plates in my mouth. When we came out, the Kiernans wanted a drink and went into the Rose and Crown (just off Piccadilly). The public house is a very rare experience for me but I was agreeably surprised by its 'refinement'. The atmosphere was that of a suburban party before the 'eats' appear. In the bar, which was furnished in Victorian style, a large man with a face like an ox gulped beer and blew out his nostrils and cheeks till I expected to see him lash with a tail and puff smoke from his nostrils like the Bovril bulls. Another man looked like Leno as Widow Twankey and made much play with his nostrils.[16] A young couple talked 'Football pools' and two nice young girls flirted with two nice young men and a stately tabby cat stalked around sniffing disdainfully at beer glasses and deigning to sit temporarily on the laps of those women who wore fur coats. He *was* a class-conscious cat.

Monday, 31 January. To Belsize Park last night. Clowser very jubilant about the forthcoming purchase of his Highgate house and very anxious Wellings should join him.

16.   Dan Leno (1860–1904) was a famous music hall comedian who often played dame roles in pantomimes, including Widow Twankey in *Aladdin*. Evidently Gladys as a child had seen him on stage.

Tuesday, 1 February. So glad my temper is better nowadays. Didn't know how sex-hungry I was until I realised I was disappointed no strange man touched me in the Tatler. As a sop comes a phone message from Darling Charles. He invited himself for today. Good! Am reading a delightful travel book by Haruko Ichikawa – *A Japanese Lady in Europe* [1937]. A delightful short film at Tatler, 'featuring' Robert Benchley, and also one of Kew Gardens with an amusing Disney *Lonesome Ghosts*.

Wednesday, 2 February. Charles came last night and we sat talking and eating from 9 p.m. till midnight. When he was going he said 'I hope I haven't stayed too late'. Unthinkingly I replied 'I wish you were staying all night'. He fairly gasped and I foolishly apologised. Lil wrote. Met Bay at Highbury and took her to see Spencer Tracy and Luise Rainer in *Big City*, a film all [about] fighting and crookedness, followed by another, *Exclusive*, of the very same type. The American films do show up badly after the French ones. Topley lent me Stephen Roberts' book *House that Hitler Built*[17] but I prefer *I'm Not Complaining* by Ruth Adam.[18]

February's diary produced a few observations on the London scene: 'Newsagent says people are busy stealing newspapers and milk from doorsteps hereabouts' (3 February); 'Much saddened by sight of a little brown dog pinned beneath a bus-wheel in Oxford Street, its tiny white teeth bared in its death agony' (12 February); and 'Some children in New North Road have been gnawed by rats as they lay in bed! And this is Christian – and civilised – England' (23 February). There was also a notable moment of succinct self-disclosure. 'I hate habits to creep on me and I hate to grow dependent on anyone else for mental stimulus. I hurt myself quite enough when George and then Leonard dropped out of my life' (5 February).

Tuesday, 1 March. Spirits remain below par despite really lovely weather. I need a 'sex' fillip. I'm absolutely obsessed by my weight of years – and I'm not 48 yet. I see '50' Highbury Park and 52 and 48 and 46 (the latter The Chestnuts boarding house) are sold. I feel sorry for those poor old fogies at 50 – the mother over 90, the daughter 70 and cancerous, and the next daughter late fiftyish and diabetic! Mrs. Thomas will be kept busy.[19] To the Tatler tonight – very poor programme.

---

17. Subtitled *An Account of the National-Socialist Regime in Germany* and published in 1937.
18. This 1938 novel is set in a school in a poor neighbourhood. Some of the interactions among the teachers and with parents may have mirrored some of Gladys's own experiences as a teacher.
19. These were four of the nine people who were living in this house in 1936. The other five

Wednesday, 2 March. Spoke to Mr. Jay (Hoxton House staff). *He* hates the narrow walls of a schoolroom too. I had half completed a letter to Lil, 'moaning' about my hatred of my surroundings, but realising I was not the only one 'kicking against the pricks', I tore up the letter. Home to do some housework and some reading. Mr. Lucas is going to re-decorate my front room at Whitsun. I have promised to give 10s towards it. He will clear and afterwards clean the room so it's worth 10s. I do try to be patient and forbearing with the boy McKenzie at school but he is so aggravating only a saint could endure him and yet smile. His 'will to power' is tremendously strong.

Thursday, 3 March. Kerr away again and a vile looking little Jew come in his place, an offence to the eye indeed. Temper not too angelic. Fire last night at Beresford and Hicks, the cabinet makers' almost adjoining Hamond Square School.[20] *Very* warm. Article (a very feeble one) by Patrick Monkhouse in the *Evening Standard* on the use of the 'Cat'.[21] Charles wrote. He accepts for *next* Monday, the day I did *not* invite him [to a party]. However, I want him to come. I'd like him to want to marry me! Will he ever?

* * * * * *

Saturday, 5 March. Editha will come on Monday. Bought a new coat, navy blue boucle, 69s 6d. Only want a new face and I'd look fine. Despatched letter of enquiry to person advertising flat in *New Statesman* as Wellings requested last night. Wandered in St. James's Park. Beautiful weather; not a seat vacant and men in blazers and one woman in white blouse and no coat. Replied to Mrs. Jackson.

were Gladys, a married couple who appear to have been the owners (Elsie and Robin Reginald Robinson), and, probably, the husband and son of Mrs. Thomas.

20. The *Hackney Gazette and North London Advertiser*, 4 March 1938, p. 5, gave details on the reactions to this blaze. 'Families in Ivy-street and Hamond-square, Hoxton, were advised by the police to leave their homes when they were threatened by a fierce fire which was discovered at 8.30 p.m. on Wednesday in the furniture factory of Messrs. Beresford and Hicks in Hemsworth-street. They were sheltered in neighbours' houses until the fire was got under control. Over 100 firemen, with 17 appliances, went to the scene in response to a district call.' Many workmen's tools were destroyed, along with cabinets and furniture under construction, a few local residents suffered damages, and a reporter was on the scene to name names. 'Firemen broke a door in Mrs. Florence Jones's house at 1 Hamond-square to gain access to the burning premises, and the scullery was flooded by water. Flooding was also caused in an upstairs bedroom and a downstairs front room at 9 Hamond-square occupied by Miss Alice Osborne, and windows in the back of the house at 47 Ivy-street, occupied by Mrs. Rose Abraham, were cracked by the heat.' Onlookers gathered, to the frustration of the emergency services. 'Big crowds thronged into Hoxton-street and hampered the efforts of the firemen until police cars with loud speakers arrived and cleared the streets.' The blaze was under control by 9.30 p.m., but the firemen were not finally withdrawn until 6 the next morning.

21. The debate concerned the legitimacy of flogging – two thieves had recently each got fifteen to twenty lashes (*Evening Standard*, 3 March 1938, p. 7).

Sunday, 6 March. Editha phoned. She and Kiernan *will* come tomorrow. To Hyde Park this afternoon. Crowds out. Many new hats worn with elastic under the female chin. Saw the new trolley buses running today for the first time from Finchley into the City area [they were replacing trams].

* * * * * *

Wednesday, 9 March. Miss Hope wrote – as usual she's full of ailments. Beautiful weather. School more bearable thanks to an occasional few words with Mr. Jay, the young Jew who reads psycho-analysis and has interests outside the schoolroom. To the Tatler. Returning saw a very noisy Communist procession bearing banners, 'Keep out Ribbentrop' and 'Release Thaelmann'. Plenty of police with them. A very unkempt lot of foreign Jews and a tiny sprinkling of intelligentsia. If they were the ruling class, God help the country.[22] Reading *Donkey Row* – find it very slow moving, so different from American 'low life' novels.[23]

* * * * * *

Saturday, 12 March. Lovely weather. With Bay to Cambridge and walked to Grantchester. Back in the town exploring Trinity, King's, Caius, King's College Chapel and Bridge of Sighs and The Backs. Wonderful weather for March, crocus carpets ablaze, willows vivid green, catkin tassels dangling and birds everywhere. Back in Bumpstead had a full size quarrel with Bay about her callous attitude towards the anti-Nazi Austrians and what they may suffer after the Hitlerian coup.[24] But Jews, Catholics and 'the masses' mean nothing to Bay as long as *she's* comfortable. I never knew a greedier or more selfish girl. AND how she drinks; spirits, wine, liqueurs – she laps them up and demands more.

News from abroad, mostly concerning Nazi Germany, was starting to creep into Gladys's writing. Miss Hammond reported at school on

22. Joachim von Ribbentrop, German Ambassador in London 1936–1938, had recently been appointed by Hitler as Nazi Foreign Minister and was in Britain for high-level talks. Ernst Thaelmann, leader of the Communist Party of Germany (KPD), had been imprisoned by the Nazis in 1933 and was being kept in solitary confinement. Some of the demonstrators also called for the release of the imprisoned anti-Nazi theologian Martin Niemöller. They protested 'the admission into this country of Herr Ribbentrop for the purpose of carrying on his Fascist intrigues with Chamberlain and the National Government' and demanded 'that this representative of Hitler's policy of war against Spain, Austria, and Czechoslovakia shall get out'. As Gladys observed, the police presence in all parts of Central London where these meetings were held was substantial, and 'Mounted police were stationed outside the German Embassy, and police patrolled the Duke of York's steps, the Mall, and Piccadilly' (*The Times*, 10 March 1938, p. 9g).
23. *Down Donkey Row* (London: Cresset Press, 1938) was a novel by Len Ortzen. The author described the work as a 'small collection of Cockney slang' (p. 8). It reads like a lightly novelised description of traditional East End language, modes of living, and shady practices. The narrative revolves around a bookmaker, his family, and neighbours.
24. Hitler was about to invade Austria and absorb it into the German Reich, which he did the following day. The consequences for one Austrian Jew are described below, pp. 81–83.

Monday, 14 March that *'everyone in the West End was very excited on Saturday evening and the atmosphere was very tense as people waited to hear whether we should be embroiled in the Austrian coup business'. Later, 'War news beats down on one from every direction. I wish I were dead' (30 March). By contrast, the next day she wrote that 'I remain quite good-tempered at school.'*

Saturday, 2 April. On phone to Miss Hammond, Em and Editha. Wellings phoned last night. To Studio One tonight to see *La Tendre Ennemie*. An elderly man sat on my right and soon began to fidget. I always think I must be imagining things, so I stood a good deal of pawing before I whispered 'You're making a mistake – I'm not young'. He sobered down for a while but soon his legs were so intertwined with mine I had to say 'Please have mercy on my stockings'. There wasn't another seat vacant and I wouldn't give [i.e., put] any sex-pervert in charge if I could avoid it. So I sat still while he held my hand. Perhaps I was even grateful for a little emotionalism in my own barren life. But suddenly he gripped my legs between his and dragged my hand under his overcoat and thrust it between his legs – *then* I found he had opened the fly of his trousers and his penis was on my bare hand. I nearly yelled out and pulled my hand away. 'Oh let me alone', I hissed, and at the end of the next picture I whizzed out. All the same, I can't help feeling sorry for anyone cursed with such an unfortunate urge that may well land them in a prison cell ere long.[25] Eros is barricaded against Boat Race crowds tonight. Oxford won.

Sunday, 3 April. Wind very high. Bay phoned. Indoors during day, reading. Wrote to Lil. I can't make Wellings out. He told me tonight that, in the street, he slapped the face of the young woman he wants to marry. He also said he followed her car in a taxi, all across London, and it cost him £3. He also said he had engaged private detectives to trace her private address, but without success. He says her car is registered at her business address. He says he puts advertisements in the *New Statesman* about people he wants to meet – a lady whose scarf he retrieved at Queen's Hall for instance – and his 'dame' rises to the bait and replies.[26] I think living alone has turned his head. He wants to pose as something between a Rudolph Valentino sheik and a Don Juan.[27] I can't believe a word of it. One has only to look at him – 'in

---

25. On 16 March 1940 she went with two or three acquaintances to a cinema 'where a man next me squeezed my leg so hard I exclaimed "You *are* making me uncomfortable", whereupon he fled. Poor pervert!'
26. The editors found no such advertisements. Perhaps he was fibbing.
27. Rudolph Valentino (1895–1926) was a handsome silent film actor who had starred in the 1921 box office hit *The Sheik*. He was known as the 'Latin Lover' and the 'Great Lover'; his death at the age of thirty-one triggered outpourings of grief from his hordes of female admirers.

slipper'd ease' with bent shoulders and peering eyes and a horrid habit of picking wax out of his ears, a habit I loathe.

* * * * * *

Saturday, 9 April. Wellings phoned last night. He told a tale of his inamorata's having caused him to be summoned for assault – i.e. for the face-slapping he previously mentioned. He said he shall go this morning 'to see her' – not go to the Court – and that will straighten everything out. He says he finds he has known her home address all along. I think his is a case of split identity. Editha says the lady must be a *Miss* 'Arris. He says he is going to Highgate tomorrow to see Clowser of whom he has heard nothing for a week. I went to South Kensington Museum today. It is too cold for out-of-doors amusements. Concentrated on the exhibition of jewellery and snuff boxes and the modern book illustrations and sketches for stage costumes and settings. The West End full of hideosities in plaid tam-o-shanters – people up for the match.[28] Am reading *Night and the City* by Gerald Kersh – an awful indictment of London night life[29] but I sometimes wonder if these novels are any truer than the old sentimental ones of the squire and the wicked baronet who seduced the governess. Lil sent me a tea-cosy. Wandered around Brompton Square and a bird was singing joyously. There was a house to let and I wished I was a married woman with a husband and 'future' there – but there is nothing ahead for me.

---

28. Scotland were playing football at Wembley that afternoon against England (Scotland won 1–0).

29. Gerald Kersh (b. 1911) was the author of 19 novels, 400 short stories, and hundreds of articles. Many were vividly imagined tales of society's underbelly. *Night and the City* (1938; New York: ibooks edn., 2001) enjoys a degree of credibility since Kersh, as a young man in the 1930s, spent time in Soho seeking any work he could find and may well have met the sorts of people who became characters in his fiction. The novel reflects some common themes of the time – gangsterism, American-style bravado, petty criminals with high ambitions and little luck, prostitution – and highlights the desperation, self-delusions, and despair of many people's lives. Gladys was not inattentive to the realities of London's seedy side. On 29 January 1937 she had noted that 'The police are very busy cleaning up London night clubs and apparently demoralising policemen and policewomen most cheerfully and at great expense to the public in order to prove that ordinary citizens are demoralising one another.'

     Just a few days before mentioning Kersh, she had reported (4 April) that the '*Daily Mail* succeeded in preventing publication of *To Beg I am Ashamed* [by Sheila Cousins] – the autobiography of a prostitute.' This book was in fact published in June in Paris by the Obelisk Press, which noted on the back of the title page: 'An attack against the book, in the London press, of unprecedented ferocity and vindictiveness caused its withdrawal before publication.' The book's notoriety may help to explain how it came to be reprinted three times in the month following publication. It was clearly not written by a prostitute but by a professional writer, almost certainly male, who knew London well. No doubt it was produced in the hope of cashing in on the lively market in Britain for tales of scandal, debauchery, and low life. The catalogue of the British Library gives the author's name, Sheila Cousins, as the pseudonym of the writer Ronald De Couves Matthews, and notes that the book was written 'with the assistance of Graham Greene'. In the *New Statesman and Nation*, 9 April 1938, p. 616, G. W. Stonier denounced the pro-censorship views of the *Daily Mail* and *Daily Mirror*, and offered some praise for *To Beg I am Ashamed*.

Sunday, 10 April. The black dog of melancholy lies on my shoulders today. I'm short of money and have even less inclination to stir out of the house. I thought perhaps Leonard might have come today, but of course he didn't, so I've lain in a chair, reading or writing and deploring the passage of time and the passing of friends. I make no new ones. How can I? I belong to no 'body' and if I visit I am usually the sole guest while the hatred of leaving my home grows ever more pronounced. I feel as though I'm already half dead.

Monday, 11 April. Lil sent 15s for my birthday but I returned 5s. I bought a navy blue suitcase with 7s 6d. Back to Hamond Square [School] and *how* it kills me. Hewson a pig, barely speaking, Conway simple, Topley monosyllabic, Kerr bland and empty as a pricked bladder, Miss Hammond all talk and running about like a dog in a fair. To Tatler tonight, a Disney programme. One does weary of so many cartoons in quick succession. One of my ears is worrying me. It feels hot and painful. Bay wrote.

Tuesday, 12 April. Miss Hammond has scored. She has ousted Hewson and Kerr and is to have *top* class. Pickering will take her history and geography and Kerr her handwork. *I* am to have the lowest class, mostly ineducables. It does seem sinful to waste a good and enthusiastic and hard-working teacher on small mentally defective children. If she worked I wouldn't care. I never begrudged Mrs. Morton and Miss Short their pick of children.

Wednesday, 13 April. Cheque received for £24 9s 6d instead of the usual £24 15s 0d – and I had expected an increment too. I shall have to write to LCC for particulars. School closed [for the Easter break] with the usual confusion and with Mr. Pickering taking even less interest than usual in organisation. He knew I was angry because he wouldn't let me get everything in readiness for the new class. He said 'You ought to have the Poplar HT [headteacher] who complained that his staff issued too much toilet paper to the children and in future were only to give two pieces to each child, "one to clean and one to polish".' Since he says people who read psycho-analysis have dirty minds and want to wallow in filthy details, and again semi-spinsters like me always like sex-novels, I'm surprised at *his* idea of humour. I've been foolish talking so much against Miss Hammond to the teachers in the Girls' Department but I do detest her so much and she does 'run' the school. Latcham's owe me £19; balance of cheque.

Thursday, 14 April. Wellings phoned last night – most mysterious about his Easter doings. Editha phoned this morning then met me and bought me six tumblers for my birthday. She looked *so* ill, grey-faced and lacklustre. She says she will retire this Midsummer or next and live on her savings. She doesn't look as if she would *live*. I left her and went westwards – bought lingerie at Weiss's and a coatee at Stagg's. Back to Library where I met Mrs. Wilmot and she made me promise to go to tea when we go back to school. She is a fool but I'm adding even them to my visiting list for the number of 'highbrows' steadily shrink and they – the highbrows – are most unreliable.

* * * * * *

Sunday, 17 April, Easter Sunday. I am 48 today, alas! I suppose all hope of amorous incident in my life is gone – yet even now I could love passionately, given a little encouragement. Em phoned and so did Editha. Editha says she shall probably leave London when she retires. How I shall miss her! She was talking about modern and ancient history – saying how the Angles and the Saxons were the first Germans known to have found England more attractive than the Homeland. She also said she thought all the recent war talk was encouraged, so English people should say, as in the War years, 'We must all stick together', and regard any leaning towards Communism as a disloyalty to the race. Went to the London Museum [at Lancaster House] this afternoon. It was crowded. Found the Irving Exhibition interesting, also the 19th century exhibits, the portraits (engravings) of past Prime Ministers and the fashions of other days. Merry Widow hats looked more comical than Dolly Varden hats,[30] I thought, and the 19th [century] Ascot gown more ridiculous than one with panniers. Saw the striking cinema operators [members of the Electrical Trades Union] on picket duty outside cinemas in Tottenham Court Road and Charing Cross Road.[31] Saw a beautiful black and white cat sleeping in graceful abandon on an expensive amber silk-covered antique stool in a St. James's shop. Waiting for [number]19 bus outside Green Park station and a conductor on a [number] 38 bus leaned out saying 'Where do you want to go?' 'I'm waiting for a 19', I answered. 'Sorry, lady. This is a bit cosmopolitan round 'ere and I thought you was Frenchy-looking and pe'raps lorst. Sorry an' all that.'

Monday, 18 April, Easter Monday. Caught 11.40 a.m. excursion train from Paddington to Bath. To my disgust found it filled to overflowing, mostly with men who stood two deep in the corridor so a glimpse of the landscape was impossible on my side of the carriage. They all got out at Swindon where there was a big football match

30. The former, popular at the beginning of the century, was hugely broad and sometimes extravagantly decorated; the latter was a flat straw hat, with a shallow crown, trimmed with flowers and ribbons.
31. According to the *Evening Standard*, Monday, 18 April 1938, p. 4, there was 'an organised effort [by the Electrical Trades Union] to spread the strike throughout the suburbs and West End'.

being played, after talking football pools and points all the way. At Bath, made straight for the Abbey cutting through Church Street where there was a fearsome fight in progress. The combatants came out of a doorway like projectiles from a cannon's mouth; one with a bloody nose fell in a heap almost at my feet, the other pounced on him and pummelled him till some dishevelled women tore him off. I fled as from the Hound of Heaven but, like Peter, stood afar off and eventually saw the 'top dog' depart with a couple of toughs, [and] an elderly man take over the injured man while one of the women produced two special constables whom she had brought from the main road. I was therefore hardly in the mood for abbey exploration. The majority of the memorials seemed to be in memory of West and East India merchants or of invalids who came to find health and found Death instead. The east and west windows are too Perpendicular to please me but I like the 'fan' (?) vaulting of roof in the aisles. How and when do visitors find opportunity for carving initials (sometimes even full-length names) on stone figures? Anyhow, why do it? Is it a desire for immortality? Was disappointed in the Roman Bath. I foolishly imagined it would be of white and gleaming marble, forgetting that nothing gleams in this country save broken glass and frosty roads! But the town is beautiful! The Circus and Royal Crescent, Camden Crescent too, are most impressive. I hadn't time for the Modern Art Exhibition. Home on a train packed with sots. Empty bottles hurtled through the windows and a procession passed to and from lavatory in corridor.

* * * * * *

Friday, 22 April. Caught 11.05 a.m. from Paddington to Welshpool. Interesting couple in carriage as far as Birmingham – two Jews in the cinema trade – apparently engaged in hiring out films and very full of the possible success of *Easy Money* [1925 silent film] coming next week to the London Pavilion. Stelle and her husband at station. She has aged considerably but still has poise and dresses well. Her husband, though the soul of kindness, is Public Bore No. 1. He talks incessantly, all about himself. Neither are conversationalists. Their lives and interests are bounded by the local politics and their daily work. They don't read – 'listen in' – or see any reputable films but they *do* keep a *most* comfortable home.

Saturday, 23 April. After interminable arguments between husband and wife we finally drove to Shrewsbury where they gave me luncheon and then we two wandered round the town while 'Douglas' went to a football match. Stelle and I had tea at Boots'. Then we all went to the cinema and saw two footling films – one a ridiculous thing about Tarzan wherein the hero kills with his bare hands (!) a lion and a tiger, is attacked by companies of men whom he successfully beats off and he never gets a scratch, a blow or his hair rumpled!! A white woman in the jungle is carried off by natives and nearly killed and appears afterwards – still in the jungle, having escaped – in a smart Parisian outfit!!! Driving home in the dark was a doubtful pleasure. 'Douglas' has already been fined for dangerous driving and I hourly expected calamity. He drives with one hand, takes *both* off the wheel to adjust the sunshine roof, and when we head for the ditch suddenly wrenches the wheel and we're all in a heap as he swerves violently right over to the other side of the road – on a hairpin bend too.

Sunday, 24 April. An interminable morning of talk. A tremendous luncheon and then 'Douglas' drove us to Shrewsbury for the 5.05 p.m. train. Travelled in comfort and talked with an ugly, Chinese-looking woman on Theosophy. She said she was in the service of the Great Western Railway and lived at Hampstead Garden Suburb, with her mother. I shared my sandwiches with her. Wellings phoned. He's very enthusiastic about Capek's play *Power and the Glory*, and recommended the new film *Bluebeard's 8ᵗʰ Wife* – he's not yet seen it though.

A new term began on 26 April. 'These small children are wearying,' she wrote. 'They can do nothing and they stare at me like sphinxes.' On Monday, 2 May she was 'very depressed by hostile atmosphere at school and such immature minds as these children have'. The next day, 'Boy at school told his mother I kept him in and she wrote making a fuss. I kept him as long as it takes me to get to the foot of the stairs and back. I never keep children at 12 o'clock.'

Wednesday, 4 May. Mother of boy turned up but was quite amiable and Mr. Pickering spoke to her telling her she was making the boy a 'molly coddle'. To the Misses Hardwick tonight. They are dear old women and they don't seem to alter. They look no older than they did 12 years ago but life has passed them by. One has been in a Tube train once, the other not at all. Neither has *seen* an escalator and neither has seen a film nor been in a theatre, yet they don't seem preternaturally old and certainly they are kindly. In the bottom of my heart is a vague wonder if they will ever leave me anything – but I don't suppose so. I always fancied Miss Monkhouse would but she left it to strangers she hardly knew although she so often said that through me she had come to make so many friends.

Thursday, 5 May. A bad night. I dreamed of Alec Davies. I am always dreaming of people who go mad now and indeed I feel insane. School is appalling. My room is so hot – it faces west. The children are so young and so foolish and Miss Hammond is a whole thorn-bush in my side. She borrows and tries to appropriate everything of use anyone else has. She wants to alter every existing arrangement. Sometimes when her foolish tongue goes prattling on I long to spring at her throat and press my thumbs on it until her tongue lolls out on those steak-coloured lips.

This was a time when Gladys was feeling more friendless than usual. The life of a woman of a certain age on her own was not easy. 'I felt so desolate,' she wrote on 1 May. 'I think I shall advertise for congenial acquaintances again. My own seem to be slipping away from me and Hoxton offers no outlet.' A week later, another Sunday, she was missing Leonard. 'Absurdly enough, I felt sure Leonard would come today. Needless to say, he didn't. I haven't seen him for nearly five months.' Nor did he appear the following Sunday, 15 May. 'I'm terribly depressed again. I wish I could meet some men-folk.' (Leonard did, though, send her a cheque for £6 on 19 May in response to her request for a loan.)

Monday, 16 May. Editha and Kiernan came tonight. They were very complimentary about my floral dress. Ginsbury wrote a delightful note saying how much he appreciated the humour of my letter[32] and how he might use some of it some day. (How I wish I could get a chance to write myself! If only I could meet people!) Wellings phoned and gave me a long account of his love affairs. I never heard such a farrago of nonsense and I believe he's suffering from a phantasy. He says he wants to study frigidity in women on the lines of the Elizabeth play recently produced and could I explain my own frigidity!!!! I gasped. *I'm* not frigid but I didn't know anything about birth control and I didn't want a child – that's why my marriage was marred.

A few days before, on 10 May, she had written, 'My ex-husband will be 48 tomorrow – if he's alive. I should like to see him.' (Five years later, on 11 May 1943, she said much the same thing, on the occasion of his 53rd birthday. 'Where is he? I wonder – and that in kindliness.') One day that summer, 28 July 1938, she was to reflect on her failed marriage. 'Today would have been my silver wedding-day. I might easily have been a grandmother. How glad I am, I am not. I haven't paid too heavy a price for my freedom. But I would like news of George. Poor George! In retrospect I have been over every incident of July 28th, 1913. He did love me once, if only for a time. Maybe it was just sex stirring in him! I wish him well wherever he is.'[33]

---

32. Gladys had just written to him: 'His play is being televised' (15 May; television had just been introduced to Britain – it would be abandoned during the war).
33. George Langford was in fact very much alive – and would outlive Gladys by almost a decade. In 1915, when he began proceedings to end their marriage, he was a lance corporal stationed temporarily at the headquarters of the London Rifle Brigade, Wilbury, Ipswich (National Archives, J77/1218/7060). He remained in military uniform until 1919, and according to the UK Memorial Books, he was in the London Regiment and Machine Gun Corps, served in France for three and a half years, and was 'Mentioned in despatches'. On 14 January 1919, a few weeks after the annulment of his ties to Gladys, he married

Several years later, on what would have been her 31ˢᵗ wedding anniversary, 28 July 1944, Gladys revisited the issue of the break-up of her marriage, and was at that time more specific in her revelations than on any other occasion. 'One thing alone I wish – that my marriage had been consummated – but I never wish that I had had a child. I loathe the idea of childbirth as much as ever I did and I am glad I never gave my youth to the upbringing of a child who would now be in one of the Forces.' 'During one period,' she later remarked, 'I was willing to have borne Leonard a child. How glad I am I did not!' (18 August 1944).

Gladys's hostility to bearing a child was deep rooted. On 1 January 1939 she noted that 'pregnant women make me feel distinctly uneasy ... I AM glad motherhood has been resolutely eschewed by me.' 'Am so glad I never had a child,' she wrote on 6 October 1944. 'I don't like having been an inmate of my mother's womb. Much less should I have wished my own womb to be tenanted. I am certainly unbalanced on this matter.' This distaste for being pregnant – and perhaps child-rearing as well – does seem to be the main reason why her marriage to George Langford was never consummated.

Some people who knew her saw her problems differently. Her niece, Bay, once said (6 May 1937) that 'no one wanted to marry me because I cause everyone a sense of unease'. The following week (14 May) her despised brother-in-law, Herbert Challis, 'let fly the animosity of half a lifetime. He said I never gave pleasure to anyone and no one could feel pleasure in meeting me as they did in meeting him and his wife! He then proceeded to the effect that I had spoilt everything, including

again, this time to Ellen Agnes Grundy, aged twenty-five, in Lindfield, West Sussex. She was the daughter of a deceased builder; he was then living in Maida Vale. This marriage, again, did not work out. In late 1923, when they were living in Kilburn, George left Ellen (known as 'Nellie'); she appealed for a restitution of conjugal rights, and the courts sided with her petition and awarded her alimony payments (National Archives, J77/2085/5307). There is no evidence that they divorced – at least not during the later 1920s. Two years later, on 20 March 1926, George married a third time, this time in Fulham, to Violet Emily White, twenty-two years old and a schoolmistress. He falsely gave his age as thirty (he was thirty-five). They were both then living, presumably together, at 101 Talgarth Road, West Kensington. Since George was still legally married to Ellen née Grundy, he was charged the following year with bigamy (31 October 1927), tried before a judge and found guilty on 15 November 1927, and was required 'To enter into Recognisance to appear for judgment if called upon' (National Archives, Old Bailey Proceedings). Perhaps this spot of trouble induced the couple to withdraw from West London, for soon after this trial he left the capital for teaching positions in the West Midlands, first in Halesowen, then Wollescote, Stourbridge (Teachers Registration Council Certificate, 1931). It is likely that from late 1918 Gladys knew nothing about his whereabouts. Since she never mentions the possibility that he might have died in the Great War, she probably knew that he was alive when it ended, which more or less coincided with legal termination of their marriage.

George Langford died on 25 July 1981, aged ninety-one, in the John Radcliffe Hospital, Oxford. His death certificate described him as a retired school teacher and his usual address as The Cottage, Islip Road, Bletchingham, Oxfordshire. His third (though perhaps never legalised) marriage had lasted; his wife, whether only in appearance or in due course actual, and sole heir in his will, Violet Emily (née) White, died in January 2003, aged ninety-eight.

We are much indebted to Ann Stephenson, Caroline Barron, Paul Klein, and Jerry White for their work in helping to rescue George Langford from obscurity.

my married life. When I said perhaps my ignorance or innocence had caused me to embark upon an impossible matrimonial arrangement, he declared no one else started any differently from what I had done at my age. Nonsense.'

Sunday, 22 May. Very pleasant weather. An early midday meal, then went to Kenwood. Sat on the Terrace reading *Cockney Past and Present* by [William] Matthews.[34] When a musty old man and woman arrived I grew restless. The old woman smelt of decay. Her finger nails were broken and dirty; she ate biscuits carried loose in her grubby hand-bag and she talked, oh, how she talked! She grumbled about the passers-by, their clothes, their walk, their manner of speech. Then she held herself up as a model of all the virtues till her frail old husband was nearly frantic. 'I could kill you when you go on and on', he said viciously, and I felt so murderous I had to get up and walk round the grounds. When I returned and sat down to read I got into conversation with a middle-aged couple from Eastbourne. The man managed Cave's Café, near the Gildredge [Eastbourne]. His teeth were obviously false but he was well groomed and seemed pleasant. His wife was the usual shapeless mass of middle age.

* * * * * *

Wednesday, 25 May. School again. Tonight to Old Vic. Met Wellings there – by accident. He *does* look a boob – sauntering in, head held tortoise-wise and with his pronounced stoop. Bored me all over again with accounts of his love-affair. He says he has written to Prof. Ernest Jones [student of Sigmund Freud and writer on psychoanalysis] the whole story and Jones (like a good Welshman and businessman) professes interest and suggests that Wellings and – or – his lady love should go to the Professor's clinic in Gloucester Road. Wellings is quite mad. He told me some long rigmarole of how he supposed the lady had been raped by her father, a professional cricketer, and how this incident had made her masochistic in her dealings with Wellings. Then he maundered off into an account of his manageress's symbolical suppressions of words in her typewriting. We walked across London Bridge and I hopped away as fast as I could lest he should invite me for Sunday night. He says Clowser is annoyed with me and I must have hurt some secret spring in his nature. I don't know how. I've always been most considerate of him. *He* hasn't always spared *my* feelings.

---

34. This 1938 book is subtitled *A Short History of the Dialect of London* (reprinted by Routledge & Kegan Paul, 1972). It was conceived by its author as an attempt to rescue the Cockney dialect from growing obscurity, and to grant it the sort of scholarly attention that, in his view, had been accorded mainly to provincial dialects. Matthews, like Gladys, was born and grew up in the East End; she on numerous occasions complains of what in her view were inaccurate portrayals of Cockney characters in films and on the stage.

* * * * * *

Thursday, 9 June. Wellings phoned last night. He *is* mad. He had met a kennel-maid in a Cotswold village in charge of two dogs called Moses and Solomon. He said 'You can, of course, read the owner's mind from the choice of name, can't you?' 'I suppose he was either derisive of the Scriptures or else the dogs had long snouts.' 'No,' says Wellings solemnly. 'He was expressing his sex-longings. Moses was a *father* of his people, Solomon the *husband* of innumerable wives. Everyone gives animals names suggested by his sub-conscious.' 'Don't be so silly,' said I. 'I had a cat, Archibald – what did *that* express? My sister has had Peggy, Primrose and Nonnie among dogs – names hardly expressive of sex-longings.' He's getting as bad as John Bunyan with his 'sin against the Holy Ghost'. He wants me to get Hazlitt's *Liber Amoris* from the Library for him if I can. Bother! Miss Hammond told me she'd had facial treatment and advised me to indulge. Since her face is as full of blackheads and her skin as oily as ever I'm not moved to emulate her. Her 'will to power' still flourishes. She says she could not board a tram this morning so she appealed to a lorry driver to give her a lift. She is full now of accounts of a man named Cyril who is supposed to be her latest follower. She never produces one. The accounts of the Japanese raids on China are appalling [Japan had invaded China the previous year]. It does seem as though the countries suffered less under their old despots than they do under their republican leaders, Germany, Spain, China and Austria. Am reading and enjoying *The Verney Letters and Memoirs of the 18th Century* [1930].

Gladys's spirits were often low during the last weeks of this teaching term. Her social life was unsatisfying and her job unfulfilling; she was sometimes ill or very tired, and often bored; one night she dreamed she had committed suicide – 'It was a disappointment to waken and find myself alive' (29 June). On Sunday, 3 July she resolved to boost her morale. 'Strengthened my self-respect by reading over a few love-letters and testimonials. Some of the latter ought to guarantee a candidature for heaven.' She rarely heard from Leonard and had not seen him for months. 'He'll never come here again,' she lamented on 29 June, 'love-making is over for me. That accounts for my depression.' Her prediction, however, turned out to be wrong.

Monday, 18 July. About 4 p.m. yesterday Leonard phoned and said he could come to tea. I nearly had an apoplectic seizure from joy. By the time he arrived I was in my new grey suit only I was too florid to look really nice. I was enfolded in his arms and passionately kissed as soon as my sitting-room door closed on us. We had tea, talked, and then, yes, though I'm 48, retired to my bedroom for tempestuous love-making. We forget our years when we are together; indeed he grows younger as he grows more passionate. My beloved! How I idolise him and how negligible all other men appear beside him! He drove me to Finchley and I raced back to cut sandwiches for school before I darted off to Wellings. I was so exhilarated I laughed at nothing all the evening. A pleasant evening and only at the last did W. refer to his mysterious love affairs. He tells me Clowser was robbed of £7 in a Brighton bar this weekend. I've done my good deeds for today. Met Mrs. Morton, who looks as young as ever, for tea, then called at Pyrland Road where I stayed for 1½ hours.

3

July–October 1938

Perils Ahead

The school term ended and Gladys was at leisure. On 20 July she had supper with Editha, who 'says her husband is always studying pictures and advertisements of women in evening dress and underwear, such as are so generously sprinkled over the pages of newspapers and monthlies'. On Sunday, 24 July she took a boat to Greenwich. 'The inhabitants of Greenwich always make me class-conscious. They are a hideous lot. The women have lost most of their teeth and all of their contours. The men look brutalised.' On the way home she 'Saw a swarm of bees that had settled on a traffic light at the corner of Pentonville Road and Upper Street. Several policemen were keeping back the crowd and a man with net, gloves and hive was preparing to remove them.' On 26 July, after shopping in Caledonian Market, she observed that 'Poor people do waste money on indigestible food! Practically every draggle-tailed woman and almost shoeless child sucked ice-wafers, chewed spearmint, drank highly-coloured soft drinks or cracked peanuts.' While Gladys seldom lived within her own financial means – indeed, she routinely borrowed money from friends and relatives – most of her discretionary expenditures were for what she saw as intellectual essentials, that is, films, plays, and concerts, and, to a lesser extent, eating out. Her books probably came mainly from public libraries. 'I have badly overspent so must pull in my horns,' she observed on 19 August; this, indeed, was her normal condition of existence – though as a rule there was little evidence of pulling in her horns.

Saturday, 30 July. Postman awakened me about 7.20 a.m. with violent ringing of bell so I fell down the bedroom doorstep and nearly fainted. At 9 a.m. comes the window cleaner unexpectedly so I go down to greet him with a knife! He *did* laugh. I met Wilmot this morning looking very old and grandfatherly, also Vera Mannering with a bad eye and the customary grievance. Les wrote. Bay phoned. Met Mr. Gaye outside Covent Garden Theatre at 2.15 p.m. The heat had made him decide against the Ballet. Instead he whisked me off in a taxi (!) to Regent's Park Open Air Theatre to see Gladys Cooper in *Lysistrata*. The setting is delightful. A cloudless sky, a background of trees in full leaf and brown birds flying hither and thither. The play was entertaining but I didn't like the grotesque masks. Ellen Pollock was excellent but Philip Merivale as the uxorious husband ought not to have uncovered a slightly bald head when his helmet was removed. I thought his neighings and pawing of the ground like a full-blooded stallion absolutely vile.

Imagine my amazement after the play when Gaye invited me to go to his home for tea! In the old days that would have amounted to a declaration! We found the house empty so had to wait till the maid returned to make tea. Meanwhile he played the piano for me, ranging from Chopin through Schumann to Beethoven (unfortunately breathing heavily meanwhile). The idea flashed through my mind, 'This is the male bird showing off before the old hen'. His dog was a particularly unpleasant little beast – all over my new clothes. The home (except the bathroom, which was distinctly 'mucky') was exactly like I expected – overcrowded with a medley of furniture and innumerable knick-knacks in cabinets. There was a conservatory, where I had tea, and the house was a little dark and stuffy and closed in from the world but all the same it was a home – and a home where the decencies were respected. I stayed till 7 p.m. and he walked as far as the Spaniards Road with me. I was foolish enough to suggest if he should ever feel inclined to go anywhere on a Saturday afternoon for a couple of hours I'd like to join him, paying my own expense. I don't think he favoured the idea. I don't love him. My heart misses no beat at sight of him. I note his need for a shave, his fleshy neck and fat hands. It is Leonard's leanness and cruel passion that carries me off my feet, and for whom I could leave the world behind – perhaps! But I *much* prefer Gaye to Wellings.

Sunday, 31 July. To sit in this flat today is to imagine one is a palm in a Kew hothouse! As the Georgian and Carolean ladies might have said, 'I'm all of a muck-sweat'. It was nice to hear Em's voice over the telephone wire today. Have written letters galore including one I hope Mr. Gaye finds gratifying.

Monday, 1 August, Bank Holiday. Hell will have no horrors for me after this flat. Milk turns bad, butter rancid and the cat's fish makes the whole house mephitic.[1] 'A garden is a lovesome thing, God wot!' – and don't I echo that view?

Tuesday, 2 August. The day before I go on holiday always gets frittered away. Thus today, hair-cut, both libraries, and westward to buy

---

1. She had, of course, no refrigerator; few people did.

dressing gown. In Shaftesbury Avenue I met Ginsbury who took me to coffee at Patisserie Valerie. (He didn't like the coffee there!) He told me all the theatrical scandal, pointed out [the actress] Cathleen Nesbitt who went by in a car in Dean Street and then accused so many other people of homosexuality I know that must be a practice of his.

Wednesday, 10 August. This gap is due to my having been to Chester for a week with Bay. I gave £4 towards her expenses and paid some extras. It has all been a great mistake for neither of us enjoyed ourselves. I had forgotten in 13 years apart what a horrid girl she was, savage-tempered and selfish. She *has* tried to keep her temper, but *why* should she want to be ill-humoured on holiday with someone who tried to please her in every way? She says I treat her like a baby. *I* think she criticises me unduly. She doesn't approve of my style of dress, my speaking my mind nor of my dislike of ugliness. We were very disappointed in the town, which is very 'slummy', and our accommodation was on the outskirts so we always had to make the unpleasant journey. The landlady was the most voluble (though very kindly) spinster I've ever met. Her father had a perennially wet nose. They had three dogs whose hairs garnished all our food. On our first day we went to Colwyn Bay. I was much depressed by the desolate mining areas through which we passed. The next day we went to Llangollen where the atmosphere was that of a hothouse but I thought the Glen by the Old Ladies' House very attractive and the canal pleasure boat trip (to the Horseshoe Falls) a delight. The next day we went to Bangor via Bettws and Capel Curig – a lovely ride – and Bangor is a delightful town or rather Garth is with its quaint pier and a view of Anglesey. We had our hands read here. The fortune teller told me someone elderly for whom I cared would die when I was about 52 and I should then settle down to a peaceful future and enjoy a few small, but very small, legacies. She also spoke of a great influence that had entered my life at about 25 and that would be with me as long as we both lived.

The weather broke next day so, after a night of storm during which I had tea with the two men in the house, all of us in night-clothes and dressing-gowns, there was nothing to do next day but explore the Cathedral and visit the local repertory theatre where we saw the world's worst company as *Double Door* [by American playwright Elizabeth McFadden]. They mowed and mouthed, undulated and gibbered, till I nearly had hysterics. Next day we walked in the Duke of Westminster's grounds, Eaton Hall, a horrid house reminiscent of the Albert Memorial. I loved watching the hares, squirrels and rabbits at play. When we reached Eccleston Ferry there was no boat available so we had to walk to the village, where we missed the bus and begged the use of a villager's w.c. Then we walked to Chester but an awful storm arose. I've NEVER before been so wet. I had to buy a new hat, macintosh and gloves that night before I could go to the pictures. Today we walked to Guilder (?) Sutton [i.e., Guilden Sutton] before leaving. Saw an elver in the village stream. On the return journey a most unpleasant boy in *our* carriage drove me into the next where a most *pleasant* man was alone. Bay wouldn't join me so from Wolverhampton to Oxford he and I talked – sense and nonsense. He told me he was 54, born in Colehill and now living in Liverpool. We discussed the depressed area and modern young people. It is good to be home again.

* * * * * *

Saturday, 13 August. Bay wrote. Em on phone. She offered to sell me her piano for £8 or £10. I want a radiogram. Met Leonard at noon in City Road. He drove me to Bognor giving me luncheon by the way at the Southampton Arms. For once, much as I love him, we were out of sympathy and I found it difficult to find a point of contact. He had brought some poems he had written in Gilbertian style about Charlie. He told me of the excellent speeches he'd made at various functions and he talked much of his children – of their innumerable ailments and their scholastic attainments. He says he'll drive me down again next Friday. I felt queerly remote from him. Came back by coach to Victoria for 6s. Had a glass of port by the way.

Like most Londoners, Gladys knew a few parts of the great city – then the most populous in the world, with around eight million people – very well, others not at all. 'What a mine of surprises London is!' she wrote on Monday, 15 August. 'In my journey to Dulwich Art Gallery today I discovered Dulwich Village, a rural spot one would never have suspected lingering in South London. I thoroughly enjoyed my exploration of the district. Dulwich Park was attractive – it was so "well-groomed".'

Wednesday, 17 August. Last night I met Wellings at 7.30 p.m. at Leicester Square Station. We went to the Samovar, a dismal café in St. Martin's Lane, empty, smelling of paint and having practically nothing in stock because of the renovations. The coffee looked and tasted like dishwater. I wasn't much in sympathy with Wellings. I get so annoyed by his persistent attempts at psycho-analysis on small evidence. His latest theory is to explain Coulson's alleged wistfulness by his lack of success with women. *I've* never noticed the wistfulness. Coulson seems a much more attractive person than Wellings who picks his nose, mumbles his words, and broadcasts fragments when eating. Editha phoned this morning inviting me to eat there tonight. She is full of their discoveries about 'graft' in provincial France. Met Nancy McMillan. She is breeding again. Miss Sidebotham, the red-haired girl at Highbury Crescent, is married. I doubt if *her* husband got a virgin.

Thursday, 18 August. Enjoyed my visit to Editha's last night. They were very full of accounts of their holiday in France. They seem to think Democracy is not so firmly established in France as they could wish but that Communism is very active there. Personally, I can't see how they can, in three weeks' holiday in a tiny place, have accumulated enough data to allow them to form a true opinion. They had [been] much amused by a Crusader – a supporter of a religious group at Cambridge approximating to the followers of [evangelist Frank] Buchman, the Oxford Group leader [of what became Moral Re-Armament].

This morning, on the phone, Leonard said he was going to Felpham today so I could go as far as Bognor with him if I could meet him by 12.15 p.m. I did and we had a glorious afternoon together. We drove through the sunshine to Kingston, ate a good luncheon at the Toby Jug and then he said he'd make a detour so I could enjoy the country-side, so we travelled all through Haslemere, Midhurst and then another side-tracking to Goodwood and to see the Duke of Richmond's house. Finally I left him at Bognor but coach service didn't offer a good run so I returned by train. At Victoria, four hefty uniformed policemen and about eight plainclothes men stood close to the barriers scanning closely faces of all leaving the train. I, with several people, stood awaiting developments but they pounced on no one and three of the uniformed men then interrogated a taximan. Why don't the authorities employ some *little*, ordinary men as detectives? The plainclothes men are so evidently police in undress uniform. Five women out of seven at the seaside are now wearing coloured kerchiefs on their heads, like Irish colleens. These are becoming to but few. I'm re-reading *Journal of a Disappointed Man*.[2] Lil wrote.

* * * * * *

Sunday, 21 August. Re-reading *Barbellion's Diary* has made me decide to leave mine to British Museum – or any other authority who will accept it.[3] It *is* good. Phoned Editha to arrange for a party on September 20th when all my friends can discuss the experiences of their

2. She is referring to W. N. P. Barbellion, *The Journal of a Disappointed Man* (London: Chatto & Windus, 1919), which was followed by the same author's *A Last Diary* (London: Chatto & Windus, 1920). They were reprinted in 1984 in a single volume by the Hogarth Press. See the following footnote.

3. Gladys as a writer may well have been inspired by Barbellion's diary, which was something of a literary sensation at the time of its publication. Barbellion, the pseudonym of Bruce Frederick Cummings (b. 1889), wrote for posterity and wanted his diary to be published. Like Gladys, he was opinionated and acerbic – and felt his genius was under-appreciated. He may have been right. He was a skilled naturalist, employed by the Natural Science Museum in South Kensington until ill health necessitated his resignation. A self-confessed introvert and egotist, he knew his days were numbered. He had for long been frail and suffered from the then little understood disease of multiple sclerosis; he died at thirty years of age. He had a publisher – Gladys did not. He was confident of his skills – Gladys only sometimes so. For her he seems to have been a literary role model. He apparently wrote and rewrote with a view to his intellectual legacy. Gladys occasionally revisited her own diary and, as this passage shows, wanted it to have a more-than-private importance.

summer holidays and their hostess can maintain a smiling silence since she doesn't travel in Europe. Tonight went to the Gaumont, Haymarket to see the new Carole Lombard film, *Fools for Scandal*. Farcical but *very* funny. Fernand Gravet, whom I have seen in French films, outshines William Powell at his own game. Walked back to Blooms-bury. Am fretting very much at being 'on the shelf'. I do try to 'count my blessings' as the hymn exhorts me to do, but I want masculine company and I want a home, not just this roosting place.

Monday, 22 August. Breakfasted in bed – with the cat – to celebrate last day of holiday. To both Libraries. There's a new huge pylon to be seen from the street-corner. It towers over the distant house-tops and is apparently at Hampstead or Highgate. Bay wrote, also Lil and Em. To Tatler tonight. A good informative film, the *Land of Rhodes*, an amusing one, *The Zoo and You* including Mabel Constanduros as Gran'ma Buggins. I can NOT think why these music hall and BBC Cockneys don't study their models more closely. The type Mabel Constanduros portrays ceased to exist 15 or 20 years ago. Even in slummy Hoxton I've not seen an old woman in a bonnet since I've worked there – about seven years.

Tuesday, 23 August. School re-opened. Ugh! The warm day and the removal of our school blinds made the heat oppressive and the odours pronounced. Kippers and fried steak and onions from nearby houses, soiled clothes of small boys, paint not yet dry, and the cheap perfumes favoured by Miss Hammond bowed down the air. Workmen perambu-lated the place. Some sing, some whistle, some spit, some sniff and quite a few cry 'Oi! You silly bugger, what're you doin' of?'

Wednesday, 24 August. Very warm. No sun-blinds at school now. Workmen, children and yapping dogs in a healthy rivalry as Kings of Noise. I get nearly frantic – and of plays and films there are so few new ones I've nowhere to go at night. Wellings goes away for a week on Friday.

Thursday, 25 August. Last night *was* wearisome! A defective water pipe and a bed that squeaked both called for attention so my evening leisure was frittered away. Today the heat and the noise of painters and the householders near the school quite exhausted me. I was so tired I could hardly crawl home. We have forms from the LCC relating to the forthcoming arrangement for paying teachers by crediting their banking accounts with their salaries. The LCC will open accounts for those of us who have no accounts of our own. Mr. Pickering brought me [Alexander] Woolcott's *While Rome Burns* [1934; a book on the theatre]. Another apparent case of scabies at school.

* * * * * *

Sunday, 28 August. Stayed at home all day, partly through lack of means, partly because no attractive new films are showing, partly because I want to see several forthcoming shows. Re-read some diaries of 1932/3/4. They certainly *are* good although I note with surprise how full they are of incidents illustrative of sex-hunger. Reading psycho-analysis and realising what is the matter with one doesn't seem to cure the complaint.

Monday, 29 August. Not quite so ill-humoured at school today. Papers, wireless news and every placard full of hints of trouble in connection with Czecho-Slovakia.[4] I do get terrified with all this talk of war. To Boots and the Free Library. The former is so poor nowadays, I shall not renew my subscription. Miss Hope wrote – full of ailments as usual.

Tuesday, 30 August. Lil wrote. Bay came. She has a troublesome cough but was very amiable. I sold her a frock for 5s, gave her an umbrella, a pair of gloves, a vest and knickers. I shall be glad when the Czecho-Slovakian trouble is ended. It gets on my nerves. I'm continually dreaming of war.

Wednesday, 31 August. Letter from Marjorie Rosenberg. Mrs. Rosenberg's maid, Agnes, has decamped. No details given so I suppose Mrs. R. upset her. They've never loved one another. I've never liked Agnes. She's too 'pushful'. Letter from Wellings. He's full of an account of a meeting in a train with a farmer's wife whom he invited to lunch on the train with him and who, he insinuates, found him so alluring she invited him to visit her at the farm where she lives. I was very annoyed because he wanted me to go to Finsbury Park and count the passers-by, working out an average for each side of the road so he could calculate the possibilities of a shop he wants to rent there. He suggests Friday or Saturday evening. I think this an impudent request for if it's a working evening I, at 48, don't want to go to stand about for half an hour, and if it's a leisure day I don't want to waste my time, spoil a whole evening, going there between 7 and 8 p.m. Phoned Editha. She's coming on Tuesday in next week.

* * * * * *

Saturday, 3 September. Wellings wrote again. He must be losing his reason like Hazlitt. He says he visited the woman he met on the train and the husband was very suspicious. He, Wellings, has psycho-analysed both host and hostess, to his *own* satisfaction, deciding there

---

4. Hitler was demanding that the mostly German-speaking Sudetenland region of Czechoslovakia be absorbed into the German Reich.

are unsatisfactory marital relations between the two. He now talks of writing to the woman and giving her an account of his *own* love affairs to help her straighten out her own (surmised) sexual troubles. He's becoming a megalomaniac, thinking he can play the Almighty to casual acquaintances. To the Lyric last night. Saw Charles Morgan's play *The Flashing Stream*, a peculiar but most entertaining play, quite different from the usual run. Margaret Rawlings is one of the best of the younger actresses but she is now dressing her hair in the new unbecoming way with curls on top so she looks quite plain. Felix Aylmer has a fat part but I think Godfrey Tearle is too old now for playing the part of a man emotionally wrought up by love. Went to the Academy Cinema to see *Uncle Moses*, a film produced by the Yiddish players. I thought the story very weak, the leading characters of paste-board quality – only Schwartz really good and the old man who took the part of the old father from Russia. Many side turnings on the north side of Oxford Street have street performers on Saturday night – a sword performance, a man in chains, a girl artist all there tonight.

Sunday, 4 September. As usual I'm frittering away the day on the bare likelihood of Leonard's coming. I always do. Bay phoned inviting me to go walking around Amersham next Saturday. Went tonight to Highgate and walked across the Heath to Hampstead Heath Station. I delight in Pond Square. I wish I could afford a house there.

Monday, 5 September. Suffered from a bad spell of rage at school today. I think I get over-wrought with playground duty, drill in the afternoon and the continual noise in the street outside. I could feel myself getting more and more frenzied but I managed to keep my hands off everyone although one boy said 'Oh, you terrified me when you screamed at me'. Teaching is the world's worst job for me and when continual talk of war and its horrors are in the air, I feel I can endure no more. Mrs. Dunlop sent me a card from Germany. I'm glad. I like her even if she is an adventuress as Mrs. Osborne alleges.

Tuesday, 6 September. Not quite so evil-humoured. Wellings phoned last night and said he would take me out – as his guest – on Thursday. Editha came to high tea. She was fretted because a fond mother had been to school complaining because Editha would not let her child wear a ring in school. Editha, like Miss Monkhouse, is theoretically a keen supporter of individual rights but woe betide anyone in her power who wants to do something different from what *she* wants. I tried to see if she would consider sharing a house with me, but no, when she retires she wants to get right outside London.

Wednesday, 7 September. Temper slightly less inflamed. Mr. Hewson, by his uncouth behaviour, annoys me. Nearly overpowered by the hypocrisy of school prayers. Kerr, a Jew, conducts the Christian prayers. *He* keeps his eyes open, wandering about punching boys who fail to close theirs. He exhorts *them* to be reverent but he usually laughs and talks with other teachers through the prayers! On phone tonight to Mrs. Rosenberg, Latcham's (I talked at great length to young Mr. Latcham), to Fowler and Piggin's and Em. I have to play for the boys' singing at Open Day.

Thursday, 8 September. Met Mr. Wellings at 7 p.m. and although I felt very tired before, I brightened up then. We had a snack meal at the Samovar where the waitress forgot her acquired accent (bastard Russian and embryo Yankee blended) and told me in good Cockney all her woes – 9 year old child and invalid husband to care for, 11½ hours working day and wearisome customers. We [were] very enthusiastic about a book of Fabre's he's reading in the Penguin series – I must re-read him.[5] We went to the Berkeley Cinema and saw a very far-fetched French thriller. I never care for Secret Service stories and as the companion picture was Laughton's *Rembrandt*, I wasn't very pleased. Saw a film of Butlin's Camp. It was Stanmore/Margate carried to the nth degree – and Lil thought I ought to go there.

* * * * * *

Saturday, 10 September. Met Bay at noon. Lunched at Lyons' Corner House,[6] thence to Uxbridge and so by coach to Amersham. Laden with a picnic basket that weighed very much, we crossed field paths, through Shardiloes Park to Mop End, blackberrying by the way, and using a private wood for a w.c. by the way. Saw hares and rabbits galore in the beech woods. I sat by the wayside while Bay gathered mushrooms in a field, then began a toilsome return to Amersham via Coleshill. I was handicapped by a hole in my stockings which exposed my toes to undue friction. Stiff and tired when we regained the coach route, Bay gave me supper and I came home, laden with flowers as midnight chimed. Still this awful tension over the Czech question.

Sunday, 11 September. It was on a Sunday 24 years ago today that I was taken to a workhouse ward when George was torturing me over breaking up our married life and taking away our home. I thought then

5. *Social Life in the Insect World*, by Jean-Henri Fabre (1823–1915), was translated by Bernard Miall and published by Penguin Books in 1937.
6. There were three Lyons' Corner Houses: one – the original – on Coventry Street, one on the Strand at the corner of Craven Street, and the most recent one at the corner of Oxford Street and Tottenham Court Road. These were huge, multi-storey establishments that catered to a wide range of tastes and incomes. The Coventry Street Corner House could accommodate at least 4,500 people – perhaps at its peak as many as 9,000; the Oxford Corner House in the 1930s claimed to be the largest restaurant in the world, and had a staff of over 700 (Bird, *First Food Empire*, chap. 9). Corner House menus and advertisements from the 1930s may be found in the London Metropolitan Archives, ref. 4364/02/022.

I could not go on. Now, I see how trifling each individual's hurts are! Em phoned. Reading Jane Welsh Carlyle's *Letters* – very entertaining because malicious and also because so self-revealing. She reminds me a little of myself with her continual headaches (but *not* with regard to her blue pills), her diatribes against her acquaintances (but *not* in her unhealthy devotion to her niece Jeanie).[7] Outside Uxbridge Station yesterday I saw the most dejected looking beggar I've seen for a long time – a slender youngish man, very dirty and unkempt and with such deplorable shoes that his bare feet were almost on the ground. He was playing a gramophone.

Monday, 12 September. Suddenly the weather has changed. It was 79° in the schoolroom this afternoon. The result was an appalling medley of odours – discharging ears, dirty feet, a diarrhoea victim and unwashed hands galore. I got so hot my feet swelled, my head swelled and I was on the point of collapse. Very unfairly I wrote a long screed to Lil saying I was contemplating suicide. I've written again tonight in a more cheerful strain. Perhaps Jane Welsh Carlyle's humour has suggested mine since I'm re-reading her *Letters* but I'm afraid Hitler is really responsible.[8]

Tuesday, 13 September. War fever raging as in 1914. Placards, wireless, everything going over and over the question. I feel utterly wretched and unsettled. Add to this a heat-wave that makes existence at school most wretched. Went westwards tonight but a full Disney programme at the Tatler kept me away. Saw a fight in progress in

7. Jane Carlyle's often opinionated and sometimes acerbic letters had been published in two volumes in 1903, *New Letters and Memorials of Jane Welsh Carlyle*. In a letter of 16 August 1843 she reported a disdain for school teaching that would surely have been noticed by Gladys. A friend who was apparently seeking a position as a governess, a Miss Bölte, according to Jane Carlyle, 'is a woman of too much mind and heart for being made into mince-meat to indiscriminate boarding-school Misses – at a "small salary" too. Ach Gott. Better one good sixpenny worth of arsenic once for all, than to prolong existence in *that* fashion! I at least should choose arsenic if in her place; and I estimate her quick determination too highly not to believe she would do the same' (I, 128–9). (It is not clear whether Gladys was reading this edition or that published in 1924 and edited by Leonard Huxley, *Jane Welsh Carlyle, Letters to her Family, 1839–1863*.)

8. In a letter of 28 September 1845 to her husband, Jane Carlyle, who lived in Chelsea, wrote that 'yesterday was rainy and dreary enough to set one on reading *The Purgatory of Suicides* (had there been time for it)'; and on 13 May 1850, after reporting some housekeeping she had done, she jokingly wrote, 'God defend me from ever coming to a fortune (a prayer more likely to be answered than most of my prayers!); for then the only occupation that affords me the slightest self-satisfaction would be gone! and there would remain for me only (as Mr. C. said of the Swiss Giantess who drowned herself) "to summon up all the virtue left in me, to rid the world of such a beggarly existence"' – and she then went on to recount an attempted suicide that she knew of. (Both references are from the 1903 edition of her letters, I, 175 and II, 16–17. *The Purgatory of Suicides* was a long poem by the Chartist Thomas Cooper, published in 1845.) 'To keep up the appearance of being alive is just as much as I can manage,' she lamented on 15 April 1856, a time when she was physically ill, 'complicated with dark apprehensions' (II, 88). It is easy to see how Gladys saw her as something of a kindred spirit.

Soho Square so fetched a policeman, then departed myself. Not getting concert tickets or anything else while this uneasiness persists.

Wednesday, 14 September. Wellings phoned last night and asked me to go out with him on Thursday. Perhaps it will dispel my gloom. War rumours fly from mouth to mouth. The King is coming back to London.

Thursday, 15 September. Met Wellings at 7 p.m. To the Samovar – as usual. A lot of talkative young women eating there. I hate the place. He aggravates me because he is so slow. He cannot decide what we're going to do or where we are going. *I* wanted a theatre, he a film, but as he always wants to come out if the film isn't to his taste I wouldn't go as I loathe wasting 2s 6d, so to the Queen's Hall where we missed the first item – *Rosamunde Overture*. Mr. Chamberlain has flown to Germany to meet Hitler. Things less like war. A blackboard fell on my head and stunned me temporarily.

Friday, 16 September. Lil wrote. Mr. Chamberlain, speaking from Heston, newly returned from Germany, said he is seeing Hitler again in a few days and the latter will come part of the way to meet him to save him so long a journey. He spoke warmly of the Fuehrer and so I suppose Czecho-Slovakia will be sold. Poor Czechs; but oh, to be spared the horrors of war. I am very selfish but I love peace and I'd rather offer a pinch of incense to Lucifer himself than have the horrors of war in England. War would have added horror for me now for there is talk of our taking school children under cover with two days' rations and a rug. To leave my home and my cat, live under canvas and perhaps get verminous would be Hell itself to me. The new nurse commented on the cleanliness of the boys in my class.

Saturday, 17 September. Mr. Wellings phoned last night. He said Jew-baiting was going on at Piccadilly Circus on Thursday night by young Fascists of the hooligan type. Somewhat relieved by the war news, I went out to buy a frock (I bought *two*) at Russell's, had luncheon at Lyons' brasserie and was just buying goodies for Tuesday's party when I met Miss Williams, from Hamond Square Infants' School. She enlarged on the plan for decanting children during war time, said we should go to Outer London and then be despatched to safety zones in the Home Counties. War news not so good now and Jew-baiting going on here in the East End. Oh, where will it all end?[9] I had such a fit of crying in Mrs. Lucas's kitchen tonight I thought my head would burst.

9. An attempt by the British Union of Fascists early in the summer of 1937 to process through Jewish districts of the East End had been prohibited by the Home Secretary (*Hackney Gazette and North London Advertiser*, 23 June 1937, p. 5). Attacks on Jewish shops and

Sunday, 18 September. News bulletins keep popping up all day – 10.30 a.m., 1 p.m. and 4 p.m. Em phoned. No news from her. Bay phoned, grumbling as usual about the incapacities of the telephone operators. She says she has been away from the office a day with neuritis in her foot. She wasn't particularly sympathetic about my fear of the decantation scheme yet she had a nervous attack when moved from one office to another!! Finished reading Herbert Hodge's *Autobiography*.[10]

Monday, 19 September. Lil wrote. France and Britain in agreement, poor Czecho-Slovakia in despair. No one will safeguard the minorities when the Germans have a grip on it. The cloven hoof of my selfishness is evident to all. I want peace for my own people and chance what comes to other nations. I want to be left at home and I most emphatically do NOT want to take care of other people's children in case of evacuation of London. Departing in commandeered tube trains to outer London, then going to stay in distant hotels, doesn't appeal to me at all but I dare not say anything. Lottie wrote. She has a cold so neither of them will come tomorrow. How silly! Editha phoned. She is rabid at world news. She wants England to fight and prophesies absorption into Germany for us if we don't back Czecho-Slovakia. Then Bay phoned, all jubilant because war is staved off a little longer. Have invited Miss Tedbury for tomorrow. Charles has accepted. Em phoned. She says Margie was in Whitehall last night and told of mobs of people crying out 'Down with Chamberlain! We don't want friends of Hitler!'

Tuesday, 20 September. Met Vera Mannering. She, like everyone else, except our staff, has been given directions for evacuation. My party spoiled by the feeling of unrest. WAR, war, war! On and on goes

inflammatory speeches against Jews were reported in September 1938 (*Hackney Gazette*, 19 September, p. 5 and 28 September, p. 5) and the issue of Sunday trading – only Jewish shops were allowed to open that day – was the cause of much grumbling against Jews in 1938–1939 (*Hackney Gazette*, 23 September, p. 5, and below, p. 82n). One BUF meeting in Dalston on a Monday evening, 26 September 1938, resulted in the arrest of the speaker for 'using insulting language' against Jews deemed likely to breach the peace; some 150 people were said to be present, a quarter of them Jews. A police inspector 'thought it desirable to intervene as the crowd became disorderly' (*Islington and Holloway Press*, 1 October 1938, p. 3, and 8 October 1938, p. 5). (The first of these press reports also featured prominently photos of local preparations for war: three of people queuing for gas masks, three of defences being constructed against air raids, and one of an anti-aircraft gun on the back of a truck.) Tension was building – and Gladys certainly felt it – along, no doubt, with many others.

10. Herbert Hodge, *It's Draughty in Front: The Autobiography of a London Taxidriver* (1938), is an example of writing about an 'ordinary life' that appealed to Gladys. Hodge, born in 1901, was brought up in poverty in Lincoln by parents who no longer got along. By the 1930s, after a series of casual jobs, he was a London cabman – and an observant one: 'A man can't drive a London cab for ten years without realising the motivating urges of human beings are Greed, Fear, Vanity, and Lust' (p. 281). On 17 September 1937 Gladys was reading another book in the same vein – Dave Marlow, *Coming, Sir! The Autobiography of a Waiter* (1937). It is unsurprising that she was soon recruited to write for Mass-Observation.

the talk. Editha behaved like Lady Macbeth in the sleep-walking scene and exclaimed 'Oh, Gahd! To think we've come to this!' She went on telling us how she's 'agonised over Stresemann'[11] and was generally 'soulful' like Sybil Thorndike as St. Joan. Leo seems more at ease. Miss Tedbury pleasant.

Wednesday, 21 September. It still seems 'touch and go' for war. I can't get peace of mind. I know I'm unutterably selfish but I can't help it. If only I could summon the courage to gas myself!

Thursday, 22 September. To school this morning with a violent head-ache. Spoke to Mr. Pickering and burst into tears so he sent me home to go to doctor's. The latter gave me a certificate for neurasthenia and then told me I needed a rest. He told me I was too introspective and too concerned with matters intellectual and I must relax. He said I should probably have been healthier had my marriage been a normal one. I wonder? To St. James's Park this afternoon. A glorious day and it was crowded but everyone was talking of war. Great tension again prevails. Hitler's demands grow larger and faster. Rumour says he wants the Ukraine. It seems England's day is done as a first-rate power. Most people's sentiments now are veering round in favour of war as this 'petty Colossus' must be tumbled or bestride us all. I do think it foolish of the Communist Party to put the 'Jew-i-est' Jews as salesmen of their papers in the busiest streets. A pavement artist outside Glave's old shop had a most attractive monkey in coat and trousers. The little creature squatted in the middle of the pavement with arms akimbo or rushed at folks who paused to watch, demanding alms mutely. I cannot settle to anything. I can't even decide to have Lallie destroyed as I think I shall do if war breaks out.

Friday, 23 September. On phone to Em this morning. To Library and met Micky Read. She has returned to teaching because she hopes to be sent away with the school children should war break out – in order to get away from her husband. I went to Kenwood this afternoon where [Benjamin] Britten passed me, looking madder than ever. War clouds *most* threatening. Miss Hammond phoned tonight giving details of new evacuation scheme for school children. I'm too unwell to go at the moment, of course. My head is driving me mad with pain but I must get blanket and rations ready for emergencies.

11. Gustav Stresemann, Foreign Minister of Germany between 1923 and 1929, was seen as a liberal politician with whom other European nations could have constructive relations. He was co-winner of the Nobel Peace Prize in 1926 – and died suddenly of a stroke in 1929, thereby weakening (it was thought) the Weimar Republic, which the Nazis were determined to destroy.

1. Islington High Street, c. 1934, near Angel tube station. Looking north.

2. Islington High Street, c. 1934, looking south. Gladys often travelled this route.

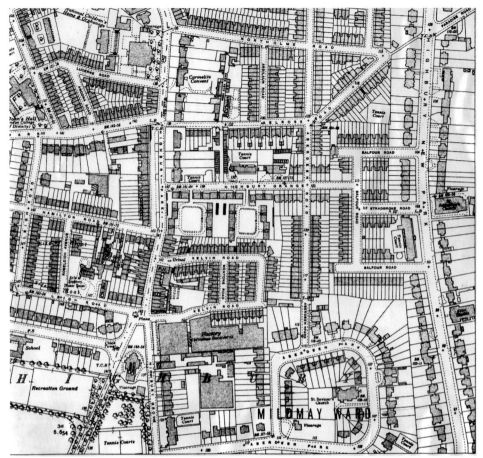

3. Gladys Langford's Highbury. During most of the time of her diary she was living at the west end of Northolme Road (top centre). In 1936 she had been living at 50 Highbury Park (slightly left of centre); in early 1940 she moved to Highbury Grange, just around the corner.

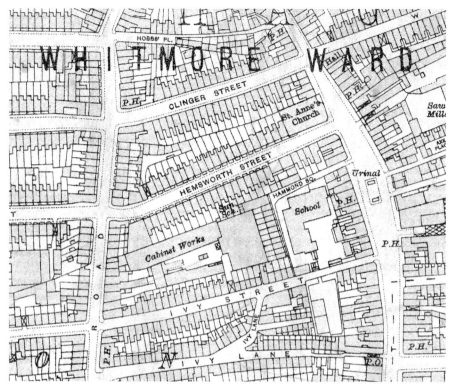

4. Hamond Square School in Hoxton, where Gladys taught. The main north-south arteries in the area are Hoxton Street to the east and Pitfield Street to the west (formerly St. John's Road). The fire reported on 3 March 1938 occurred in the furniture works immediately to the west of the school.

5. Hoxton Street, nos. 263–265, c. 1930, showing an entrance to Hamond Square, with the school in the background.

6. Gladys Langford and her then husband, George, July 1914. She was then 24.
This is the only known photograph of her.

7. Caledonian Market, 1935, about a mile north of King's Cross Station. Gladys occasionally shopped there – one of London's principal outdoor markets.

8. Bacchus Walk, off Hoxton Street, just south of Hamond Square, c.1930. This terraced housing was typical of the district.

9. Hackney Central Library, Mare Street, c. 1939. Gladys, a great reader, often borrowed books there.

10. A corner hardware shop on Kingsnorth Place, c. 1934, a typical back lane in Hoxton.

11. Astoria Cinema, Seven Sisters Road, Islington, 1936. While Gladys, an active film-goer, occasionally attended the Astoria, she was more likely to patronise tonier venues in the West End.

12. Essex Street, running off Hoxton Street, in the 1930s, one of the roughest streets in London.

13. 72–90 Highbury Park by Northholme Road, where Gladys lived at number 4.

This was Gladys's Highbury neighbourhood in the later 1930s. The photographs, although taken in 1969, show buildings that had not changed much externally during the previous thirty years.

14. 14–18 Northolme Road; number 4, to the left, has a similar frontage.

Saturday, 24 September. Met Bay at noon and tried to arrange my domestic plans for her to carry out in the event of my being carried off to look after the evacuated children. I shall give up this flat, have the telephone removed, warehouse my furniture and Bay will take my beloved Lallie. She and Joan Sutton persuaded me to lunch with them and I finally left them and went to look at the crowds in Downing Street and finally to St. James's Park. They, thinking I was melancholy and unwell – as I am – tried to track me down, which they did and discovered me in the Park. After that we again went to Downing Street where film photographers were busy and murderous looking men were selling *Daily Worker*[12] literature and quite a few people were prepared to pick quarrels.

Sunday, 25 September. Mr. Wellings phoned last night to enquire as to my welfare. He is still very positive war won't occur. He says Hitler, had he been determined to fight, would have done so ere this, and that war will not come for a year or two. He urged me to do nothing drastic about breaking up my home at present. He also thinks it would be better to leave Lallie here, and pay for him. Joan Sutton phoned.
Later. Went westwards tonight. First placard I saw said 'Hope rises again', next said 'Grave news, Czechs fighting Poles'. That was enough to send my spirits down to zero again and home I came to listen to the news. This hour to hour anxiety is upsetting my mental balance seriously. Bay phoned. She's worried because they talk of sending Miss Wilshin outside the danger zone. Lots of people in the depôts trying on gas masks. Notices say they will be available at polling stations.

Monday, 26 September. No good news. Queues outside those places where gas masks are being fitted. Windows being blackened, kerbs being whitened; everywhere talk and rumours of war. Little knots of parents outside the schools where notice of preparations are being given. Library girl and grocer's wife both tearful at the thought of what may happen to their pets. Little gaiety among street traders. Roosevelt is said to have cabled Hitler asking him not to use force, but what does Hitler care for Roosevelt? I was hateful. I told Em I wouldn't stay with her while Bee was away. (I hate Kathlyn so much.) Em is so good-natured – although she didn't bother much when mother was dying – it seems cruel to disappoint her. I think I shall stay on Wednesday and Thursday. Lil wrote, also Mr. Ginsbury. The latter says Clowser speaks warmly of me – I wonder if Mr. Wellings made mischief? Parliament is to meet on Wednesday.

Tuesday, 27 September. Mr. Wellings phoned last night. He still thinks there will be no war BUT today booklets were left at each house

---

12.   Organ of the Communist Party of Great Britain.

telling people what to do in case of war and men are digging trenches on Highbury Fields.[13] Em on phone, also LCC medical officer's representative. The latter told me I had permission to leave London and that the LCC doctor would not want to see me. I mentioned the blackboard's having fallen on my head on the 15th and I was told to ask the doctor if this had had any adverse effect on my health as, if that were so, sick leave would not be deducted from me. I have written to Mr. Pickering, Challis (since Lil suggested I should stay there for a while) and to Fowler and Piggin's, whose account I settled. Bay came. She has St. Vitus' Dance again.[14] She says point blank all she cares for is Mary Wilshin! Lil wrote a second time urging me to go there. Mr. Chamberlain broadcast. His speech sounded as though he was throwing the Czechs overboard. If Hitler would yield one jot, all would be well – as far as war is concerned. Air Raid Precautions require volunteers still.

Wednesday, 28 September. News blacker than ever. Mrs. Lucas's son called up – Naval Reservist. Plans for general evacuation in progress. Trench-digging everywhere. Long faces, tearful women in streets. To Weiss's for dressing-gown. Police vans with loudspeakers in Shaftesbury Avenue directing folks to nearest gas-mask station. To Em's. Bee full of plans for getting the family away. His wireless braying through the news again and again. To bed exhausted and the night traffic along Eastern Avenue kept me awake all night.

Thursday, 29 September. Chamberlain, Hitler, Daladier and Mussolini meet at Munich to dismember Czecho-Slovakia politely. We all see a ray of hope for *us* – none for the Czechs. Plans ready for billeting, willy-nilly, folks on villagers and country people. Poor Lil! I went walking in Epping Forest this afternoon. Trees changing colour, so lovely. Men digging trenches, so ugly. Saw Crowe Hall, Woodford for sale, an early Georgian house. I'd like to have it. At supper time a neighbour came in to say Peace Agreement was sealed. I'll believe it if I see it in print tomorrow.

Friday, 30 September. It *was* true! A peace agreement *is* signed and war is averted, at any rate temporarily. Bee brought up tea and paper

13. Plans were announced to dig trenches in the borough's open spaces to accommodate 36,000 people, roughly a tenth of Islington's population (*Islington and Holloway Press*, 24 September 1938, p. 1). Other preparations to cope with aerial attacks were well underway by the end of the month: 'Highbury Fields is a maze of trenches', evacuation plans were under discussion, and 'nearly everyone in Islington has a gas-mask now' – surely an exaggeration (*Islington and Holloway Press*, 1 October 1938, pp. 1, 2 and 5). The Borough Council Minutes for September–December 1938 (held in the Islington Local History Centre in Finsbury Library) reveal an active commitment to work in support of ARP (Air Raid Precautions).

14. St. Vitus' dance (i.e., Sydenham's chorea) is a motor nerve disorder characterised by irregular, involuntary jerky movements of the facial muscles, feet and hands; it is caused by an infection.

at 6.30 a.m. so I should have the news. I left Em's at 10 a.m. and as I went along Eastern Avenue a workman stopped me and asked if I thought the peace would last long? Everybody talks to everybody else now, as in the days of the Great War. I was so pleased to get home. Went westwards this afternoon and to Rosenbergs tonight. Leslie is an ARP warden and so is Mr. Samuel. The latter has rigged up a gas-proof room. Mrs. R.'s new servant – arrived on the 22nd – has already given her notice. She's a nice, smart girl too. Margie has hopes, apparently, of a Roumanian Jew's marrying her. *He* has no money. Mr. Wellings phoned. He wants me to go to see *The Corn is Green* [a play by Emlyn Williams] with him on Tuesday.[15]

Saturday, 1 October. Poor Czecho-Slovakia! The Germans begin to move in today and Poland is making territorial claims. I keep thinking of the hapless people. Em and Bay phoned this morning and I invited Em here tomorrow. I only hope Leonard won't offer to come too. I don't want to miss a bout of possible love-making. It might lift this cloud of gloom that enwraps me. To the Tatler this afternoon and thence to book seats for two Queen's Hall concerts and on to the Academy Cinema to see *Prison sans Barreaux* and a companion film, *The Five Faces of Malay*. Lil wrote a very elated note because war is not to come – yet. To hear the news commentator on the films you'd think Chamberlain was Buddha, and he has such a silly sort of voice. Every time he appeared on the screen there was wild clapping. How idiotic to applaud a two dimensional figure! Mussolini was hissed but neither clap nor hiss greeted the picture of Hitler. Queer, people don't know how to react to him.

Sunday, 2 October. Em came about 1 p.m. and stayed till 5.30 p.m. I was spared Kathlyn's presence. I feel rather better today but still terribly languid. A dead day as far as social and intellectual life are concerned.

Monday, 3 October. Lil wrote at great length. I would have liked to go to her for a few days but Bay wants to go with Miss Wilshin this weekend and Lil can't entertain three at once. News broadcast interesting tonight – account of House of Commons meeting, Duff Cooper's reasons for resignation, Chamberlain's account of the peace arrangements.[16] Bay phoned. Saw Wellings' new shop. Attractive! An

---

15. She did not actually get to see this play, at the Duchess Theatre, until 17 January 1939 – and was not impressed: 'Found it very poor in quality, a few good scenes for Emlyn Williams himself but none of the other characters was convincing. The little Cockney minx who leads him astray is one minute speaking well and fluently, the next in malapropisms and with the accent of the stage Cockney – but never that of the real one.' On several other occasions she complained of unconvincing portrayals of Cockney characters on stage or screen.
16. Duff Cooper, First Lord of the Admiralty and a critic of Chamberlain's appeasement policy, resigned in protest against the Munich Agreement, which he saw as dishonourable and

awful gale raging tonight. Am enjoying Roger Fulford's *George IV* [1935].

Tuesday, 4 October. Miss Hammond wrote. My absence [from sick leave] seems to have given her much more work. When the day for evacuation drew near Conway stayed away for three days; so did Mrs. Dunn, and Miss Lingwood flatly refused to go with the children. Met Bay at noon and treated her to a meal. She introduced me to her colleague, Lily Goldstein, who announced in Bay's presence that Bay is not really prudish but can stand a broad joke with unruffled composure. I was surprised at Bay's choice of friend. This girl is a cheap and nasty little person with fluffed hair and decayed teeth. Went on to see Cochran's new show at the Palace – *Flashbacks* – a very entertaining show exhibiting films from 1838–1938. I found the news films very interesting. The ordinary films of entertainment were not brought beyond 1915. It is strange to see what simple things made us laugh then. The screen was certainly very much the entertainment of the subnormal in intelligence. There was an appalling storm of wind last night. I saw two trees down in St. John Street, Clerkenwell and a tree fell on a bus and killed and injured 13 people.[17] In New Oxford Street an army lorry loaded with gelignite was stranded at a traffic crossing. A similar lorry was behind it. A queue of buses and cars was behind, afraid to draw near for the lorries had chalked on them 'Keep Clear. Dangerous. T.N.T.' A bus conductor had a brainwave for no policeman was near; this young man hopped off his own vehicle and beckoned forward a long line of vehicles despite changing traffic lights. The result was a lengthy line of cars piled up in the opposite direction. Miss Tedbury phoned last night inviting me to accompany

defeatist. He argued, among other things, that Hitler's assurances were not to be trusted (*Hansard*, House of Commons, vol. 339, cols. 29–40). In his autobiography, *Old Men Forget* (London: Hart-Davis, 1953), Cooper recorded his disappointment that the Prime Minister, in his broadcast on 27 September, 'had been unable to give them [the Czechs] a word of praise or encouragement and had reserved all his sympathy for Hitler' (pp. 239–40). The First Lord's resignation was poorly received within the ranks of the Conservative Party; the tide of opinion, he felt, was strongly against him and in favour of Chamberlain (chap. 15). Cooper affirmed his support for a longstanding principle of British foreign policy – 'to prevent one Great Power, in defiance of treaty obligations, of the laws of nations and the decrees of morality, dominating by brute force the continent of Europe' (p. 246) – and his opposition to Chamberlain's popular but 'spurious peace' (p. 251).

Mr. Fred Montague, Labour MP for West Islington, suggested that Chamberlain might soon have to resign and said, 'Britain has been humiliated by the Prime Minister' (*Islington and Holloway Press*, 1 October 1938, p. 1). A later joint statement by the TUC and the Labour Party condemned the government's policy (*Islington and Holloway Press*, 7 January 1939, p. 6). In early October 1938, however, the mood in Islington was predominantly one of relief, and 'large congregations at local churches' were reported to have given thanks for peace (*Islington Gazette*, 4 October 1938, pp. 1 and 2).

17. Hoardings were blown down, trees uprooted, and wooden fences demolished. The gale resulted in a 28-year-old woman being knocked down by a bus in Dalston and killed (*Hackney Gazette and North London Advertiser*, 5 October 1938, p. 3 and *Islington Gazette*, 5 October, p. 3).

her to the Royal Photographic Society's Exhibition tomorrow. Wellings phoned and we've postponed our theatre outing until Thursday.

Wednesday, 5 October. Miss Hammond phoned last night and invited herself to visit me – curse her! She said 'I'll bring my own sandwiches', knowing full well I'd not permit that, so now I'll have to spend good money feeding her. I had to spend yet more good money (a) on the doctor (b) on Miss Tedbury. Dr. Russ doesn't advise my returning to school next Monday. Says 'Why hurry?' and declares congenial company would do me more good than anything else. Met Miss Tedbury. *What* a hideosity! Lank dark hair, a pitted face, a skinny body and a costume – something between poppy and brick red, a hat of a more alarming shade, cocked over one watery eye. To the Exhibition and found it most fascinating, especially some stereoscopic cabinets with their contents. The technical photographs of embryos, of insects' heads and bird life were most fascinating. I soon found Miss Tedbury wearisome. Her talk is all of 'Mum' and 'Jack', her brother. Her silly face worries me too. Lil wrote.

Thursday, 6 October. Miss Hammond came to luncheon and I greeted her with floods of hysterical tears. She brought a huge bunch of lovely chrysanthemums. I told her I thought Mr. Pickering might have written. He did by tonight's post. Who runs *that* school? She was very amiable and she is very generous – but I do dislike her. Went westwards in afternoon. What a lot of beggars have monkeys now! Saw a series of sandwich-men in Charing Cross Road, obviously well-dressed and comfortably placed citizens, carrying Anti-Semite banners and sandwich boards. I *DO* hope there is never persecution of Jews in this country. Unhappy people! I'm glad Leonard never asked me to marry him. I should have done so and even borne him children, I loved him so. (Queer! I notice I use the past tense. I'd hardly realised I'd stopped idolising him. I think I realise I don't matter much to him anymore.) Saw [Eleanor and Herbert] Farjeon's *An Elephant in Arcady* last night at the Kingsway. Most entertaining! Tunes based on those of 18th century composers, costumes 18th century. Poses a delight to the eye. Wit slightly salacious, very salacious at times but always subtle. I wish Wellings would buy a new mackintosh and wear shoulder straps. He looks so shuffling and futile – but he isn't. He says if his new shop prospers, his income should be about £650 per annum. Football pools are so adversely affecting John Bull 'Bullets' competition Clowser may easily lose his job.[18]

---

18. *John Bull* was a popular weekly magazine; it was running regular crossword competitions for its readers – with monetary prizes.

Friday, 7 October. London County Council has granted a day's holiday to all its schools that the children may have a chance to recuperate after last week's excitement. I went to Miss Jones's (Pyrland Road) to tea. The welcome was warm but the stench was overpowering. I nearly vomited. I often wonder if I shall be as dirty when I am old but I don't hoard rags, papers and dirty clothes nor have over-much furniture nor let my cat sleep in filthy boxes and use empty cake tins for its excretions. I nobly stayed about 2½ hours and I fairly staggered with faintness when I got into the fresh air again.

4

October 1938–August 1939

Awaiting the Worst

During the next five months or so, Gladys's moods were noticeably up and down (perhaps more the latter). She was a highly strung, volatile, intense person. Her remarks on other people were more inclined to be acid than kindly (though there were a few she praised); and her pessimism tended to outweigh her positive outlook. She was conscious of her ageing looks, and she often, it seems, felt lonely, and sometimes unwanted. She acknowledged herself to be 'peppery', and sometimes 'overwrought', not least with children at school. 'Today my rage has been absolutely ungovernable and I'm afraid of what I may do' (1 December 1938). 'I'm getting very worried about my mental health', she wrote on 11 January 1939. 'I'm only back at school two days and my temper is even more violent than ever before. I haven't smacked anybody since I returned to school but I catch myself tweaking boys' hair, pulling them along by the arm and actually gibbering at the children in my rage.' She concluded her entry this day with the plea, 'Oh, God, if there be a God, send a man into my life.'

*Gladys often had conversations with strangers; a few she liked, but most failed to pass muster. On Saturday, 29 October she went to a matinée at the Aldwych Theatre. 'The usual dull females attached themselves to me, one an ugly creature, pasty-faced and bespectacled, who wanted to tell me all about an exam for which she was working, and another, a woman about my own age or even older, seemed quite normal when she described her activities as ARP and canteen and Christian Scientist worker. Alas, having found a patient listener she went on with a recital of her success as a seductress. According to her own tale, even her journey from Northampton to London today was with possibility of an "affaire's" maturing tonight. How absurd, that middle-aged women, somewhat be-whiskered and **very** withered, should lay claim to an exciting chain of lovers!' On one occasion (6 January 1939) she 'Talked with a fat little blonde who sat next to me and was mistaken for her MOTHER by an oily Jew whom she knew in the audience.' (Gladys was aware of her own difficult personality, especially in the classroom. 'My temper is truly murderous,' she remarked*

77

on 10 November. 'I glare at the hapless children like a Medusa. I am sorry for them as well as for myself.')

Some of the contributors to Gladys's ill humour were fairly clear: the weather in December–January was often brutally cold and the pipes sometimes froze in her flat; her new oil-stove was cantankerous; she was routinely in debt and borrowing money from friends and relations; and she sometimes felt friendless and devalued. In one especially gloomy passage she lamented that '1939 is over a week old and I'm no nearer making fresh friends, finding new interests, in fact, no nearer anything save the grave' (8 January). Her mood was little better on another day later that month. 'These vile days crawl by. Slush, snow, ooze, sleet, cold winds and European war news make waking a nightmare' (26 January). 'O for a private income!' she added later.[1] By contrast, and without obvious explanation, other days were much more cheerful. 'Have been very amiable at school', she wrote on 15 February 1939; some days later she reported herself as 'Very amiable with children at school and they seem happy and gay with me' (6 March); and on 10 March she voiced a sentiment that was unusually upbeat – 'I really think I am successful with some of the children at school [she probably was] but I do get tired of them.' Her spirits repeatedly rose and fell. One day in February she wrote, 'Feel very depressed again though a pale sun shines'; the next evening she saw a 'delightfully witty' film and 'I laughed aloud again and again' (5–6 February). (Gladys was a connoisseur of clever wit, which almost always helped to boost her spirits.)

Temperamentally, Gladys was not easily made content, though she actually spent little time ruminating or sulking in her flat. During her waking hours, when she was not teaching – and this gave her only occasional satisfaction – she participated actively in London's cultural life – its theatre, films, concerts, and exhibitions; and at home she was a regular reader and sometimes commented favourably on a book that was engaging her. 'Am reading and enjoying Walter Greenwood's Only Mugs Work *dealing with racketeering and pin-table saloons in Soho,' she noted on 29 October 1938. 'I find it both entertaining and convincing.'[2] On 16 November 1938 she reported herself as 'much

---

1. On 30 January Gladys penned a typically catty description of a woman she met that day – 'I wonder if I look like that – a shabby "char" would have more style' – but she concluded with a reflection on her own pinched circumstances: 'Yet *she* can talk of her investments while I can only talk of my debts.' 'How willingly would I put my hand into almost any old man's pocket', she remarked on 12 March, 'to get the money to buy my release from teaching.'
2. Walter Greenwood's fast-paced novel (London: Hutchinson, 1938; reprinted by Howard Baker Books, 1969) portrayed the decadent world of Soho – with its gangsters, prostitutes, and pinball gambling dens. The novel may have appealed to Gladys, in part, because many of the theatres she visited were on the edge of Soho. Greenwood's extensive use of London street names and descriptions added a sense of authenticity for his late 1930s readers. Current readers might be intrigued by his descriptions of police vehicle tracking, which embraced methods that closely resembled the techniques used during the Second World

enjoying Amy Cruse's After the Victorians [1938], *the account of the birth of the* Daily Mail'.[3] *On 2 December she was reading Thomas Turner's eighteenth-century diary: 'He's a very lovable type'.[4] On 2 February 1939 she was 'gurgling over Beverly Nichols' new book,* Revue. *Very malicious!'[5] By contrast, she had no use for D. H. Lawrence: 'I was never [one] of those who fell victim to his alleged dictatorship in literature. I always thought him a charlatan' (24 January 1939).*

Gladys inhabited a world in which artistic judgments were regularly rendered. Once in a while she was praised for her literary sensibility: 'Mr. Kiernan said I ought to write a gossip column or review books as he thought my writings were better than most he read' (11 November 1938). Others were not so fortunate. On 2 February she heard from Norman Ginsbury, the playwright: 'He's very depressed over the critics' damning verdict of Enemy of the People *for the Old Vic.'[6] Gladys's diary is packed with critiques of what she saw and heard. 'I went to the Empire Cinema tonight [9 October] to see Alfred Hitchcock's* The Lady Vanishes, *an excellent thriller, moving fast, which English films rarely do. The scenes were so exciting, one sat forward in one's seat, tense with emotion. I did enjoy it although the rest of the programme was unmitigated rubbish.' She found J. B. Priestley's play* When We Are Married *'riotously funny' (30 December); and after denouncing the play she attended on New Year's Eve, she remarked on the young couples in the audience. 'They don't race up as wildly as I did when I was a girl! People have so much more of the sophisticated pleasures nowadays. They don't get as excited as George and I did in 1912 when we saw* Bought and Paid For *with Alexander Carlisle in it.'[7]*

The political news and public events that caught her attention were rarely reassuring. Reminders of the turmoil on the Continent and the strong possibility of war appear from time to time in her writing. 'Balloon barrage today and iridescent dolphin-like shapes dot the sky,' she wrote on 8 October 1938. 'People are supposed to preserve their gas masks,' she remarked later, four weeks after Munich (29 October). 'I

War to plot the movements of military vessels and aircraft (Part Two, Chapter 12). Gladys had a taste for racy and 'low life' fiction. Later, on 28 December 1939, she mentioned that she was reading *Back Street* by Fannie Hurst (New York: Collier, 1930), a novel in which a flashy young Cincinnati woman enjoys glamour and excitement for a time, but dies alone and forgotten in a European spa town.

3. Cruse's study was concerned with all sorts of popular writing, including the *Daily Mail*, and their social contexts, between 1887 and 1914.

4. Why Gladys found Turner 'lovable' is unclear. However, his diary, which details everyday life in a mid eighteenth-century village, is filled with the sort of social realism that appealed to her. Turner was observant and well-read, had an enquiring mind, and, as a shopkeeper, was at the centre of many aspects of local life. Gladys would have read the 1925 version of his diary, *The Diary of Thomas Turner of East Hoathly, 1754–1765*, edited by Florence Maris Turner.

5. This 1939 novel was rooted in the entertainment world of London, especially the stage.

6. In 1939 Ginsbury produced an English version of Henrik Ibsen's 1882 play.

7. This play was written by George Broadhurst and first produced in 1911.

never got one. I do wish I could get away from England. This continual preparation for war keeps me on tenterhooks and I'm saddened by the repeated attacks on the hapless Jews.' On Armistice Day – which she thought should be abandoned – 'The News of the pogroms in Germany sickens me. God rot Hitler & Co!' Three days later her sister Lil wrote, 'echoing all the Daily Mail *support of Hitler's diabolical treatment of the unhappy Jews' (14 November). On 28 December she met Leonard and they had tea near King's Cross. 'He was terribly dispirited. The persecution of the Jews, the bad trading conditions and the European situation were his only topics. He succeeded in depressing me completely.' The charged politics of London at this time included numerous confrontations between Fascists and anti-Fascists, some of them in Islington.*[8]

The sell-out of Czechoslovakia continued to split public opinion. On 23 November 1938 Gladys recorded that 'Mr. Chamberlain is gone to Paris today but apparently not to so warm a welcome as before for some people in the crowd cried "Down with Munich" and "Vive Eden".'[9] *'When Chamberlain appeared in the news reel,' on 14 January 1939, 'not one cheer greeted him, only stolid silence. Is he a falling star, I wonder?' A week later at a cinema 'The appearance of Chamberlain on the film was the signal for some hissing' (21 January).*

As a frequent traveller about town, whether on foot or by public transport, Gladys observed daily life and sometimes reported on it. 'Met Bay at Piccadilly,' she wrote on Saturday, 12 November. 'The women of the streets have all been cleared out of the Tube Circle now.' Among the other sights that attracted her attention were 'a street performer, apparently a tight-rope walker, assisted by a girl in trousers – unusual', whom she saw at Islington High Street (15 October); street photographers, whom she thought were increasing in numbers – 'I have been "snapped" several times today' (22 October); a woman pinned under a lorry at Highbury Corner – 'She was groaning pitifully' (9 November); and, during a cold spell after Christmas, she remarked on 'Streets crowded with women whose noses show blue under their "make up". It's a consolation to see faces as ugly as one's own' (5 January). On 30 November she saw 'in Upper Street a pawnbroker's, Barratt's, with its three brass balls illuminated inside. Once one slunk by pawnbrokers, if patronising them. Now the world goes in – perhaps

---

8. The *Islington and Holloway Press* for 6 August 1938 included a photograph (p. 1) of a crowd of around 10,000 that had gathered two nights before to hear Oswald Mosley speak at Ridley Road on the border with Dalston. 'Bands of Jews and Communists who attempted to drown [out] the speaker by the singing of the Red Flag were cleared out by the police' (p. 5). Local Fascists who marched through Islington in February were said to have been 'delighted with their reception' (*Islington and Holloway Press*, 11 February 1939, p. 2).

9. In February 1938 Anthony Eden had resigned as Foreign Secretary and later declined to support Chamberlain over the Munich agreement.

because they all do a big retail trade in goods other than unredeemed pledges.'

Daily life continued to generate material for her diary. 'Unemployed lay down in Oxford Street yesterday, demanding bigger "relief"' (21 December). On 2 December she witnessed a street scam. 'Despite the fact that, only a week ago, a man broadcast the methods with which he had repeatedly gulled the public, yet today in Regent Street a masked man in tall hat and morning coat was selling jackets for 6d alleged to contain money in excess of that sum. A huge crowd of girls was around him.' Toilet facilities did not go unnoticed. 'Had tea at Valerie Patisserie [5 November], where the basement lavatory is surely the smallest in London.' On 6 March she went with Wellings to the Gate Theatre. 'That place is so arty. The doors labelled MESSIEURS and DAMES are decorated with nude life-size figures, a man and a woman respectively, each ornamented (?) with a painfully dark fig leaf suggesting pubic hair rather than covering.' School, too, was the setting for an occasional surprise. On 15 February, 'While looking out of a window at school in play-time, a ball from the playground caught me in the face and nearly sent my false teeth down my throat! I have an inartistic lump on my lower jaw now.'

Jewish refugees were, if not exactly flooding into Britain, at least becoming more prominent in British daily life, and thus, predictably, subjects of comment and curiosity, even hatred. On 22 December 1938 Gladys heard from one acquaintance of her 'Gentile friend who is forfeiting half her monthly salary to support a Jewish refugee family after paying their fares here. The man has been so badly treated in a concentration camp he is too ill to work and is in a nursing home. Lil wrote, railing against the Jews as usual.' ('She's full of forebodings about the advent of possible refugees,' Gladys wrote of her older sister a few weeks later, on 10 February. 'Challis is Jew-haunted, [and] sees the shadow of Moses in every menace.') On 23 December, Gladys visited the wealthy Rosenbergs, whose new maid, 'Rosa, is a Jewish refugee, an ex-secretary speaking and writing six languages. She was driven out of her office by the Nazis with a revolver at her head. Her old parents were in a concentration camp for 18 days, and returned to find every valuable taken and every stick of furniture smashed. Her fiancé, to whom she should have been married in October, is deported – but to Shanghai, and it's doubtful if they'll ever meet again. She has been since August with a Roman Catholic colonel who worked her nearly to death, telling her daily how the Jews have only themselves to blame and how much she ought to be grateful for finding shelter in England. He seems to have been a positive sadist. Then she went to a couple with a baby who worked her from 6 a.m. till midnight, then woke her up for baby-minding. I gave her 2s for her Xmas box.'

Gladys's diary provides testimony as to the mixed feeling in England in 1938–1939 concerning the arrival – and, in some eyes, the alarming presence – of these refugees. On Monday, 16 January 1939 she reported that 'There was a collection taken in all cinemas and theatres on Saturday and 10% of receipts were made over to the Refugee Fund. Apparently this does not meet with general approval and there was a demonstration against it in Piccadilly Circus and Leicester Square on Saturday, trouble with the police and thousands of hand-bills distributed declaring refugees were taking away English people's jobs.'[10] *Gladys admitted to mixed feelings herself on 27 January, when she was again at the Rosenbergs. 'Rosa, the maid, delighted as her fiancé is to come to England from Germany. I can't help thinking the influx of Spaniards, Czechs and Jews is rather alarming. Possibilities of jobs for our own unemployed must be lessened by these invading hosts but their plight is so pitiable where can they go?'*

Anti-Semitism was pervasive in pre-war Britain and, for the most part, socially acceptable; and Communism injected a newer voice of hostility into public life. According to Gladys on 28 January, 'England seems to be getting politically minded like all the European nations. I've seen several hammer and sickle signs on walls today; on other walls appear Union Jacks and a label "Isaac Hore Belisha must go".[11] *The local paper tells of yellow spots on Jewish shops in Islington.*[12] *Lil wrote – all about the Reds (of whom, of course, she knows nothing). She also told of a village meeting with the Vicar as chairman and when an opponent spoke against the Vicar's views, that worthy announced: "If you speak again, I shall pronounce a blessing".'*

Rosa made one more appearance in Gladys's writing, and her remarks highlight the ease with which tensions might arise between

---

10. Much alarm was expressed about the prospect of refugees taking jobs that Britons deserved (*Islington and Holloway Press*, 7 January 1939, p. 7; 14 January, pp. 4 and 5; and 28 January, p. 7; and *Islington Gazette*, 25 January 1939, p. 1). One strand of this argument was that charity should begin at home, and that aid should be directed to alleviate distress in Britain (e.g., industrial unemployment; the national unemployment rate was around 12 per cent) rather than abroad.

11. Leslie Hore-Belisha (b. 1893) was Secretary of State for War in Chamberlain's administration; he was also Jewish and fairly widely distrusted.

12. Fascists were suspected of doing this spotting on shop windows, which was reported in Upper Street, Essex Road, and Caledonian Road (*Islington and Holloway Press*, 28 January 1939, p. 1; p. 3 reports chalking of the letters 'P. J.' – for 'Perish Judah' – on a wall in a 'particularly Jewish neighbourhood'). The Fascist campaign often attacked 'Sunday trading tricksters', that is, Jewish shopkeepers who were able to open on Sunday by legislative right while others had no choice but to close. In Stoke Newington, Bethnal Green, Hackney, and other parts of East London the British Union of Fascists exploited the resentment of local hairdressers, grocers, and other retailers towards Jewish businesses.

Local studies of Fascism have shown that rank-and-file members were commonly drawn from unemployed and irregularly employed members of the working class. When these men found work, their memberships were liable to lapse. These tended to be localities where the Conservatives scarcely existed, the Liberals were in decline, and Labour seemed to offer little in the way of recovery, thus leaving the BUF as a viable political option. An informative discussion of these and other issues pertinent to the later 1930s may be found in Martin Pugh, *'Hurrah for the Blackshirts!' Fascists and Fascism between the Wars* (London: Jonathan Cape, 2005), chap. 11.

the newcomers and their hosts. This 'Viennese refugee maid is "in bad odour" – she has such frequent and lengthy phone calls from fellow refugees and she complains so much about English food. I was annoyed with her when she sneered at the stodginess and bad cooking of the English.[13] *She and her friends were glad enough to get here. I don't mind grumbling about England myself but I don't care to hear foreigners indulge in contempt of my native land' (3 March 1939). One assumes that such 'misunderstandings' must have been found in thousands of relationships between foreigners and the native-born in England in the late 1930s.*[14]

Occasionally this winter a day's diary entry was long and detailed.

Tuesday, 31 January, 1939. Council sent a small cheque as they are re-adjusting salaries, making them payable at the month's end in future. Met Wellings at the New Restaurant and Clowser was there. He

---

13. Rosa was not the only refugee servant to balk at English cuisine: see Lucy Lethbridge, *Servants: A Downstairs View of Twentieth-century Britain* (London: Bloomsbury, 2013), pp. 244–5.

14. On 13 January 1940 a diarist for Mass-Observation (#5363) had lunch at a home in Elstead, Surrey, and a visitor there said, 'she is glad to get away from home and German Jewess, refugee, whom she "adopted" before the war, and now can't stand, she is so pushing and ungrateful'.

    While a casual anti-Semitism was widespread in British society at this time, it could often co-exist with genuine sympathy for the plight of the Jews in Nazi Germany and other parts of Europe. The British government, which was often as ambivalent as ordinary citizens, avoided articulating clear and comprehensive policies on refugees. The Home Office studiously failed to keep its own statistics on the sensitive issue of Jewish immigration, partly to retain its freedom of manoeuvre on the issue, partly because there were so many divisions within the government and among senior civil servants.

    Louise London's *Whitehall and the Jews, 1933–1948: British Immigration Policy, Jewish Refugees and the Holocaust* (Cambridge: Cambridge University Press, 2000) presents a nuanced and balanced view of this complex and controversial issue. She concludes that while the British government did help to save persecuted Jews, this was done very much on its own terms. Refugees received only qualified welcome. Broadly, the government wanted to pick the best and the brightest of Jewish refugees. To be admitted to Britain between 1933 and 1939, Jews had first to satisfy the government that they had guaranteed financial support or that they could re-emigrate or had significant intellectual capital or commercial know-how. Women might be allowed entry if they were prepared to be domestic servants. As one contemporary authority put it, 'The only occupations open to refugees without a special permit from the Home Office are domestic service, nursing, and a limited number of places (at present 1,000) in agriculture. Special permission to work is available for persons who supply a kind of skill or ability not readily available, but the limitations have been very strict, and permission to exercise trades and professions is generally subject to consultation with professional associations and trade unions' (John Hope Simpson, *Refugees: A Review of the Situation Since September 1938* [London: Royal Institute of International Affairs, August 1939]. p. 69). It is estimated that some 90,000 refugees were admitted to Britain between 1933 and 1939, around 90 per cent of them Jewish; almost 80,000 refugees remained in the country when war broke out in September 1939 (*Whitehall and the Jews*, pp. 11–12).

    Walter Greenwood's 1938 novel *Only Mugs Work*, mentioned by Gladys on 29 October 1938, observed that the criminal underworld had found a profitable new line of work by smuggling into England Jews fleeing from Nazi oppression in Austria. The novel suggested – quite plausibly – that large sums were charged to facilitate illegal entry, and that the hapless refugees were sometimes later blackmailed as well (Part One, Chapter 2).

came over to speak and gave me the *Evening Standard* with a review of Ginsbury's play in it – not a kindly one either. Then I learned Coulson had married an actress. To the Old Vic to see *She Stoops to Conquer* [by Oliver Goldsmith]. I don't care for these revival plays. Margaret Yarde has such a wild manner (as in *Poison Pen* [1939 film]) one wonders if her sanity be reeling. To Charing Cross Corner House for coffee and ices. Walked to Piccadilly. Horror-struck to find Leicester Square and the Circus one teeming mass of people, most of whom moved slowly along chanting 'We want arms for Spain'. I have never seen so many police, mounted and on foot. I could not help noticing what seemed to be a huge preponderance of foreigners in the crowd. There were also the hooligan type in plenty, flat noses, broken and blackened teeth and smelling of dirt. Lots of these were trying to provoke orderly pedestrians to quarrel. The subways had their chanters too. I was terrified and I think Wellings was very unchivalrous in that he didn't trouble to see me into a bus. I had difficulty in getting into one and when I did, it was stuck fast in a sea of people, taxis and private cars. I didn't get home till after midnight. Wellings says he met Charles and he isn't coming next Tuesday [to Gladys's supper party]. He also met Miss Sidebotham (now married) and Griffiths.

* * * * * *

Friday, 3 February. Fog! Met Bay at Piccadilly. Ate at Lyons' – vile, coddled food. Few people at theatre. Play, *Gaslight* [1938, by Patrick Hamilton], quite good although I don't admire Gwen Ffrangcon Davies and I thought the Detective an unconvincing figure. Dennis Arundell looked exactly like the old photographs of my Uncle Harry. Entered into conversation with my neighbour and exchanged sweets and cigarettes with him. He said he was a great grandson of Charles Dickens and was 19 and in the Navy and that his ship was to escort the King in his forthcoming trip to Canada. He was very perturbed by the results of an accident (motoring) he has recently sustained in which his nose was broken and the shape of his face altered. (He had a vile, blotchy complexion.) He said he was only in the gallery because he'd omitted to go to the Admiralty for an advance of pay. He was very class-conscious and quite horror-struck because I wasn't impressed by the difference between the Merchant Service and the Navy and because I dared to say I thought the men in the trawlers and whalers had more courage and less reward. Tottenham Court Road and Leicester Square Tube Stations suffered explosions this morning. IRA activities suspected.[15]

There was a significant new development in Gladys's life in early 1939: she started to write for the social research organisation Mass-Observation, which had been set up two years before to foster a sort

---

15. See also below, 2 and 27 July 1939.

of social anthropology of contemporary Britain. 'Am much enjoying reading Mass-Observation in Britain,*' she noted on 8 February. 'I am offering myself as a voluntary Mass Observer.'*[16] *This was to become a serious undertaking for her. 'At last my Mass Observation paper has come and I hope to send in a report' (22 February); two days later she was still busy 'on my Mass Observation manuscripts'; and on 2 March she posted what she had written to M-O's headquarters. This writing for M-O, as we shall see, was to continue through much of 1939 and significantly enlarge upon what she had disclosed and would continue to disclose in her private diary about her views, her past, and her social life.*[17] *Her submissions to Mass-Observation inform all of the next chapter and much of chapters six and seven.*

As the year advanced, tensions, both private and public, became even more pronounced.

Thursday, 16 March. Feel very neurasthenic, weak in knees and depressed. No new acquaintances, no new experiences and I felt too tired to go westwards for a cinema. Phoned Bay. To Library. Hitler is already arresting masses of people and enforcing laws against the unhappy Jews in dismembered Czecho-Slovakia.[18]

Friday, 17 March. A mother to see me at school today. She was quite pleasant but I *had* been unduly tart with the boy. To Rosenbergs tonight. Clarrie and Mr. Freeman there. Her repugnance for her elderly husband is apparent in her every movement and gesture. She has aged *very* much and is no longer beautiful while he is more like Punch than ever. I spoke heatedly to him with reference to his sneering at my interest in Mass Observation, pointing out to him any one person's choice of interest was as good as another's as long as it hurt no one and my interest in sociology was every whit as laudable as his mania for card playing. Leslie came in later. He and Mr. Samuels as air raid wardens were full of plans in case of enemy attack, for war is in the air again now that Hitler has seized Czecho-Slovakia. We all 'listened in' to Mr. Chamberlain's speech, and to me the first half of it sounded like self-defence, the second half like jingoism.[19] Wellings phoned. Clowser is already seeing less of Coulson since the latter's wedding.

---

16. The book she mentions, *Britain by Mass-Observation*, was a Penguin Special that appeared in early 1939. It was written by Charles Madge and Tom Harrisson, two of the founders of M-O, and included essays on people's attitudes during the previous autumn's Munich crisis, astrology, and 'Doing the Lambeth Walk'.
17. Later that month she was actively in search of information. 'Persuaded all my male colleagues to give me information for my Mass Observation Economic Conditions dealing with clothes. Very busy on that and the Crisis Directive reports' (22 March).
18. Hitler, breaking his pledge of the previous year, had just ordered German forces to occupy all of Czechoslovakia. This action was a further blow against Britain's policy of appeasement.
19. In this speech delivered in Birmingham, the Prime Minister did indeed find his own conduct

Saturday, 18 March. Lil came today. She bought from me my green coat and a blue hat. I took her to a local café for a meal. Bought a cheap blouse and knickers. Escorted her to Piccadilly Circus, then I went on to the Marble Arch Pavilion to see the new English film *I Met a Murderer*. I liked the outdoor scenes very much and James Mason was splendid. I should think he'd prove a film star. I didn't care for the heroine, Pamela Kellins. She's very Jewish looking and ran badly, kicking out her legs sideways. Feel uneasy at the thought of possible war. Lil said a village woman nearly struck Challis in her righteous wrath because he laughed at the plight of the Czechs.

Sunday, 19 March. I can't sleep or settle to anything with another Crisis in being. *How* I loathe that word! Broadcast news, placards, conversations in the street revolve around the hated Hitler. *How* I wish I could leave England but I haven't a cent. There'll be nothing for it but suicide if war breaks out. Hundreds have sought death, surely I can too! Bay on phone. We are going to Mañana[20] next weekend.

* * * * * *

Tuesday, 28 March. *Still* talk goes on about Crises, Joint Action, 'putsch in the East' and falling markets. How I loathe Hitler! I wish he might die a death of lingering agony, in exile, the butt of nations. If only one could feel at peace! Madrid has fallen [to Franco's forces]. I wonder if Alfonso will be reinstated?[21] What a waste of life that Spanish Civil War has been! Wrote to Lottie. Am enjoying John Gray's *Gin and Bitters* [1938].[22]

Wednesday, 29 March. These days *are* devoid of incident for me. Wellings phoned last night. Tonight I went alone to the Tatler.

Thursday, 30 March. Still talk, talk, talk of possible war and preparations for it. How I long to die! Met Wellings at the New Restaurant – why does he like that place, I wonder? It's *very* ordinary. We went back to his flat to 'listen in'. I didn't enjoy the Bella Bartok item but I did like the Bizet Symphony no. 1. Wellings is very positive that war will not come, that the preparations are a 'ramp' – to lessen the number of unemployed and to increase the wealth of the great industrialists, just as Hitler's regime did in Germany.

Friday, 31 March. As fast as one [thing] soothes my fears, another strengthens them. Today linen labels were being made for each child in

---

to be blameless. His concluding words spoke vaguely of the need for Britain and other
democracies to defend freedom (BBC Written Archives Centre, typescript).

20. This was the name of her sister's house on Camps Road in Helions Bumpstead, Essex.
21. Alfonso, the theoretical King of Spain, had been deposed in 1931 and was living in exile in
Rome.
22. The autobiography of a novelist (b. 1901) who had lived mainly in London.

case evacuation should come. England has promised to support Poland – so has France. To Brondesbury where Leslie makes preparations for going to America and Mr. Samuel to understudy him as air warden. The latter, like Wellings, predicts that there will be no war but that Italy will be allied to France within three months. His brother is acting as an Observer for Mass Observation. Mrs. Samuel didn't come up. She doesn't like me. Mr. S. promised to send me an invitation to a film trade show and also to get a philatelist friend of his to value my stamps. I met Nancy McMillan on the train. She has two children now and her father has obtained work while Pat, the young cousin who was such a demon, is now in the Air Force.

* * * * * *

Monday, 3 April. To Em's last night. We sat in the semi-darkness, which I abhor. This morning I was infuriated almost to the point of a seizure to find Mr. Pickering is abrogating his own rule of never keeping a teacher to a class for more than a year by keeping me in the bottom class yet another year while Miss Hammond luxuriates in idleness at the top class again, he taking History and Geography for her. Most of all was I incensed by his saying 'Of course, it's very awkward for me to arrange – Conway can't take the Infants and *you* can't take music or hand-work.' As I *do* take music and *did* take musical appreciation, this was very feeble and as I'm the only one on the staff who takes *any* interest in current affairs, has any knowledge of modern drama, English literature or art, it seems an appalling waste of a teacher to put me on MD [mentally defective] children and then leave me there indefinitely. Then, to add to my tribulations, Air Raid Precautions arrangements swamped me. I'm almost distraught at the thought of being sent anywhere from 'The Wash to Land's End' with children from whom I may not escape for years. I'm writing to the London Teachers' Association tonight to see what can be done. Lottie wrote.

* * * * * *

Wednesday, 5 April. I never remember 'breaking up' [for holidays] with so heavy a heart! Shopkeepers, everyone, discuss the probability of war. Directions in radio news and to schools is 'Teachers leave their addresses for instant recall if necessary' and children are told where to attend and what to do should emergency arise. I almost wish something *would* happen to ease the tension. All this is too much for me. I think I shall throw up my job and chance starvation. I also think to sell up so that I have a pound or two behind me. I feel wretched and can settle to nothing.

The Easter holiday brought Gladys little pleasure, despite the fine weather, mainly because 'WORLD EVENTS mar everything ... No wonder one teacher, a man, has committed suicide rather than face

Evacuation! I *carry a razor-blade about with me to use in case of emergency and my head bubbles like a witch's cauldron. Bay snaps at me over the phone for selfishness, points out I'm not the only one threated by upheaval. That's true, but I'm the only one mattering to myself. Who cares for me besides?' (Easter Monday, 10 April). She wrote of war talk, prayers for peace, and sirens sounding, and (13 April) a 'Crowd of people in Charing Cross Road bearing placards "Chamberlain Must Go", policemen keeping them moving'. An appeal to traders and consumers from the Jewish People's Council to boycott German goods caused a storm of controversy in the* Islington and Holloway Press *on 15 April 1939. There were charges that such pressure would only bring war closer, 'and it will be the young Englishman who will have to do the fighting'. In the next week's issue (22 April 1939), 'Islington Jews Hit Back!', particularly against the claims of James Shepherd, a local Fascist leader.*

Saturday, 15 April. To London Teachers' Association Office this morning. The Deputy Secretary says I can refuse to go with children on the Evacuation journey but I must go to the school unit when it is established. He says if I resigned, in all probability, in due course, thanks to the National Register, I should be called back to the service but I should by then have lost all my rights and privileges in the profession, so go I must for teaching, but he says the Council will give billet, one person per room. Sat in St. James's Park and now I've a fine cold.

Sunday, 16 April. Bay phoned; otherwise my Sabbath calm – and gloom – was uninterrupted. I ought to be ashamed of myself – as soon as war threats are temporarily silenced I start whining about my personal loneliness. I've certainly had enough of fourteen years' unrelieved loneliness. Went westwards but was unable to get into the Carlton for *Love Affair* so had to have 6d worth of Tatler, which was mainly Disney cartoons. Am reading [Geoffrey] Boumphrey's *British Roads* [1939] and enjoying it greatly.[23] Subconsciously I'm remembering I'll be 49 tomorrow and thinking how little I've done with my life, wondering whether George remembers me (I doubt it) and thinking how much I am changed from the girl of 14 who, at a soirée, decided to commit suicide when life held no more for her. Life might hold much yet [for] me if only I had a man in tow.

Monday, 17 April. My 49th birthday! On phone to Editha and she was very bitter about my refusing to go with the evacuated children.

---

23. Gladys liked to read books as soon as they were published – this one had appeared only in January 1939. She also liked works of non-fiction that she could relate to the present. Boumphrey (p. 7) offered 'the point of view of the realist ... who regards the past primarily as an approach to the present, as a text-book from which may be drawn many lessons of value in shaping the future'. This perspective was to her taste.

She said she had always thought I was ridiculous and so did other people. To the Carlton to see Charles Boyer and Irene Dunne in *Love Affair*. The first half was excellent, the second ridiculously sentimental. Mr. Gaye phoned saying his leg was too bad for him to come. I *was* disappointed. Miss Hope sent me an ash-tray. Marjorie and Mr. Haffner arrived first. He *is* like Charles Boyer. He is very charming and at leaving he held my hand fast and said I need not grieve over grey hair as I was very charming to any man. Very pleasing if quite untrue. Dunlops, 'Middleton' and Lottie arrived. Leo was in an impish mood. Mrs. D. wore the same dress as usual. Mr. Wellings very supercilious when Marjorie talked. Small wonder. She *is* a fool.

Tuesday, 18 April. School re-opened and I felt – and looked – ghastly, knowing I had to tell Mr. Pickering I refused to participate in the Evacuation Scheme. Whatever I've thought or said about him in the past, I must now withdraw for he was most sympathetic and said he quite realised I was unfit in health and had been for months. I don't know if he mentioned the matter to the others but they've said nothing. To see Mrs. Jackson tonight. She's more unbalanced than I am. Like George III [who was often mentally unstable], she talks continually and incoherently. I could hardly make sense of what she said. Nellie is to marry a German but there has been a long wait because she has had to prove the Aryanising of all her relatives. Phoned Em and Bay; the latter is nearly as depressing as I am myself. Wrote to Lil inviting myself for Whitsun.

Wednesday, 19 April. Lil and Stelle wrote. Feel rather better. This new class is not so lethargic as some I have had. Mr. Pickering has been notified he has to apply for headships of other schools as our numbers are falling so fast. Met Mrs. Morton and after tea walked from Clapton to Amhurst Park with her. Upper Clapton Road is so altered as to be almost unrecognisable. My rent is raised by 6d weekly as Mrs. Lucas's rates have gone up. I am not pleased.

Thursday, 20 April. Griffiths ran after me this morning and again tonight, talking a long while. There's not much teaching in schools nowadays. All the morning one fusses over collecting money for milk and giving the stuff out. All the afternoon I was trying to get details of parents' wishes for possible Evacuation Scheme.[24] We spend thousands

24. Evacuation persisted as a concern. A few weeks later, on Wednesday, 17 May, 'All my dinner hour wasted in listening to details of forms to evacuees to fill in when we teachers do our voluntary duty at the schools this weekend.' Parents were being encouraged to register their children for evacuation, and on Saturday, 20 May Miss Hammond phoned Gladys to report that 'they had only about 18 people there yesterday [the 19th] for registration for Evacuation Scheme for mothers with children under five. Apparently it was the same all over London.' Hamond Square School was open for twelve hours on Saturday and 'only 32 people came to register! What a fiasco! People are no longer war-minded, despite press

of pounds on education but children know less and less on leaving school. Islington Borough has wasted £8,900 on digging trenches last autumn, deciding they are unsuitable and filling them up again. Dozens of steel shelters lie red with rust by the roadside.

Friday, 21 April. Mr. Pickering says the teachers have to work in relays on May 19th and 20th as ARP voluntary workers, giving parents assistance in filling up forms relating to Evacuation. I've had trouble enough with those of 44 children today, but I offered to do two periods instead of one as I'm shirking the actual Evacuation journey, if it ever occurs. To Brondesbury and boredom as only Marjorie and Mrs. R. were present. Sent down the stamp album to Mr. Samuel for valuation. Mr. Wellings phoned. He has fallen off a bus and hurt his arm.

Saturday, 22 April. To my astonishment Darling Charles (Mr. Gaye) phoned this morning to invite me to a matinée. I met him at 2 p.m. outside the Westminster Theatre, where, from dress circle seats, we saw T. S. Eliot's *Family Reunion*, founded on the Orestes myth, with a chorus of aunts and uncles. I found it most confusing and not at all entertaining although I liked Catherine Lacey's performance. My escort then took me to tea at Zeeta's at Victoria where we sat and talked till 7 p.m. He has four sisters living with him, I find. He is a fireman for ARP but will only act in the service of his bank. He says pressure is being brought to bear on the 'under thirties' in the service. We discussed Mass Observation. He says his sisters want to leave London and he will live in lodgings for a while then join them. He speaks strongly against marriage. At night I went to see the new play *The Women* [by Clare Boothe], which is very amusing, teeming with wisecracks, but very coarse. I'm surprised the Censor passed it. I met Marjorie Rosenberg and her friend Addie there. I also [saw] Kenneth Smith in the distance.

* * * * * *

Saturday, 29 April. Drew salary from Bank, paid electricity bill. Viewed flat in Woburn Square – two backrooms overlooking mews, one a very small room. House well kept but the stairs narrowed before the 3rd floor was reached. An attractive district [near Russell Square], to me, but if war came I'd have to be evacuated, furniture as well as self. To Staggs to buy a coat, 49s 6d, maize-coloured. To Patisserie Valerie to eat and then to Warner Theatre so see *Yes, My Darling Daughter* [1939]. May Robson is excellent. Home in the rain, much writing of letters. No time for reading. Crowds in West End for Cup Final.[25]

campaigns, and won't be until another crisis arrives' (Sunday, 21 May). As many sources from 1939 attest, there was a vast lack of enthusiasm for evacuation.

25. Portsmouth played Wolverhampton Wanderers at Wembley in what would be the last FA Cup Final until 1946. Portsmouth won 4–1.

Sunday, 30 April. A vile day! Heavy rain and cold prevails. Bay phoned, inviting me for next Saturday. Mr. Wellings phoned last night. Read with avidity Wyndham Lewis's *The Jews, Are they human?*[26]

Monday, 1 May. Raining all day! Met Griffiths this morning. Mrs. Dunn is dying. I knew it. Death was in her eyes the last time I saw her. Very disappointed at receipt of jumper Em has been knitting for me. I had thought of it as being of royal blue and a soft wool. It turns out to be a grubby Wedgwood colour, the bouclé type, big and ungainly so I look an apple-woman in it. I must keep it now as she has gone to so much trouble in knitting it. Phoned her but she was out. Sent Lil another 10s. The Bloomsbury landlady wrote offering me the large 3rd floor room and another on the 2nd floor at £8 per month.

Tuesday, 2 May. Home from school but not allowed to have tea in peace. Up comes Mrs. Lucas so I couldn't even enjoy the evening paper. She squatted here 'twaddling' while I felt increasingly murderous. Then Em phoned. She waited till Em had finished – then talked on so it was late before I got to the Academy Cinema where I saw an excellent French film, *I Was an Adventuress* [1938]. I was so late home that Wellings had phoned five or six times before my return. He wants me to go out with him on Thursday.

Wednesday, 3 May. Lil wrote again. I am *very* irritable at school. This afternoon a woman – a Mrs. Smith – came up complaining that the child had developed St. Vitus' Dance because I had smacked him so much. I *have* smacked his finger tips but I have never caned him. She admitted that she herself beat him so unmercifully she was often afraid she'd get into trouble about it. She said she'd kept him at home now and declared that I'd kept him in to wash up for me for nearly all the dinner-time. As I only have a cup and saucer and plate, and I wash them myself, *that* wasn't true. She said the boy had fallen on his head in the hall yesterday, but as I neither took drill nor was there an

---

26. This 1939 tract by a prominent writer was an attack on anti-Semitism (which also took pokes at English class-consciousness and neglect of the poor) and at times an attempt to explain it. Some of his assertions had more pithy elegance than depth. 'Unless one is phenomenally interested in the Jews as a people, the antisemite is unavoidably a bore' (p. 30). 'The antisemite is a gentile of disordered mind who has become what he is by brooding upon a bogey, rather as children used to develop epilepsy at the time Napoleon Bonaparte threatened an invasion of England' (p. 35). Lewis had by this date repudiated his earlier admiration for Hitler. (Gladys may have enjoyed, among other things, this short book's barbs against various aspects of English culture, such as its philistinism and the celebration of athleticism. 'One of the most obvious forms of "toughness" is to be perfectly impervious to the seductions of fine prose, good acting, or a beautiful picture. As Englishmen we are better able to form an opinion about all this than are the Germans. For we have in England what is left of the stupidest – the most pathologically dense – military aristocracy that the world has ever seen. The Junker is a highbrow compared to our lot' [p. 80].)

assembly, he wasn't *in* the hall. To Pyrland Road tonight to see the 'old ladies'.

Thursday, 4 May. Here beginneth my 20th year of Hell! – Teaching! It would have begun only I didn't go to school I had such a raging headache.[27] Met Wellings and saw the Czech film *Innocence* with him at the Phoenix. It was poor, slow-moving stuff and had hardly any English subtitles.

The prospect of another war was ever-present. Not much learning was going on at school. 'All the ARP activities rob the children of hours of education' (24 April). On Sunday, 7 May a 'May-Day procession of workers passed here. They had bands, blood-red banners and posters. The latter included "No Conscription", "Chamberlain must go", "Unite with Russia". They, the marchers, all seemed very young, and were very sprightly and smart. Good luck to them if they can create a "brave new world" but I expect they'd be exploited by their leaders as we all are.' On 12 May she 'Noticed from the train window sections of air-raid shelters dumped in back gardens of Kentish Town and Camden Town. What a ramp it is!' 'I've dropped 8lbs worrying about the war,' she reported on 18 May.[28] The prospect of war cast a shadow over Gladys and many others of her generation. On 24 June she 'enjoyed Terence Rattigan's play After the Dance *very much, not because it was so good a play but because it dealt with the tragedy of getting old for my poor, war-scarred generation (I can't realise I could so easily have been a grandmother by now) and all the 1915–1920 popular songs make my heart ache for the dead past'.[29]*

Gladys's personal life was still mostly coloured by sadness and regret. 'I wish Leonard would write' (9 May; he did on 16 May). On 11 May, 'George is 49 today. How I should like to see him! He is in my mind the day long.' New clothes were expected to help perk her up. 'How I wish I were young enough to look attractive in all this finery. Now I can pay for it, but then I could not. I was married in a second-hand costume' (13 May). The purchase of new shoes led her to remark on her feet – 'Mine are *deplorable. No wonder George always said I ought to keep my feet hidden from the public eye when they were unshod. Like Isabella of Castile, I must try to remember to cover*

---

27. 'How much I envy people who have leisure to live and work at their chosen employment,' she wrote on 21 June 1939.
28. In the borough of Islington preparations for war were well underway, including the provision of bomb shelters, and there were debates about the merits of the various proposals (*Islington Gazette*, 7 February 1939, p. 1; 7 June, p. 1; 16 June, p. 1; 27 June, p. 2; and 29 June, p. 2).
29. One diary entry that was more buoyant stemmed from an evening at Sadler's Wells on 27 April 'to see Lord Berners' new ballet, *Cupid and Psyche* – a riot of colour, costumes gorgeous in colouring, music gay, a real antidote for war news. It was greeted with vociferous applause and the composer took a series of calls. There was a crowded house. When Jupiter gave the Nazi salute, the house rocked with gusty laughter.'

them when I am dying' (20 May). Sometimes it was hard to summon
up this sort of wry humour. 'I am lonely. I feel so niche-less' (4 June).
By contrast, two days before she had met three (apparently younger)
men and enjoyed 'a riotously jolly evening'; and one day the following
week she reported that 'I do feel well and I look quite youthful. I wish
I could meet more people' (8 June). Leonard, this month, was ill and
in bed. 'I doubt if he will ever come to bed with me again. Strangely
enough, I'm not so upset as I thought I would be. He has slipped out
of my life so much of late. It is nearly six months since I saw him' (9
June). As for Mr. Gaye ('Darling Charles', on occasion), with whom
she spent the evening of 13 June talking, 'I am afraid I get no further in
making him aware of me as a woman. I should say he is rather under-
sexed. He is very anti-Freudian in opinion.'

There was one brief change in Gladys's life in June, for on the 20th
she was 'Sent home from school unwell'; the next day she went to 'Dr.
Colin Russ who gave me a certificate for nervous debility', and she
was granted sick leave until 26 June and thus could put aside for a few
days her cares as a teacher.[30] Her questioning mind continued to be
active, on matters large and small. 'Why are men persuaded to fight in
capitalistic struggles? The newly married couple in the flat below sup
nightly on fried fish. How can romance and rancid oil keep company?'
(27 June: the Barbers had recently left).

Thursday, 29 June. Lil lent me £8. Prize distribution at school. Very
funny. The LCC member, Mrs. Girling, made the presentation. She has
a mouth like a badly driven horse, a figure like a cottage loaf and feet
like Little Leah's. The chairman of the school managers is an equally
ugly dame with a wide and gummy smile, a double squint and thick-
pebble spectacles. There was also a rubicund female with flat feet,
a jaundiced looking young man, ill-nourished and crafty-looking, a
buxom young woman who looked a virago and a Punch-like old man
with no teeth and a slobbery mouth. Mr. Pickering put on soft soap
with a shovel. The chairwoman in her speech said 'We hope every
year that Mrs. Girling *won't* be able to come. We know how busy she
is!' She never noticed her negative till the audience laughed but Mrs.
G. looked murderous though I doubt she reads Freud's *Psychology of
Everyday Things*.[31] Out with Wellings tonight. He's very cantankerous

30.   The log book for Hamond Square School in the 1930s indicates that Gladys had occasionally
      been absent because of 'Nervous Debility' or 'Neurasthenia', with easily the longest
      previous absence being sixteen days in September/October 1938. The current sick leave
      had no formal termination prior to the log book ending with the school's evacuation just
      before the outbreak of war (London Metropolitan Archives, EO/DIV4/HAM/LB/2).
31.   The book's title is actually *The Psychopathology of Everyday Life* (1901; later published in
      various English editions, the first being in 1914). Its topics became part of the intellectual
      fodder of urban cosmopolitans in the 1930s. They included slips of the tongue, forgetting
      proper names, misreadings, stumbles in writing, bungled actions, and superstitions, most
      with a heavy emphasis on sexuality, repressed and otherwise.

nowadays. Two of his manageresses are leaving him. I think he over-works willing horses. He has had bailiffs as his Hammersmith [library] branch because he won't pay the rent although he's had concessions from his landlord.

* * * * * *

Sunday, 2 July. Bay phoned. After an early luncheon went to Hyde Park to see the review. Took up a good position opposite to Dorchester House and saw Queen Mary, the King, and Queen, and the marchers excellently. Huge crowds there despite showers, all very orderly. There were airmen, Auxiliary Fire Service, Mercantile Marine Reserves, Ambulance Corps, ARP workers from all over the British Isles. Tanks, mobile units, cyclist messengers, nurses – they went by in an unending stream. I can understand the recruiting value of such a march past. Even I felt I ought to be doing something for the state – but really, those ridiculous tin helmets deter me.[32] Anyhow, I shall be with the children, I suppose, only it seems shabby to leave the dirty work to others. Of course, there are those who love to don uniform and be officious and official at the same time. Bombs at London, Midland and Scotland stations – the IRA again, I suppose.[33] Norah Waln's book almost persuades me one ought to fight for democracy if Nazism grows too powerful.[34] Offered service to St. Francis Humanitarian Hospital.[35]

32. Under the headline 'Citizen Army of Defence', *The Times*, 3 July 1939, p. 14d, carried a long, detailed, and rousing report of this parade of 20,000 men and women, members of both civil defence services and fighting units. 'Many Hyde Park demonstrations have been held on Sunday afternoons, but never has there been one more memorable than that of yesterday. … This time the people were joined by their King and Queen; and in another special sense this demonstration was in sharp contrast to many which have been held in the Park, for, where they were sectional, this one was eloquently expressive of complete national unity.' The marchers were said to have been in good humour, with many signs of patriotic enthusiasm. 'So,' the account concluded, 'in a typically British way, had national readiness to resist aggression been demonstrated.' Five photographs of the review were featured on p. 18.
33. 'Considerable material damage' was done by these explosions, which resulted from bombs placed in suitcases in seven railway station cloakrooms – in Stafford, Derby, Birmingham, Coventry, Leicester, Leamington Spa, and Nottingham (National Archives, EF 5/38, a list of the many IRA incidents in 1939 up to early July). The IRA's bombing campaign, which was designed to force the British government to withdraw its presence from Ireland, had been launched at the beginning of the year: see J. Bowyer Bell, *The Secret Army: The IRA 1916–1979* (Cambridge, MA: MIT Press, 1980), chap. VIII. On the first day of June Gladys had gone with Wellings to the Curzon Cinema 'but felt uneasy lest IRA enthusiasts should be bomb-dropping there'. On Saturday, 24 June, 'Coming home, my bus missed by a few yards the IRA bomb at Piccadilly Circus. There have been several thrown tonight. The bus conductor was green with fright and an old man alone in the vehicle was distraught.'
34. Waln's *Reaching for the Stars*, she had written the previous day, '[is] very quietly written but an awful indictment of Nazism'. It was published in 1939 and subtitled *An Account of Experiences in Germany and Austria from 1934 to 1938*.
35. Later she confessed that 'I am in search of social contacts rather than "good works"' (10 July), and her visit there, at 19 Red Lion Square, four days later, was not reassuring. 'It is a dismal, stuffy place; it seemed the sort of place one might go for an abortion. The secretary was small, very "refined" and very simple. I got the impression that the place was run on commercial lines for Dr. Oldfield's benefit [he ran it]. Anyhow, it's a cranks' stronghold

Wrote to A. J. Marshall, author of *Black Musketeers*.[36] Saw a man outside a public house in Theobalds Road with a young fox on a chain!

Monday, 3 July. Evacuation schemes sole topic of conversation at school. Result – frayed nerves and ill humour for me. My visitors necessitated much running about. Micky Read (Mrs. Sueddon) bursting to tell me about her matrimonial discontents and her imaginary illnesses but I successfully evaded both recitals. Em looked hideous in a straw hat more suitable for a child than for a sexagenarian, Kathlyn white and fat like a snail[37] and Bay in good fettle. She, Bay, is offering her services for the Blood Transfusion Scheme. Does this gratify her guilt complex, I wonder?

* * * * * *

Wednesday, 5 July. Letter from Lil. Our cousin Annie in Australia, aged 73, has just married for the *fourth* time and the bridegroom has given her a lovely car for a wedding present. I wish I knew how she did it. Wrote to LCC for details of sick leave 'in hand'. I wish I could get a breakdown pension. My poor mind is in such a ferment. I feel distraught. Met Vera Mannering, worried by 'Evac' preparations.

* * * * * *

Friday, 7 July. Lil sent a *very* amusing account of the farcical air-raid rehearsals at Bumpstead. She says Mrs. Waters' school is to be evacuated to the East Coast – near Lowestoft! To Rosenbergs. Leslie off at once to Air Raid Wardens' meeting. Only Mrs. Rosenberg left so I was bored to extinction. Leonard was brought back to London today, with a nurse in attendance. I really feel if he were a poor man he would have been cured long since. Rosa, the Viennese maid, told of family tragedies. Both her grandfathers were shot dead, one in Hungary by a drunken Anti-Semite as he sat at table on Yom Kippur. The other's body, riddled with bullets, was dumped on his own doorstep at a Sabbath sunset. Em phoned.

* * * * * *

Wednesday, 12 July. Em on phone. Lil suggested my going to Mañana but it was a very half-hearted welcome, so I shan't go. To St. James's Park to see the debutantes but was too late. Saw only soldiers marching instead. Indeed, you'd think England was at war, with baby-

---

and I didn't like the "atmosphere" of the place; there was a furtive quality about it. It is a hospital for digestive troubles, these to be cured by fruitarian diet.'

36. Marshall's 1937 book is subtitled *The Work and Adventures of a Scientist on a South Sea island at War and Peace*. It is based on an expedition to Espiritu Santo Island in the New Hebrides – and includes a preface by and accounts of certain field activities of Tom Harrisson, one of the founders that year of Mass-Observation.

37. Gladys's usual harsh words about her niece were tempered later this month, after a lunch at Em's – 'Kathlyn is distinctly improved' (31 July).

conscripts marching, gun-carriages on the tram-lines and auxiliary fire service and ambulance personnel everywhere. I wish I could leave England. Not very amiable at school.

* * * * * *

Tuesday, 18 July. Letter from Stelle but no definite invitation. Spoke to Marjorie Rose on phone. Leonard has now had an X-ray photograph but the ulcers are not gone and he may need an operation. Clarrie is about the same. Marjorie has no ailments at the moment. To Russell's. Bought green macintosh for a guinea. Had a 1s 6d dinner at Lyons Shaftesbury Avenue branch. The waitress told me her troubles. (I'm Public Listener no. 1.) She has a spot on her lung and has to go to a sanatorium for four months. She says her pay is 11s 3d weekly and deductions are made for laundry, uniform and caps and aprons. Unless she makes 6s or 8s daily in tips she can't live free from debt. She says parties at one table she abhors as the tip for six or eight people is rarely more than 1s. She hates to see two women come in together as it means they sit over a meal discussing dress or diseases, keeping out other clients with other possible tips. She says 'Street-girls are the best. They'll give lavishly then they have done well.' She pointed one out. 'She's getting on now but she puts a brave face on it and never gives unnecessary trouble.' She says waitresses are paid 5s or 2s 6d prize if they sell the most drinks, but, she added mournfully, 'If you say "Would you like anything to drink?" half the diners say "Yes, a nice glass of water, please, miss".'[38]

* * * * * *

Wednesday, 26 July. Broke up today but I never remember a less exciting breaking up day. What with the bad weather, the recurrent Crises and the IRA threats, pleasurable excitement has become a thing of the past and always ours is an unfriendly staff. Miss Hammond and Conway shook hands but Kerr and Topley walked off without a word and had I not come out as Pickering did, he too would have departed without farewell. To Hardwicks. They seem well. Time stands still with them. The house is very silent so I felt oppressed.[39]

Thursday, 27 July. To Library and Town Hall. Met Wilmot. At 2.15 p.m. met Wellings. To Welwyn – like me, he's not very favourably impressed with the Garden City. Enjoyed my day with Editha [who now lived there] but her husband *is* a poor thing. Lil wrote. She *isn't* coming to London tomorrow after all as she fears IRA activities.

---

38. Gladys did not write in her diary between 19 and 23 July inclusive, part of which she spent with Lil and Challis in Essex, which included a day trip to Felixstowe.
39. 'I do deserve a legacy from one or other of the old dames I cultivate,' she had written two days before. 'I'm very short of money.'

They have bombed Victoria and King's Cross cloak rooms.[40] Wherever you go now, aeroplanes drone over your head.

Friday, 28 July. Today is the 26th anniversary of my unfortunate wedding day. If only I could forget! Wrote to Lil reproaching her for her letter to Emmie. This afternoon went to the Aldwych to see Ram Gropal and his dancers, a feast of beauty. The Eagle dance was exquisite. The Kite dance was delightful. The Cobra dance was impressive. The lovely serenity of the dancers seemed to permeate the audience, who were silent and motionless during the dances. I never before realised (despite Watts' paintings) how beautiful was the human back. To Rosenbergs tonight. Leslie had bought his mother a magnificent silver fox cape. Need I say she was not satisfied and wanted it enlarged. I think I have outlived my affection for her. I hate to see her eat peas from the spoon with which she is serving them, pick out chocolates or biscuits and put them into other people's mouths, and nag that maid steadily. She is the most dogmatic woman I know and she is usually wrong. Marjorie is mad on sex. She drags it into every conversation and uses it to explain every illness and discomfort save her own. She refers to me as being quite abnormal – a sort of 'Colonel' Barker. This does irritate me. IRA bill ['Prevention of Violence (Temporary Provisions) Bill'] rushed through the House.[41]

* * * * * *

Tuesday, 1 August. Weather remains so unsettled no plans for holidays seem worth making. Rain, wind and thunder come every day. Bought a jumper and a blouse at Selby's. The shop-girl who serves me keeps her figure but begins to shew her age despite lipstick and dyed hair – perhaps because of it. Had an awful nightmare. Thought I was at the New Restaurant with Clowser and Wellings and the latter kept teasing me about talking too much and too fast, 'like mad George III'. I was so angry I rushed out, meaning to go home but the Italian waitress urged me to return, saying 'You can't afford to lose any more friends'. When I went back, Wellings and Clowser had gone and there were crowds of people at each table, all wearing gas-masks. They crowded round me, gibbering and shouting in foreign languages, when I noticed they were skeletons in suits with grinning skulls behind the masks and their skinny fingers were crooked, ready to clutch me and throttle me. I was so terrified I felt dying from shock when I wakened.

---

40. One man was killed and fifteen injured by this explosion. 'Thick clouds of smoke poured from the building as passengers scattered in all directions. ... Women near the scene of the explosion had their dresses torn off by the force of the explosion' (*Islington Guardian*, 28 July 1939, p. 5).
41. Among other things, it permitted the expulsion from the country of people not ordinarily resident for twenty years and suspected of violence. It was thought that recent offences had been committed by IRA leaders from Dublin. For background, see Bell, *Secret Army*, pp. 160–1.

Wednesday, 2 August. Lil wrote. Still it showers but at last the barrage balloons have gone from the sky. Em phoned. War conversations and prognostications make me ever more fearful. I look at my beloved cat and wonder whether I'd better have him destroyed – but I love him so much! To the Aldwych again to see the second programme of Ram Gropal. He is exquisite – and what a vogue he has. The gallery was packed with Hindus and intelligentsia.

Thursday, 3 August. To the doctor's this morning. Talked with him for about half-an-hour. He suggests my living in a boarding house – at any rate for a time. Rain falls steadily. Stormy Commons meeting yesterday because Chamberlain permits the Long Vacation to begin on Friday.

Friday, 4 August. Met Wellings last night. He said a small child who saw him coming down a Tube staircase cried 'Oh, look at that old man!' I'm not surprised. He stoops badly and is going bald. He walks as slowly as a rheumatic old age pensioner and when not talking frowns angrily. He looks nearly as old as I am. Mr. Haffner sent another card. More rain and yet more. Talked with Editha on the phone yesterday about H. G. Wells' new book.[42] Lil sent three letters by two posts. *Later.* A terrible fire in Knightrider Street [EC4] this afternoon – and storms. Equatorial effect of rain, hail, thunder and lightning.

Saturday, 5 August. Wellings on phone last night. He wonders if Editha would go as part-time manageress of his libraries as he is losing Mrs. Wynne. Bought *two* navy blue hats. To the Tatler and to Studio One tonight. Saw Danielle Darrieux in *Retour à l'aube* [1938]. Excellent. Also saw Disney, *Ferdinand the Bull*, which was very weak compared with his usual output. Letter from Charles. He says we must have an evening out together after I return from my holiday. Delightful prospect. I wish he would marry me!

Sunday, 6 August. Very depressed today. House is empty and silent and my every movement echoes and re-echoes. I don't want to spend money unnecessarily and there's nothing I particularly want to see in the cinemas and I hate going out on Sundays and Bank Holidays. How easy I should find it to do as mother did and stay indoors for weeks on end! I must fight against this. I wrote innumerable letters and read a pleasing novel [published in 1938] by Lewis Browne, *Oh, Say! Can You See!*

---

42. She is referring to Wells' *The Fate of Homo Sapiens: An unemotional Statement of the Things that are happening to him now, and of the immediate Possibilities confronting him*, which was published this month. 'Adapt or perish' was one of its key messages (p. 312), though Wells held out little hope that the former was likely to occur, given (among other things) the probable imminence of a crippling war.

Monday, 7 August. Gloom persists! Last night I walked around Finsbury Park and Woodberry Down. It seems criminal that the latter lovely road should be chosen by the LCC for their slum clearance plan erections. It was one of the most beautiful rural spots in the district. Of course, the idea is to introduce the Labour Vote into a sound Municipal Reform [anti-socialist] district. Today, very early, the house emptied again and silence fell. Em phoned; otherwise I'm thrown on my own resources. Sent a letter to Wellings and began one to Ginsbury.

Tuesday, 8 August. Walked the streets last night and stood at the gate till Mr. Lucas came home. Found those attractive houses in Canonbury Park South all, or nearly all, empty, ready for slum clearance flats. It's sinful to destroy such pleasant villas for great barrack-buildings. Today workmen are busy darkening traffic lights ready for tomorrow's 'black-out'.[43] Only a plus sign remains visible [on the top of the three vertically-arranged lights: she provides a drawing]. Spoke to Em. Walked in Oxford Street. Many foreigners there. I AM a fool. I spend time and money on people who don't care two hoots for me. I had planned to treat Bay to a day at Leamington and had found out times of trains and so on for the trip. As soon as I mooted the subject tonight by phone she burst out that she couldn't come as she was going to [Miss] Wilshin's. I ought to have learned when she refused the trip to Bath that she did not want to be separated from Miss Wilshin and her garden. She soon realised she'd hurt me and said she would come after all but I wouldn't give her the name of the hotel. I want no one's company as a favour. But I AM a fool for I do a lot for Bay though she has never put herself on one side for me or for mother. She's generous with goods but not with her time.[44]

Wednesday, 16 August. I have been for a week at Armathwaite Hotel, Holly Walk, Leamington. On the journey down, two elderly ladies told me the life history of their stomachs. Arrived at the hotel I had a shock. Mine host looked exactly like Father Time without his scythe and the receptionist was all twitter and toothy smile and nervous anxiety to please. The guests appeared to be only two high-bellied dames with bosoms like shelves and a languid spinster with a sepulchral cough! The town was clean, pleasant, free from slums – apparently – and the domestic architecture peculiar, ecclesiastical-phallic. Every boarding house boasted Gothic effects plus dwarf obelisks stuck on every projection. Time brought bird-of-passage guests – some very attractive, two charming girls from Vancouver; they declared I must

---

43. There was to be a trial blackout, accompanied by aerial observations (*Islington Gazette*, 9 August 1939, p. 1).
44. Gladys wrote nothing in her diary during the following seven days.

be an actress, and I never denied it. (I've been suspected of being a nurse, wife of a licensed victualler and librarian.) There was a girl who was crippled (infantile paralysis), a librarian from Minneapolis who was 'doing' Europe alone! She said to me 'You ought to travel. A woman like you ought not to let herself get into a rut.' Then there was a teacher from the North with a sister in attendance who plucked him from under my nose whenever our conversation became too prolonged. This man said I ought to be psycho-analysed I am so restless. Then there were people coming and going from the North with all of whom I fraternised. Indeed, I've not been so flattered since I left Metwell and my inferiority complex is put to sleep for a long while. I needed this fillip to make up for lack of friendliness at Hoxton. Another sop to my vanity was the offer by Mr. Wellings to engage me as his subordinate in running his libraries – £1 for 12 hours weekly. Of course I didn't accept. I love my leisure too well. I don't care to work for a friend. I am too unstable to commit myself and I could earn more money in less time in Evening Schools. I went to Warwick Castle – had a very facetious guide and not enough time to view the pictures. Visited Kenilworth. Motored to Broadway, through the Cotswolds and on another day to Edgehill and Sulgrave Manor. Spent hours in the Public Library. Returned redder and rounder than ever to a spate of letters including one from Lottie, another from Lil, card from Leo. While away Leonard wrote offering a loan. Ginsbury wrote, Editha and my own people of course. Phoned Bay who is ill. Taking her to Trent Park tomorrow.

Back in London, Gladys, whose physical health was better, ruminated further on how trapped she felt. After relaxing on a trip by boat from Richmond to Teddington on 18 August, she imagined a better life. 'How I should like to live in one of those houses with lawns sloping down to the river. If only I could get free from teaching!' The next day international politics intruded. 'More threatened crises! Oh, how I long for peace or, if not peace, escape from teaching so evacuation didn't hang over my head.'

PART TWO: 1939–1940

5

March–July 1939

Writing for Mass-Observation

In February–March 1939, Gladys volunteered to serve as a writer for Mass-Observation, the social research organisation set up in 1937 to lay the foundations for 'a science of ourselves', and Gladys replied to several of M-O's 'Directives' (she is Directive Respondent no. 1286), which were (as a rule) monthly questionnaires about a wide range of issues, personal, social, historical, psychological, and political. She answered some of these questions in considerable detail and in so doing disclosed a lot about her tastes, her background, her values, and her current circumstances, sometimes well beyond the facts recorded in her diary. In May she described how she managed her wardrobe and her purchases of clothes.

For the last four years I have kept an account of my spendings on dress. The average sum is £52 per annum.[1] I do not wear 'best dresses' for most of my friends are of the Bohemian type who either wear 'arty' clothing or sports wear. I myself wear woollen suits of different weight when at school or jumpers and skirts. I do not possess gowns suitable for evening or semi-evening wear. I pay 37s 6d or 45s 9d for suits, 8s 11d or 12s 11d each for blouses, 12s 11d to 18s 11d each for jumpers and an average of a guinea each for woolen coatees, usually of Viennese or Czecho-Slovakian manufacture. For coats I usually pay from £3 10s 0d to £4 4s 0d each but my last coat cost only 49s 6d as it is very light in colour and is only intended for wear during the few weeks of summer.

I usually buy two or three hats at 12s 11d or 15s 11d each in a year and a couple of small 'pull-on felts' at 4s 11d or 6s 11d each for wearing on wet days or in cinemas or theatres so that I need not remove my hat in the latter places for I hate showing my iron-grey hair. For gloves I pay 8s 11d or 10s 11d for a fleecy lined pair (I object to the use of fur lest the animal should have been trapped) of gloves for winter

---

1. Her annual salary was £324; after deductions for income tax and superannuation, her actual monthly pay was £24 9s 6d.

wear, 4s 11d for fabric gloves for summer wear, but I usually have two pairs of kid gloves at about 8s 11d per pair given to me at Christmas. I pay 2s per pair for lisle stockings and have about fifteen pairs in a year. I cannot afford good silk stockings as I am a heavy wearer and I detest the cheap and nasty variety of foot-wear. I pay from 25s 9d to 32s 6d per pair for shoes and have about three or four pairs a year since I do not wear slippers in the house but the new crêpe sole shoes of foreign make and low price have won my allegiance this spring. I am not including the cost of cleaning clothes which would probably be another £2 10s 0d per annum, but the figure quoted at the beginning does include shoe repair.

When about to purchase clothing I decide the limit I can afford, descend upon the stores I patronise (I find it wise to deal at the same shops and ask for the same assistants as a rule), and give in a few words an idea of what I want or ask for something in the shop window I am practically certain will suit me for I hate (a) wasting time shopping, and (b) giving unnecessary trouble to shop assistants. I never read a fashion page. I detest exaggerated styles. I never shop by post so I do not read advertisement pages. Women's papers are written for nitwits. I avoid them. I do look in West End shop windows for the artistic effects are often pleasing and the lovely colours are a joy after the drab effects of a working day in Hoxton. The shop windows supply a sort of 'Russian ballet' touch to my brisk walks from one place to another. The few women friends I have rarely mention dress and I never discuss it with acquaintances although I may ask a candid relative to comment if she thinks my choice unduly youthful in effect.

As previously stated I have no 'best' wear but I wear my newest things for theatre wear, visiting friends, or when on holiday. I rarely wear things a second season; the exception would be a jumper or blouse. Woollen suits I find best for day wear as they do not crush. I prefer to pay a fairly good price (proportionate to my salary) for clothing and wear it rather longer than to buy cheap and shoddy stuff that is crude in colouring and bad in cut. I always regret buying a cheap article.

I should describe myself as being suitably dressed and becomingly (according to my age). I wear navy blue and white, black and white, green and black and navy relieved by gay stripes. I hate to wear a jumper or suit that I am likely to see on anyone else. I favour the severe or tailored styles because I am not of a frivolous type and never have been and I keep the etceteras – gloves, handbags, handkerchiefs and scarves – to match each outfit. I wear no jewellery or ornament of any kind. Had I more money to play with I should have no difficulty in buying suitable clothing. My great trouble is the buying of hats. One wearies of the mannish type and the ultra-fashionable is absurd on a heavy face with a pronounced nose.

I feel much lighter-hearted in a new suit or with an occasional lapse into a [Greta] 'Garbo hat'. Indeed, I often go out to buy a new article to relieve my inclination towards melancholia. I am troubled if I look dowdy when visiting my wealthy Jewish friends, gleeful if I find I have favourably impressed a woman friend, grateful if a man comments favourably and impishly delighted if I get something that makes a youthful colleague of the same sex envious. On the whole, I think I seek to impress my men-friends favourably. I dress carefully for any interview when I 'have an axe to grind'.

A few weeks later, in June 1939, she wrote to M-O (again in response to its Directive) about social class, and disclosed some of the nuances and subtleties in trying to understand this central reality of English culture.

I consider I belong to the 'upper lower class'.[2] My father was originally a sawyer but had his own timber yard by the time I was born. My mother for a short time was a machinist but spent most of her life, until her marriage, with her parents at home. When my father died my mother drifted into very 'low water', turning from shop-keeping to machining which she continued until she was eligible for an old age pension.[3] Although, from six years of age until I was married at twenty-three, I was permanently under-nourished, usually shabbily dressed and never having a shilling to spend in waste, I always regarded myself as belonging to the *upper* lower class as, though bread and salt might be my dinner, we always kept a 'parlour' with no bed in it. I might buy 'kag-mag' [inferior, 'rubbishy'] meat or 'specked' oranges but I wore gloves, even as a child, when shopping. We sat down to a properly laid table, used no slang or bad language, I attended a private school, and afterwards, thanks to a scholarship, a Secondary School, and we aspired – well, there was no limit to our aspirations. I do not think income has anything to do with class. I earn £324 per annum but I still feel painfully akin to the lower classes although most elementary teachers regard themselves as belonging to the professional classes, even to the ranks of the minor deities.

I move in rather a different class from my parents' associates, quite a different set from that of my grandparents. Both paternal and maternal grandparents came from Essex peasant stock. On coming to London all four of them became poor but (I think) honest working class folk. One grandfather was a 'top' sawyer, the other a 'Peeler' policeman and then foreman over a small gang of dock labourers. The upward trend began

2. She had first written 'upper lower middle class' and then, after deleting 'middle', wrote in the margin: 'A Freudian would sense assumed humility in that deletion.'
3. Her mother worked as a seamstress and Gladys on one occasion (29 April 1943) was explicit in her appreciation of what she had struggled to achieve: 'I realised too how much I owed to her during those long years when a sewing-machine held her in thrall.'

with my parents. My father was a very ambitious man and did well in the timber trade but lived riotously. His associates were mainly monied business men. He was a keen Conservative, read a lot and travelled fairly widely. My mother was ambitious for her children. She stinted herself of food and firing that I might be educated for teaching.[4] As a child I 'cultivated' acquaintances and neighbours who read much or talked well. Secondary School made contacts with my social superiors possible and from that time onwards I have tried to be a social climber – not necessarily into monied circles but into cultivated society (not very successfully from a variety of reasons). My present circle of friends includes several cranks or enthusiasts, usually with a bias in favour of drama or literature, and many Jewish people in comfortable circumstances.

I feel at ease with the Bohemian type, be its origin what it may,[5] with my equals and with the artizan and shop-keeper and 'decent working man' type. I am very uneasy with the middle and professional classes lest they despise me for my accent or for the hundred and one tiny details that doubtless 'give me away'. I am inclined to boast or to refer unnecessarily to my humble origin in order to anticipate adverse criticism. I get on very well with the successful business man type. I notice this particularly on holiday when I usually stay at country inns or commercial hotels. I think I identify such men with my father whom I greatly admired. My closest friends are mostly of my present class rather than of my childhood's class. This sounds a contradiction. I mean their monetary position is mostly about equal with my own but their origin was not so humble.

Exceptions. (1) A Jewish family and their intimates, some of whom reach the super-tax level. They have been my friends since the war years when I worked as confidential clerk for one of the 'clan'.[6] (2) A

---

4.   Several years later Gladys mentioned that 'my poor, hard-working widowed mother never sent me out to work as a child', as, implicitly, might have been expected (9 April 1944). On 12 November 1936 she had remarked that 'I *am* grateful I am not and never have been below the subsistence line, never known dirt and disease. Only mother's marvellous struggle saved me from this. She toiled to give me an education.'

5.   On 1 February 1943 she reminisced about these social circles that she been connected with in earlier days: 'Am reading *Half My Days and Nights* by Hubert Nicholson [1941; a reporter's autobiography] and am very nostalgic in consequence. His description of parties, lectures, plays recalls my own twenties and thirties when I was surrounded by people who argued persistently, dabbled in the arts and were self-constituted dramatic and literary critics.' One passage in this book (pp. 137–38), evoking a mood of the later 1920s, describes the sort of milieu that attracted Gladys: 'It was a huge and beautiful flat in one of Clifton's fine old houses [the author was then living in Bristol], packed with people always, mostly middle-class or upper-middle, with a small sprinkling of working-class members. They ranged from energetic communists to timid right-wing liberals. There were university professors, authors, painters, even a big business executive or two. They had play-readings and short talks and lots and lots of discussion; and I have never found any group of people anywhere among whom the level of discourse was so high, the quality of debate so good. It was extremely stimulating.' This was the sort of society that she aspired to be part of.

6.   This was the Rosenberg family.

man of middle-class birth, a journalist, poet (almost unknown) and now proprietor of several circulating libraries. He is very literary, politically minded and appreciative of all the arts.[7] (3) A man of middle-class birth, an Anthroposophist, mystical, much travelled in Europe.[8] (4) A Jewish playwright, of the middle classes, very well-read and enthusiastic about all forms of arts.[9]

I married a man of my own class but I thought he was as ambitious as I am and imagined we should climb socially. His position as a schoolmaster was 'safe' and allowed opportunity for some advancement. I should not, even as a young woman, have allowed myself to consider matrimony with anyone who would have kept me in the poverty-stricken condition in which I was reared. I am at present fond of a man whose birth is superior to my own, whose position is assured and pensionable and whose family numbers no black sheep among its members, and I rather think my affection is conditioned, perhaps born of the fact that he would lever me upwards.

I have no children but had I any I would not, under any circumstances, send my sons to a public school or even to a boarding school. I know too much of sadism among teachers and children. I should send boys and girls to a good Secondary school, co-educational if possible.

The working-class attitude to money varies considerably. (I work in Hoxton, so I know something of the subject.) Casual labourers and people who are in and out of work frequently are thriftless. They know they can never *really* provide for a rainy day so they spend as they get. The artizan type or the municipal employee generally has a little money 'put by', but there is a third class with wages so low, though they may be regular, as to make current expenses absorb total earnings. The last type usually pays into various clubs[10] and buys furniture, clothes, bicycles, etc., by Hire Purchase terms. I should think the middle classes are the meanest with their money. They live in fear of going down the social slope and in hope of going up it and their money is their lever so must be hoarded. The casual labourers seem the most generous with their scant money but many people of all classes are ostentatiously generous, usually because they suffer from an inferiority complex and for one reason or another want to buy prestige. I should imagine that the 'black coat' class and the middle class think most about money because both are so anxious to 'Keep up appearances'. Almost everyone seems to have a pet economy.

Gladys went on to describe her own tastes, habits, and preferences.

---

7. This was Gladys's frequent companion Arthur Wellings, a bachelor, aged thirty-seven in 1939, with a much older half-brother as his only near relative.
8. This was Charles Gaye. Referring to 'darling Charles' on 9 November 1936, she wrote: 'How I wish he would marry me.'
9. This was Norman Ginsbury.
10. Funeral insurance through burial clubs was particularly widespread.

I moved to Highbury fourteen years ago because many of my friends then lived in the district, because it was accessible to my work and for Central London and because it had romantic memories for me. Incidentally, I liked the suggestion of 'fallen glory' in the fine old houses once inhabited by 'merchant princes'. I am now thinking of removing to Highgate or Hampstead since the district is changing. Factories and working-class flats are superseding Georgian houses and their lovely gardens or Victorian dwellings with their 'carriage drives'. I think I am different from my neighbours when I hear their radios blaring jazz music, when I see the women folk gossiping by the hour and overhear their conversation – garbled news from their daily paper, scandal and 'home-and-baby' discourses; or when I see them dishevelled and grubby, shopping about in dirty slippers or with frowsty [i.e., slatternly, unkempt] dusting caps atop of their 'permed' hair.

I hardly ever go into a public house save for an occasional mid-day meal in a luncheon room above stairs. On the rare occasions I am persuaded to go in (there speaks the prig), it is to a saloon bar in town, any bar in a country inn, although I note the yokels resent the advent of a 'townie' in the common bar in small village hostelries. At cinemas, if I can get westwards before 1 p.m., I pay 1s 6d which is the charge for practically any seat in the house; otherwise I pay 2s 6d but only 1s if I go locally, which I rarely do. I pay proportionately to my income – not more – because I am a film- and play-addict and want to see as many of each as time and money allow.

I am *very* sensitive about my accent. I was unmercifully teased by the mistresses (never by the girls) at Secondary School about my ã-s and i-s. A Scottish friend made me wary when saying 'saw' and 'sore', 'raw' and 'roar', and so on. I am also very nervous about using foreign words as I am not musical and so uncertain of pronunciation unless I have heard the phrase scores of times. I have a foolish habit of spelling the word rather than saying it, as though to show my listener I am not a fool since I can spell if I cannot say words. I have changed my manner of speech. It has not the slightly nasal whine of my sisters' although it had in my early youth. I have turned my natural Cockney into what is apparently a Midland accent since I am often asked if I come from Leicestershire!

She had a little to say about the word 'mate', which 'is a common address among friends in Hoxton and is often used to address me by friendly parents of school children, stall-holders and occasional bus-conductors. Children in the East End use the word invariably for "friend". Thus: "Me an' my mate wen' to the Tahr" (Tower).'

A few weeks later, in July, she wrote to M-O about 'Age differences', and this subject gave her an opportunity to compare and contrast social attitudes and practices and living conditions at the beginning of the twentieth century with those that prevailed in the later 1930s.

I am NOT representative of my own or of the succeeding generation in health, as I have never spent a day in bed in my life. My contemporaries fainted more often, wept more frequently and were more hysterical than my juniors are. My contemporaries spoke vaguely of 'indigestion' or 'being unwell'; they did not drag constipation into drawing room conversational topics, and they suffered recurrent disabilities in silence. They wore more clothing, used more perfumes (but much, much less cosmetics, if any) but bathed much less and changed their underwear less frequently. They visited the dentist less frequently and otherwise pretty young girls used to have badly decayed teeth, whereas I find younger women now wear false teeth when necessary quite unblushingly.

Again, I am NOT representative of my period, for my mother, in an age of over-eating, insisted we should always rise from the table with a desire for 'a little more' instead of achieving repletion even when funds permitted a well-spread board. It was impressed upon me that I must eat bread and butter before cake – unless I 'rode in my own carriage'. I must NEVER accept a third helping. I, with many other children I knew, was allowed to sip a little beer, even a little brandy and water from my father's glass. Every effort must be made to secure a hot dinner on a Sunday. Stewed eels, hot boiled beef and pease pudding, flooded with watery gravy, were all purchased from local cook-shops. (It was a working-class district.) From the confectioner I used to buy brandy-balls, bulls' eyes, fig-toffee, aniseed balls and liquorice comfits – also Cupid's favours, i.e., lozenges with love phrases imprinted thereon. None of these 'dainties' seem known to my juniors who eat wrapped toffees and boxed chocolates.

Hot potato cans stood at every street corner whereas now it is the roast chestnut vendor. Ice cream 'jacks' sold water-ices in coloured glasses to children whereas Wall's and El Dorado representatives now supply all ages and sexes. Cornflour blancmange and stewed fruit appeared on Sundays in summer and suet puddings, currant and roly-poly were favourites but no young woman I know nowadays will touch suet puddings lest her figure should suffer. She eats salads whereas I never saw one until I was eighteen. I was always advised not to eat raw green stuff by my mother lest I should inadvertently swallow 'some creature that would eat everything I ate till I starved'. We took a pint of milk on Sundays for a pudding. I never remember drinking milk until I was a grown woman. Cereals and grapefruit I did not know, but pickles appeared on the meal table twice a day when funds were plentiful. Gin-drinking was confined to old women or women at a low-class funeral – because it induced tears I was told. No 'nice' girl of my generation went into a public house. My brother always used to say, 'When I take a girl out, I ask her if she'd like a glass of port. If she says "Yes" I never take her out again because I know she's "no good".' (He would now be 60, if alive.)

We wore corsets – most of my girl friends tight-laced but I anticipated the modern hatred of whalebone. If we were bold we wore 'peek-a-boo' blouses, revealing a V-shaped expanse of neck under net or gauze. Feather boas we coveted and with these we made as much play as Miss 1939 does with her silver fox furs. We wore hats weighed down with flowers or stuffed birds, perched on 'bandeaux' and speared with hat-pins on hair puffed out with horse-hair 'sausages' or wire-frames if our own locks were scanty. Curling pins made hideous those of us who had not naturally curly hair whereas today my juniors are 'permed' or 'set'. My girl friends went to a hairdresser about once a year, usually for a Christmas party effect. My sisters used to clip my hair and singe the ends with a match and to this day I wash my hair with ordinary soap and water while my young friends use shampoo powders or have a 'dry shampoo' at a hairdresser's. I was never allowed to appear outside my bedroom door unless and until I was fully clothed lest any male member of my family should see me. Today, mixed bathing and sun-bathing alters that rule for the present-day folks.

'Having a good time' in my youth meant being sought after and taken out by many young men, and being officially engaged by the early twenties at latest. An occasional seat in the gallery or pit of a theatre, frequent walks 'in the gloaming', some 'spooning' (I never hear this word now)[11] at picnics or on the river, a fortnight's holiday with all or some of the family. (One never went away with a fiancé. It was considered to be 'too much of a temptation'.) Parties were the red-letter days of our lives. There were Christmas parties, wedding parties, engagement parties, birthday parties (but no candles on cakes then). For weeks these were planned and one *must* keep the sexes equal in number or with superfluous males if one wanted a success. Then there was the escorting of the females to their homes. My juniors deride such parties, I find, and the idea of a compulsory escort arouses hoots of laughter.

A few months later, in July, she replied to a M-O questionnaire about dancing, which she no longer did, with a recollection of her mixed pleasures. 'The first dance I attended was in December 1908 when I was eighteen. It was a College dance (both sexes attended the training college). We had talked of it, planned for it, practised for it for weeks and I was very excited. On the eventful night, the ladies' cloakroom was heaped with wraps and crowded with girls in new *dresses, changing shoes for dancing slippers and pinning on sprays of flowers. I wore my shabby everyday coat, a rabbit-skin fur (1s 11½d), a premature Christmas box from an obliging sister, and a secondhand frock, quite unsuitable for the occasion. I can remember now how deplorable I*

11. To cuddle or fondle.

looked in walking shoes with bows sewn on askew to suggest dancing slippers, a drab grey dress and with no kindly face-powder to lessen the shine born of cold winds and yellow house-soap. I thought I should be ostracised but my fellow students were not snobbish. Neither were they sparing of comment on my poor performance as a dancer' – and she went on to recall jocularly her ineptness. 'Despite the adverse criticism, I romped through the Lancers, "sat out" some dances with partners who talked well, and came home under the stars at midnight with two attendant swains, each of whom invited me to his forthcoming Christmas party. All very un-modern of course!'

She remembered her early months of marriage.

My husband earned £100 per annum in 1914 when I married him.[12] We paid 8s 6d weekly for a nice flat (or 'rooms' as we then called them) in Clapton. Our home (furniture and linen) cost us less than £60 in cash. We were a typical 'upper lower class' couple. I had 30s weekly for house-keeping. Out of this I paid rent, lighting and firing, bought my clothes and found my own spending money. I was impressed as a child with the idea that money was valueless as compared with leisure but this was an heretical idea.

Most of my contemporaries sought employment that was 'safe' and 'had a future'. That accounted for my being trained as a teacher although I loathed the idea of such employment.[13] The Civil Service (even if it meant a post office counter-hand) was 'nice'. It was very derogatory to have a relative who was a factory hand, and even a shop-girl was not 'nice'. The great hope was to be able to retire. Pocket money for children was scanty but the rare pence bought much more. Cheap sweets were 6ozs or 8ozs for a penny. One accepted a farthing [quarter penny] gratefully but the child of today almost refuses a proffered penny. We were always expected to contribute towards the household expenses once we began to earn but I find this is not very usual today among my present acquaintance. I gave 6s out of 8s weekly and 12s out of 18s, buying a mid-day meal out of the 6s retained.

HOME was sacred. You dared not criticise its sanctity in pre-War days. It was a place for which one longed in absence, to which one returned with joy. One had a niche in it, but there are few 'homes' today – unless it be among the Jews. A large family with the resultant widespread social contacts made Home exciting enough without radio or gramophone. Rarely an evening passed without a visitor (whose coming and going was carefully timed to exclude meals unless he or she had an official invitation). There were books to lend or exchange, songs to 'try over', books to read aloud round the fire; but I am assured

---

12. They were actually married in July 1913.
13. In the 1911 census Gladys, still living with her mother, is described as a 'London County Council Teacher', though she seems never to have written about her pre-Great War teaching.

none of these things have charm and appeal today. One did not leave home at Christmas but returned to it, with offspring, if any.

Father's word was law. Sunday dinner was torture as Father's criticism of conversation (topic as well as language) was severe as well as arbitrary. Mother was Father's understudy. She vetoed slang and swear-words. She silenced conversation even faintly suggestive of sex or religious doubts. She decided who was to be cut off the visiting list but she appealed to Father for leniency when late home-coming and lent latch-keys were involved. Elder sisters and brothers (oh, how many I had!) must be treated with deference, must be served first at the table and obeyed unhesitatingly in the absence of parents. In most families toys, books, umbrellas and even clothes were communal property but not in our house where permission must be sought from the owner ere a pen-knife was borrowed or a ball bounced. Loyalty to one's own family loomed larger than loyalty to the Royal Family. Individual disgrace or shortcoming meant family disgrace. Husband and wife never visited separately but the husband went out alone, for unfaithfulness in husbands was as common then as now.

SEX was taboo. One 'finished at the neck' according to my mother's idea. If we had abdominal pains, she rubbed embrocation on our throats!! Tuberculosis would have been countenanced but not appendicitis. Babies were not referred to until they were in existence. Menstruation must neither be mentioned nor eased. One entered matrimony in a conspiracy of silence. So horrible was marriage in my mother's eyes that she refused to attend a marriage of any of her children or receive them in her home for months after their marriage; perhaps that is why four out of the six marriages were failures. She had had thirteen children in quick succession which probably accounts for her phobias. Contraceptives were unknown to many married people; now girls in their teens are glib in their reference thereto. Our great horror was to be regarded as 'fast'. The 'glad eye' was not funny. It was shameful. Visiting a w.c. when a male – brother, fiancé or stranger – was about was iniquitous. In 1911 when out with my future husband, I asked to be excused and for days after wondered, nay, even enquired, if he 'still respected me?' Young men who went into a lavatory when visiting women friends were 'not nice', than which nothing more damning could be said.

When I was young, my mother impressed on me I must *never* take any present (other than flowers or sweets) from any young man of my acquaintance, nor must I allow him to take me out 'lest he has stolen the petty cash or money from his master's till' in order to do so. This view was most unusual. When War came and I had escaped from the thraldom of my mother's views to some extent, I accepted expensive presents and submitted to being 'treated' to theatres, picture galleries, outings of all sorts by fellow workers and clients of my employer but almost always my escorts were Jewish and were monied people who would have been horrified had I attempted to pay my own expenses. Nowadays I allow my male contemporaries to pay my expenses if they invite me to dine or wine with them, or to join them at theatre or cinema, but since I entertain them to supper parties at home I feel under no obligation. If I agree to allow myself to be taken out by my juniors I insist on a 50/50 arrangement as I feel a young man cannot get much 'kick' out of escorting a middle-aged woman. I still however accept gratefully but without expostulation 'treats' from Jews, though they may be my juniors, (1) because they are so very generous, (2) because they are victims of a national inferiority complex, and seem to get some gratification in playing host to a friendly Gentile. I never openly pay for fares, tickets, etc. when out with a man, but settle at the end of the day with him. I find few women of my age attempt to pay their own expenses but many young women (25–35) expect to go out on a 50/50 basis unless they are engaged to be married to a man. Most women accept drinks, ices, confectionery from a male escort without qualms.

Of my immediate acquaintances so few drink more than an occasional glass that hangovers are unknown. They get intoxicated with ideas and speech rather than with alcohol. I know a few young women who boast of their 'morning after' feelings and who look ghastly while they gleefully recount their symptoms. These are under 35 and *very* few in number. (I ought to add my acquaintance among women is *very* limited.) Of my acquaintances among women over fifty, everyone regards excessive drinking as disgusting in women, deplorable but not disgusting in men.

Gladys had numerous Jewish friends and acquaintances, and on one occasion in 1939, in reply to M-O's February/March questionnaire on anti-Semitism, she provided a relatively full account of these social relations, at least as she construed them when her mood was cool and analytical.

My opinions of Jews are based on the fact that I worked as a confidential clerk in a Jewish firm from 1915 to 1920 and that about a third of my friends are Jews. I find them much more stimulating than Gentiles as their interests and their hobbies are so many and so diverse. They are usually widely travelled and many are keenly interested in the arts. Their home life appeals to me. Family affection is very strong among them and comfort and kindliness seem to enfold the 'stranger within their gates'. They are free from snobbishness and treat their employees and servants as human beings, sharing jokes with them and identifying themselves with their employees' concerns and interests. They have, however, no appreciation of the rights in regard to free time of their employees. The man I loved is a Jew but he always inveighed against mixed marriages, saying that the children of such marriages grew up to despise one side of their family, so he married a Jewess.

Her opinions of Jews were certainly mixed – and seem to have become more severe by the 1940s. 'I may like Jews but not as colleagues,' she wrote in her diary on 5 February 1940 after teaching. A few weeks later she and a few others were visiting Mrs. Rosenberg in hospital: 'I can see how Jews make themselves distasteful. Tea was brought up to us and we took possession of the waiting room as though we were an invading and successful army, turning out its normal occupant, a dreary looking female who looked like an ant found under an upturned stone' (27 March 1940). She made some flagrantly anti-Semitic remarks in 1945 that are hard to reconcile with her earlier professions of warm feelings towards Jewish friends. On 11 April that year, after being in the West End, she described the Jews she saw as 'rowdy, exhibitionist, noisy and gorging – oranges, sandwiches, sweets and leaving disgusting litter trodden into the floor. Sympathised with Nazi attacks on Jews and wished their efforts had been worldwide. (How I dislike Jews now I am out of love with Leonard. I do not even care for Mr. Jay as I once did.)' Later in 1945, on 2 October, in the chaotic aftermath of war, she observed that 'Jews are landing illegally in Palestine. DAMN the Jews! I can understand the Nazis tormenting them. Why can they not merge with neighbouring people?' Such sentiments sound much like those of Lil and Challis and certain voices in the popular press that she had deplored in the late 1930s.

6

August–September 1939

The Current Crisis

Winston Churchill's teenage daughter Mary wrote of the late spring and early summer of 1939 that 'We were on a countdown – and more and more people were beginning to realise it.'[1] By August Britain was manifestly on the verge of yet another major war, and this alarming prospect affected individuals in different ways. Certainly, not many people were enthusiastic about military action, and few were heroically inclined or optimistic. The possibility that the bloodshed and mass slaughter of 1914–1918 might be repeated, perhaps with even more disastrous consequences, was horrifying. During the last week of August Gladys was actually writing two diaries: one, as usual, for her own eyes only; the other for Mass-Observation (she is Diarist no. 5350), which had just suggested that its volunteers might start journals about their personal experiences of the 'Crisis'. This chapter reproduces all of her daily entries from 24 August, when she was about to go on sick leave, until 22 September, inclusive.

Thursday, 24 August. Em sent cream but it was too sour to eat. Had a sleepless night so went to Dr. Russ this morning. He gave me a certificate for psycho-asthenia and advised me to go to the Maudsley Institute for treatment.[2] I dread the stigma of that and asked him instead to suggest the Council doctor should see me. This he did. I phoned the London County Council and have to see their doctor at 1.30 tomorrow. Then I phoned Miss Hammond to prepare her for the worst. Chamberlain's speech doesn't sound very hopeful. It's all like last September's hateful nightmare being repeated. Britons are told to leave Germany,

---

1. Soames, *A Daughter's Tale*, p. 115. Gladys's response to the ominous Nazi–Soviet Non-Aggression Pact was, 'What frauds politicians are! Nazis and Reds combining! Hitler will marry a Jewess next!' (22 August 1939).
2. The usual name given at this time to Gladys's illness was 'neurasthenia', which would probably be seen today as clinical depression and/or anxiety. The Maudsley Hospital in Southwark specialised in the treatment of mental illnesses.

Americans told to leave Britain. RFC men[3] are on Highbury Fields. Overheard snatches of conversation. One woman to another, 'War, war, everywhere. I'm sick of war-talk.' Another woman, 'And all the street lamps have been darkened'. A child, 'My mother won't leave the radio. There she sits all day, waiting for news.' In the Library, the gas-mask notices are up.

Later. Poor Bay phoned. She is nearly as distraught as I am myself. Miss Wilshin will have to go to one place and she to another if war breaks out. She wants Em and Kathlyn to go there. She loves her house so much she is terrified at what may happen to it. She says all the people in her office expect War now. I'm writing for news of Wellings.

Friday, 25 August. Wellings phoned last night. He is still positive there will be no war but that Russia is the predestined victim. To County Hall. Wept copiously and hysterically before the Doctor, who phoned Dr. Colin Russ and they both agreed on Maudeley treatment for me, while I am to absent myself from school until Michaelmas Term unless I feel so well that I ask her to see me before that date. Tonight I went to Dr. Russ and he's given me a letter to the physician-in-charge at Denmark Hill. Walked from Westminster to the Bank via Whitehall, Strand and Fleet Street. Bay on phone; she's still perturbed. Miss Hammond on phone. *She's* going back with her arm in a sling. How absurd is the BBC custom of summarising news before giving it in full! Are we *so* dense?

M-O. Nightmares and recurrent neurasthenia, almost collapsed. LCC doctor gives leave of absence till October. Says I must go to Maudsley Hospital for treatment. Hang on the end of radio news. Keep making wild plans. Worried because my niece, a Civil Servant (aged 37) and very neurotic, looks like breaking down under the strain of being sent she doesn't know where for she doesn't know how long. My sister (aged 66) in an Essex village nearly distraught at the thought of having evacuees thrust upon her. Went to Kenwood to escape war-talk. Place almost deserted. Phone talks at night with my niece.

Saturday, 26 August. Felt somewhat guilty seeing parents and teachers on their way to schools re-opened for emergency. Saw several children with franked postcards in their hands, evidently to announce their arrival to parents when they reach the area to which they are being evacuated. Notices on the walls give details about air-raid warnings and signals of gas-attacks; pavements are whitened but people don't seem so overwhelmed as they did last year. It's that old tale of the boy and the wolf. The German envoy or ambassador – whichever he is – has flown to England with Hitler's peace plan. I believe Wellings is

---

3. She must have had the Great War on her mind and been thinking of the Royal Flying Corps, by the 1930s the Royal Air Force (RAF).

right and that there will be no war. Have been reading [Arthur] Calder Marshall's *The Changing Scene* [1937]. He almost makes me think of joining the Communist Party only I realise all parties are equally shifty to suit their own purposes.[4] Walked in Kenwood tonight. Sent for NOX lamp, 2s 2d.

Later. The unfortunate teachers have to go to school tomorrow *too* and have a rehearsed evacuation on Monday. How my colleagues must hate me for being absent! News announcer states 'There is now better feeling between Japanese and British. The Japanese soldiers have recently begun to salute the British policemen again.' How unutterably absurd!

M-O. Feel guilty because my teacher colleagues are recalled and working but I feel bordering on lunacy, remembering newsreel pictures of bombardments. Cannot read or settle to anything. Notices about air-raid warnings garnish every blank wall and some shop windows. Grocers show emergency boxes and Air Raid Precautions provision boxes at different prices. I do not buy because I believe it is a ramp. Salmon for the cat has leapt from 3d to 4d a tin. On the whole people do not seem as overwhelmed as they did last September. A friend tells me he has paid 2s 2d for a NOX lamp and bought 8s worth of black paper for his shop windows as 'Black-outs' will persist as rehearsals, if not for air-raids. He says 'There will be no war. Russia is the predestined victim.' (He is 37 and owns a small chain of 2d libraries. Reads international politics carefully.) Very amused by BBC announcer who reports better feeling between Japanese and British now. 'Japanese soldiers have been seen to salute British police officers.' (This may not be a word-for-word report but it's the gist of his sentence.)

Sunday, 27 August. Rumours abound. Everyone talks in terms of ARP. To Dorothy Neale's (Mrs. Collins') for the day with Bay and Miss Wilshin. Bay is distressing, a mass of St. Vitus' Dance. Dorothy very calm and very full of her ARP activities. The husband, Percy Collins, is very namby-pamby. Round-eyed, toothy, dressed like a sidesman in chapel, said he found accounts much more interesting than dealing with people in Relief work!!! I grew very bored just with eating and sitting. The others played whist in the evening. They have been to Sweden two or three times but have nothing of interest to tell you about it, only enumerating the names of the people they met. I have had a sudden revelation. I *know* that if I wanted to free myself from nerves I should send in my notice to school and earn a living some other

---

4. This 1937 book by Arthur Calder-Marshall (b. 1908) was dedicated to 'Those who prefer to understand the society in which they live' – Gladys was clearly in this enquiring mould – and included chapters on drama, films, fiction, education, and material necessities. Its perspective was decidedly anti-capitalist and class-conscious. Gladys was not as a rule sympathetic to left-wing politics.

way. Phoned Em. Now *she's* starting to worry. Noticed that Dorothy continually referred to this place or that place 'where we slept'. I also noticed that Percy made many references to pretty women in offices and shops who pleased him.

M-O. Visited acquaintances at Enfield (husband a Public Assistance Officer, wife ex-Civil Servant, both in their thirties). They were full of accounts of their ARP activities. I felt disgusted. It was another form of social activity to them instead of a waste of money and effort. Why didn't people get equally busy about our own 'Distressed Areas'? They mean more to me than Poland or Czecho-Slovakia does. Democracy and Despotism seem much alike, as Sydney Smith remarked long ago. My niece (the Civil Servant before mentioned) rushed to the radio for the 6 o'clock news. She also quotes an astrologer in her favourite Sunday paper. Someone comes in and says her friend, who is a Territorial, was shipped to Africa yesterday.

Monday, 28 August. International news no better. Life is wretched and the days seem so long. Children rehearse evacuation. Sandbags obscure windows of big buildings. Everyone talks to everyone else – and the heat is intense. To Regents Park this afternoon, reading DORA [Defence of the Realm Act] regulations, a *hundred* of them! Lil will get distraught when she reads billeting regulation. I keep trying to decide what to do. I shall give tentative notice on Thursday. I want to leave here and I want to get Lallie away out of danger. Today a man in Downing Street caused a riot by throwing over people's heads a suitcase full of black rubber balls bearing peace slogans on them. A woman has been 'grievously injured'.

M-O. The days seem so long while we wait for news. Sat in Regents Park. An Irishman, 'down-and-out' apparently, said 'Twenty-five years ago we had a war to end war. Now there's another coming. I'm sick of politicians. Someone's going to make profit out of the poor b_____s who die, I bet.' Everybody talks to everybody else – they always do in times of crisis.

Tuesday, 29 August. Dreamed last night. I was sorting rags swarming with maggots, to make shrouds for evacuated children. This morning dreamed I heard a bell ring and a voice said 'It is Colonel Death come to billet corpses on you. Don't keep him waiting. He can be very unpleasant.' I thought I opened the door and a figure in black just like [the actor] Conrad Veidt stood there. I wakened to find myself in my dressing gown on the doorstep. To Maudsley Hospital Outpatients' Department. Closed. Hospital patients evacuated. Saw the almoner who phoned Dr. Russ for me. I have to see him tonight. Lots of people are carrying cats about in baskets, evidently to be destroyed.[5]

5.   On several occasions Gladys had expressed concern that, if war came, she might have to

M-O. I seem to see such a lot of people taking cats about in baskets, evidently to be destroyed, as the people are obviously not going on a journey. Went to Maudsley Hospital but the Outpatients' Department closed last Friday and I could get no treatment. I was told the indoor patients had been evacuated. My landlord has made a black extinguisher for the sky-light. I am going to see the new Lincoln film or I shall go crazy, waiting for news. Dreamed last night I was sorting rags in which maggots were crawling to make shrouds for school-children. This morning I dreamed I heard a bell ringing with a beautiful deep note. I thought someone said 'It's Colonel Death come to billet corpses on you. Don't keep him waiting. He can be very unpleasant.' I thought he looked like [the actor] Conrad Veidt – when I wakened and found myself in my nightdress and dressing gown on the doorstep.

Wednesday, 30 August. Didn't see Doctor last night. Went out with Wellings instead as I felt needed a change. We saw *A Girl Must Live*, English film but played much faster than is usual in English films. Lilli Palmer was very good. Ginsbury's play is running at Buxton.[6] To Dr. Russ's this morning. Was horrified to find Maudsley authorities had suggested I should be sent as inpatient to LCC hospital for treatment. I declared I would kill myself rather than go in. Finally he decided to suspend judgment and put me on parole to do nothing rash and to see a nerve specialist if I felt worse. Went to Em's. I *wish* I could get a break-down pension and get another job to supplement that amount. Sometimes I think I will resign and keep my sanity. Phoned Leonard. He says he has tried several times to get into touch with me but in vain. He will come to discuss matters with me on Friday, international affairs permitting. To Em's. No good going there as paying guest. I should go crazy with Bee around.

M-O. Ammunition on London Fields camouflaged with green leaves. Men at work piling sandbags on road across Hackney marshes. My sister, an Ilford housewife, has bought 4lbs sugar beyond her usual weekly purchase. She says a grocer's wife told her there were big stores of other foods in the country but not much sugar. Her husband is writing to all sorts of country addresses, particularly to Cornwall, for 'hidehole' addresses. I am glad I am not in school just now – children are wild with excitement. I saw crowds of them at London Fields climbing over sandbags, swarming over fire-floats of London Auxiliary Fire Services, shrieking and dancing like dervishes in the gutter. Open-mouthed crowds gaped around the entrance to Victoria Park through

---

destroy Lallie, her beloved cat. Many people did euthanise their pets during the early weeks of the war.

6.   This was *Viceroy Sarah*, produced by the Old Vic Company. It was very favourably reviewed in the *High Peak News*, 2 September 1939, p. 6. Its run was short-lived since, with the outbreak of war, the theatre was closed – temporarily.

which lorries loaded with war materiel were manoeuvring. My friend says trade is still very bad in his 2d libraries. He says 'The men seem more "windy" than the women. Women seem to realise there's not much action when there's so much talk.' An acquaintance tells me of a young man travelling in pencils, office-desk equipment, etc. who has been hitherto paid £2 weekly and commission now being told he can only work on a commission basis as he has not had an order for more than two weeks. I also hear the dyeing and cleaning trade is stagnant.

Thursday, 31 August. Paid Em £2 19s 0d. Drew £21 for self. Gave tentative notice here [4 Northolme Road] in what *I* thought was most courteous terms. Up came Mr. Lucas white with passion, very insolent about my wanting to leave them in a hole and so on.[7] I was flab-bergasted. I meant to be nice. He would not accept my notice and so I have to leave on Thursday next. Felt so sure Bay would let me put furniture in her garage and take me as Paying Guest (thought it would be a paying proposition for her). Made enquiries about a lorry to carry goods. Met her tonight to find Miss Wilshin is unwilling and so I must get in where I can. Godfrey, the butcher, *is* considerate. He said he'd get me a lorry or do anything he could to help. Yet I buy hardly anything from him. Miss Hammond wrote, also Lil, Stelle and Miss Monkhouse and Miss Hope. Murray phoned. Told me not to worry. To go to them if I liked. Em is distraught. Lil is on end. Children are to be evacuated tomorrow. Some Civil Service people are to go. Traffic will be held up tomorrow. Special ARP practice tonight. Reservists called up. I don't know what to think. I feel quite mad. Not many people at the Zoo.

M-O. Gave notice here tentatively. Landlord insolent – would not accept that arrangement. Says I must go next Thursday. He's furious because he will not be able to let easily. Everyone leaving London who can. Tried to get goods warehoused. Depository full. Bustled around trying to get goods taken to my niece's at Ickenham. Lorries not easily obtainable. Emergencies make some people charming. Butcher, with whom my dealings are very limited, says he will get me a lorry if necessary. Many more drunken people about.

Friday, 1 September. Wellings on phone last night. Advises me to return to teaching. Then Murray phoned. Told me Mrs. Dunlop is still in Germany. Then I told him all my troubles and he said I must go to them if need arose. This morning Em phoned. Leo phoned – he's still positive there'll be no war. Then the upholsterer phoned about lorry. Then I phoned about a flat. Then I phoned Leonard to tell him not to come. Took flat in Cromwell Avenue [in Highgate]. Paid £1 deposit.

7. Landlords in London were confronting a plummeting demand for residential properties and the prospect of untenanted houses and apartments.

Then found flats below were emptying and I might well be alone there. Came back, discussed matters with Lucases; finally decided to stay on here. Hitler has seized Dantzig, bombarded Polish towns and now England and France have mobilised, cars are being commandeered and black-outs begin. Wireless drones out news in sepulchral tones all day. Much traffic in street. Everybody prepared to fight. People drunken with excitement. Green coaches used as ambulances. *What* a world! Why should women endure birth-pangs to have children grow up to be disembowelled? Leo says his wife is in Germany and she will probably regain German nationality.

M-O. Everyone (except me) seems anxious and willing for war now Hitler has taken Dantzig and bombarded Poland. Streets are crowded with people and they are all drunken with excitement. Two shop-keepers told me they are selling extra quantities of cigarettes. People keep nervously lighting and smoking cigarettes. Sad little parties of children trail along towards the station for evacuation. All the neigh-bours hammering plywood for their windows. Paid £1 deposit on a flat in Highgate, then forfeited it and decided to stay on here as everything seems so unsettled and I didn't want to find myself in a strange house. Some nurses who lived in the Highgate house were giving notice as they would be scattered. My friend was out all night doing ARP work. He is a Jew. Saw Green Line coaches rigged up as ambulances. Traffic congestion is marked and travelling along the roads in black-out condi-tions is perilous. The bus conductors seem the only cheerful people. I wonder if outdoor life improves their temper? Hydrants are marked with a broad yellow splash. Now Mussolini is the Hero 'soft-soaped' by nations. Ugh! What frauds all politicians and party leaders are.

It was almost a fortnight later that Gladys resumed writing in her private diary, but excepting three of these days, while she was away from London (6–8 September), she did continue to write for Mass-Observation, and the following entries are from this diary.

Saturday, 2 September. Decided at last to leave London. The dark-ness is awful. Found difficulty in getting a car but local tradesman offered to drive me into an Essex village after his shop had closed. We had a nightmare journey driving in the dark on an unknown road, the driver being very fatigued having spent the previous night driving relatives to safety zones. How everyone enjoys brief authority, espe-cially if it entails wearing a uniform! ARP workers in those hideous steel helmets that make all wearers look ridiculous popped up from the darkness again and again with exhortations and warnings delivered in authoritative manner, or with unsought, unasked directions for our journey.

Sunday, 3 September. In this tiny village [Helions Bumpstead] one does not, alas, escape from the braying wireless set. Many cottages have it on at full blast with the news, repeated again and again. If only one could escape from the 'vain repetition'. My host echoes – in strident tones – the *Daily Mail* views. These, like the views of some other newspapers, have veered of late, but strangely enough, the devoted reader never seems to notice any change of view, just mouths afresh whatever 'his' paper tells him.[8] I am disgusted with mankind. [War was officially declared this morning.] They cheer for Edward VIII or George VI, Chamberlain or Churchill, War or Peace, as instructed. The old men are the most belligerent. It is as though they *wanted* to sacrifice their sons.

Monday, 4 September. I wonder if these air-raid warnings and 'suspected' approaches of enemy aircraft are part of a plan to scare us into agreeing with anything our Government may choose to do? I don't feel I can believe *any*thing. Could only buy three candles at the village grocer's. School children are billeted in the next village. It seems strange to see them carrying little cardboard boxes everywhere – their gas-masks. *I* don't carry one for I have none. I hate the very look of the things. Air-raid warning given in next village early this morning. I am told that *none* of the wardens heard the summons so did not foregather. Aeroplanes keep passing over this house at long intervals, usually at a very high altitude.

Tuesday, 5 September. Every time a passer-by is seen on the road outside my hostess calls out 'Any fresh news?' Everyone has a tale, a rumour, a report. The butcher is not sure about meat supplies. If only the wireless news would cease and people would talk of something else! I notice that none of the reports in the newspapers seem to be signed. 'From our own correspondent', 'From a special correspondent' occurs again and again. I dread nightfall. Darkness and stuffiness then prevails.

Saturday, 9 September. Circumstance and health have made a break in entries. I am amused by people in this tiny village and in neighbouring tiny market town [Haverhill, Suffolk] who carry gas-masks

8. The *Daily Mail* consistently advocated right-wing causes. Its powerful proprietor, Lord Rothermere (1868–1940), had openly supported Hitler, even visiting him as a guest in January 1937; and the *Mail* published as unquestioned fact much Nazi propaganda. It had also enthusiastically endorsed Oswald Mosley – at least until violence at fascist rallies prompted a more muted tone – and its reports of Communist activity during the Spanish Civil War were flagrantly biased. The *Mail*'s manipulative approach is discussed in John Simpson, *Unreliable Sources: How the Twentieth Century was Reported* (London: Macmillan, 2010), especially chapters 9, 10 and 12, which includes some comparisons with the somewhat less doctrinaire policies of Beaverbrook's *Daily Express*. The *Mail*'s sudden change of heart in September/October 1939 is discussed on pp. 322–3 of Simpson's book.

with them wherever they go. I should imagine the likelihood of needing them here is inconceivably remote. Almost everyone one meets repeats what one has already read and heard ad nauseam about the war. It *was* a treat to have a tradesman call who was jocular as ever and non-topical. I am told a few of the Londoners here and in neighbouring villages are thinking of returning home. They find rural life boring. I think I shall return next week. I find the darkened stuffy cottage rooms unbearable and not at all healthy. I feel 'doped' when I waken here and I'm sure if germs are about I shall catch them. I feel so disconsolate and depressed. The village store is busy and the local postal staff overworked, thanks to the influx of visitors. Rumour is busy with tales of evacuees. Some folks are indignant at the behaviour of the children, others get worked up over their relatives – elderly, sometimes aged, people who have children or expectant mothers thrust upon them. I feel sorry for the evacuated and receivers alike. It is a terrible hardship for old people or poor people already crowded into small dwellings to have an influx of unwanted guests.

Sunday, 10 September. Fewer people carrying gas-masks today. Several women having to do laborious outside work because their husbands are Territorials or Reservists who have been called up, or, in one case, an ex-policeman who has returned to duty.

Monday, 11 September. More tales of discontented evacuees. Child from a neighbouring village said to have set out for London armed with three pairs of socks and a gas-mask. He was found by the police. Woman with two small children billeted near Bishops Stortford was accorded so chilly a reception by her hostess she went back to London with her husband and will ask the authorities for another allocation. From teacher friends I hear of *their* trials. The children are unruly, foul-mouthed and dirty in some instances. Some have infectious complaints. The villagers are perpetually on the teacher's doorstep asking her to discipline, give first aid to, or wash and de-louse their charges. All the teachers seem to have received good billets. The amusing thing is the gusto with which nonentities assume temporary officialdom. *They* will not want the war to end. From a grocer friend in London comes an entertaining account of how customers whisper their requests over the counter as though rationing had already come. Accounts of antagonism amongst near relatives also reach me. Boxed up together, sharing narrow quarters, not sure how long their trials must last, edgy through nerves, they quarrel, reproach, and are embittered with each other.

Tuesday, 12 September. Cooler weather means closed doors, fewer echoes of neighbouring radio sets and consequently less hint of war in this peaceful village. The school re-opened yesterday. Visiting grocer would not let us have more than ½lb candles, and said matches were scarce. The news of Mr. Chamberlain's flight to France gave us all cause for amusement. 'Is it the prelude to another Munich?' some ask.[9]

Wednesday, 13 September. Every time an aeroplane flies over someone declares he recognises its make or knows its destination! My hostess, whose faith in the National Government and the truth and purity of the English Press was once so profound, keeps saying 'You can't believe *any*thing or *any*body NOW'. Personally, I long for a spiritual revival. There is a lot to be said in favour of the high ideals of the Victorian age despite its smugness and hypocrisy.

Thursday, 14 September. Poor puzzled people! No one in the village seems to know what to make of this mysterious war. Unanimity is obtained only when the black-out is mentioned. Everyone loathes it and their nerves are on edge because of it. I am told a teacher in charge of the children in a nearby village was knocked down and injured by a lorry in the darkness. People do not seem to love the elementary schoolmistresses in the different districts nearby. They complain of their volubility and desire to 'manage' people.

Gladys now resumed her private diary, the first entry of which recapitulates events of the first fortnight of the month. On each day from 15 September until the end of the month, except for 17 September, she was writing both her private diary and her diary for Mass-Observation, and all her writing is here reproduced.

Friday, 15 September. Mr. Godfrey and I had a nightmare journey to Helions Bumpstead on September 2ⁿᵈ. We left at 8 p.m. He was fatigued, didn't know the road and it was dark as Hell's mouth. Men in tin hats challenged us as soon as the tiniest flick of our headlights appeared. People misdirected us when we asked questions and it was nearly midnight before we arrived. The Mañana household is peculiar for catering and the poor young man [Mr. Godfrey] had nothing but a stiff whiskey and soda and a dry biscuit to help him on his homeward journey. Beautiful weather prevailed through most of my stay. I walked into Haverhill, into Steeple Bumpstead and saw Mrs. Hewson at the Fox & Hounds at Steeple Bumpstead. She had five teachers billeted there and found them superlatively talkative. Another day I walked into Castle Camps and a mile or two on the Barlow Road. Returning, had tea at the village shop in Castle Camps, chatted with shopkeeper,

---

9. The policy of appeasement enjoyed, of course, much less support than a year earlier – Hitler's takeover of all of Czechoslovakia in March had played a major role in toughening outlooks. The Prime Minister in fact went to France for the first meeting of the Anglo-French Supreme War Council. It was reported that 'the two Western Powers have decided to act … in a unified way as if they were one and the same nation' (*The Times*, 13 September 1939, p. 6a).

an immense woman with flat feet and furiously false teeth. She introduced her husband, a lank, dark chap with ox-eyes and teeth like old headstones in a country churchyard. They showed me over their back premises and accompanied me to the scullery, where I washed, and the w.c., an earth closet the hole of which was covered with a wooden lid, gay with whorls in bright blue, yellow and red.

Then I was introduced to a customer, a small, voluble woman with a newly acquired four-century-old house. Called and like the house immensely, cream-washed walls, oak beams, tapestried chairs, log fire and calm! It was almost as though the house had a character of its own. She had a sooty mandrill in a shed turned into a cage. I went again another day with biscuits for Chico, the monkey, a sad eyed prisoner, and she invited me to tea the day before I left but I had decided already I had no use for this Mrs. Haughton. She may have travelled but she has not acquired much to relieve her natural bore quality. She is wizened and has not formulated her opinions but accepts them from the press and the radio like the rest. She now has an evacuated teacher boarding with her, an awful female from the Roman Catholic school in Eden Grove. In Lil's village is Mrs. Scott, an unkempt creature who alleges 'Ah'm an artist. Ah've a temperament, Ah can't bother about cleaning. Ah love beautiful things.' But she didn't know despite her alleged cleverness that the two cups and saucers on her mantelpiece were Sèvres. Mrs. Haughton wants me to edit some articles on country life for her. What do *I* get out of it?

When I left today Lil wept. She is so afraid she'll have evacuees billeted upon her. I came up by coach to King's Cross. (How comical policemen look in tin helmets, and how like Hamelin after the Piper's second tune looks London now with so many children missing.) I took a taxi from King's Cross. This house *is* dark. Lucases live in fear of air-raid warden's visits and no wonder; they appear for the tiniest gleam. How they love their momentary holding of power. Wellings thinks the war will soon end. I don't. Folks are enjoying themselves so much. Em and Bay on phone giving different sides of their story. Leonard wrote.

M-O. Returned to London. It's more war-like than London ever looked in 1914–1918. Policemen in tin helmets look ridiculous. There is enough sand (in bags) to make a British Sahara and London looks like Hamelin after the Piper's second tune, without its children. Shopkeepers profiteer with a vengeance. Butter is 1s 7d a pound, eggs 3d each. Drawing pins in boxes marked 1d are sold for 1½d. I am determined to be fleeced as little as possible. I will do without butter when I have bacon or jam. I will eat porridge instead of eggs for breakfast, and I am having clothes cleaned instead of buying new ones, as far as I can. The black-out in town is just as wearing as it was in the country. In the downstairs flat, the front window is shrouded with *two* pairs of curtains and in the big room is a tiny reading lamp with two pieces of paper round it. You cannot see another person's face across the room yet the air wardens have just knocked to complain of a gleam somewhere. Sheer officiousness! People of middle age begin to say 'I won't go out at night. I shall never visit my friends until the war is over.' I hope I shall not do that, but one *does* get depressed. My cat's fish, which usually costs 4d per lb, today cost 10d per lb – that is, for small fresh haddocks. I still have no gas-mask and so far no one has challenged me to produce one when I am in the streets. Every wall is unsightly with plastered posters – indeed I am horrified at my beloved London's ugliness now. She's like an awfully ugly middle-aged woman who has lost all pride in her personal appearance. The milkman makes only one delivery daily now. The man in the bottom flat never undresses now – he's so fearful of an air-raid occurring. The Southern Railway is so poorly served with trains that a young woman who leaves the office at 4 p.m. has to wait 1 hour 20 minutes for a train and is nearly limbed when she attempts to board the train.

Saturday, 16 September. Cost of living sky rockets! Fresh haddock to cat, usually 4d, now 1s. No ox liver at 10d. Had to pay 1s 4d for some pig or lamb liver, not sure which. Apples 1½d lb, tomatoes, Eng., 2d lb, plums 2d lb. Stewing steak 1s 10½d lb instead of 1s 4d lb. A few more children about. No small change apparently – two postal orders for 9s 6d each given as change at local post office. The butcher says people are returning from the country. I find the darkness depressing and making my general health deteriorate. Nine o'clock broadcast news late. At 6 p.m. I notice that, though ships may be sunk, or be alleged to be sunk, the crews are always saved.

M-O. Sleep does not refresh one now, thanks to the lack of air and light, not only in bedroom but all over the house. Called at the Library to enquire of ARP warden whether one was legally compelled to carry a gas-mask. The look of those vile things makes me want to gibber. The female who replied to my question was the usual 'toothy' type of Englishwoman in the middle-class world. Her accent was correct but her intelligence was sorely lacking. She kept saying 'I regard my gas-mask as my life-belt, so will you when you have one'. I did not point out that I didn't *need* a life-belt any more than I *wanted* a gas-mask. She kept saying 'Now you don't want to be a casualty and give trouble, do you?' Finally she said 'You can't go to a cinema without one, you know'. I retorted if the cost of living goes up by leaps and bounds as it has already done, I shan't be able to afford a cinema entrance fee, 'So I still shan't want a gas-mask' – and I still have none. Fish for the cat now costs 1s lb. Ox-liver, usually obtainable at 10d per lb, not to be purchased from my butcher, who let me have 1s 6d lb lamb's liver for 1s 4d for the animal.

It was very saddening to see poor women looking in shop windows or on stalls in Holloway Road, their lips moving as they worked little mental arithmetic sums to see what they could afford to buy. Apples, plums and tomatoes were cheap. People seem very depressed. Few talk of war but some speak viciously of Hitler. All complain of the darkness. It takes an appreciable proportion of one's leisure to shroud windows successfully. Individual shopkeepers are profiteering. Slippers that were 2s 11d a fortnight ago in the little shoe-shop opposite are now 4s 11d. No change of £1 at Post Office. Received two postal orders for 9s 6d each.

Sunday, 17 September. I've no longer any faith (I never had much) in Wellings' prophecies of a speedy ending to the War. Russian army has now marched into Poland and German soldiers are said to be coming from Eastern to Western front. National Register details are to be taken on September 29th. Identity cards will be issued. *What* a country! I wish I were dead! I don't care two hoots about any Government. I don't care who rules over me so long as I have peace. The thought of having my lovely little cat destroyed if I have to leave home worries me more than any national calamity! I daren't spend money and I'm getting appallingly depressed.

Monday, 18 September. Glorious weather! To Bay's early. Cheap day tickets still available on the Piccadilly Line. Bay very nervy and much thinner. Went into Uxbridge, bought dark lamps and paper. Nearly bought black material for curtains but am short of money. Wellings phoned tonight. He talked against the National Government and immediately the wires began to whirr. I'm sure someone was listening in. I wish people wouldn't discuss politics with me by wire. Letters from Mrs. Rosenberg, Miss Tedbury, Mrs. Haughton and Lil.

M-O. I am still going about without a gas-mask. Day returns (cheap) still issued on Piccadilly Tube. Almost everyone carries gas-mask – some women apparently have carriers to match their outfits. The exceptions are nearly all young men between 18 and 25. Prices soaring everywhere. I am told some people (mostly in poor districts) have had telegrams announcing death of their male relatives in action but I have no confirmation of this.[10] A friend was discussing politics with me (mainly to the detriment of the National Government) over the telephone wire tonight. Immediately there was much whirring and rumbling on the line. I said 'Don't discuss politics over the wire with me. I have no party feeling.' When he changed the subject the whirring ceased – probably just a coincidence. I will not buy the *Radio Times* until the programmes improve.

Tuesday, 19 September. I phoned Leonard. He says he will try to have tea with me as soon as possible. Lil wrote. HMS *Courageous* [an

---

10. Aside from naval casualties, there were few British deaths from military action early in the war.

aircraft carrier] said to have been sunk yesterday [500 lives were lost]. Prices soar: leg of beef 1s a lb, whitings for cat 10d a lb!

M-O. Obtained permit from Central Library (i.e., Fuel Control Department) to purchase coal by the hundred-weight to the amount of two tons in a year. Prices of fish almost prohibitive. An elderly slice of hake was marked 1s 6d per lb and I had to pay 10d per lb for whitings for my cat. Had to spend more hard-earned money on black-out paper and dark shades for electric lights. It seems strange to see beggars with gas-masks. Life is apparently sweet even when spent on the kerb. People seem very aggrieved at being told so little. The fishmonger's assistant and the butcher's cashier complain, say they suppose we are fighting for the interests of wealthy people, and 'Anyhow it's all very fishy'. The butcher's assistant blames the Jews. He says he wrote to the *Daily Mirror* about them this afternoon but fears his letter will not be published. 'They're too powerful,' he says solemnly.

Quite suddenly a man in a garden at the back of the house began to play on the bagpipes. My landlord was talking to me. He thought it was an air-raid warning and, turning green, scuttled down into the basement. I nearly laughed aloud. To satisfy him I gazed out in the front of the house to see nothing was happening and finally he was content to curse the 'musician'.

Wednesday, 20 September. Em phoned last night. She sounded thoroughly wretched. Spoke to Wellings. He's still convinced the Nazi party is breaking up and that peace will come soon. He says Streicher and Goebbels have already fallen. I wish I could feel optimistic. Hitler's Dantzig speech with threats seems to have made people here very nervy. My window cleaner and my landlady both referred to it. Spoke to Editha. She's reproachful because I'm doing nothing for my country – but what is *she* doing? Just eating, walking and resting. She seemed quite jubilant too when I said I looked so much older. Had a very bad night and the cat slept equally badly for he leapt up and tore my shoulder in his fright. To Dr. Colin Russ tonight. He has given me a prescription to have made up for some tablets that are supposed to 'perk me up'. Bought two cheap jumpers for winter wear.

M-O. My window cleaner is very worried. Work is so slack through people's being out of town or having plastered their windows with sticky paper to prevent their crashing in a possible air-raid. He has the rent of his flat to pay and also has to send money to his young wife and child who have been evacuated to the Leicester district. Hitler's threat in his Dantzig speech to give five bombs for every one of ours, and his mysterious hints of unknown horrors in store for us, have evidently scared people for both the window cleaner and my landlady refer to the threat with evident dread. What a lot of money is being wasted. Schools in areas to which evacuees are being sent are not open yet. They are not at any rate in Welwyn Garden City [where Editha now lived]. Evidently 'nerves' are affecting many people with internal trouble. I have heard of several cases of acute diarrhoea in adults. In one case a milkman asked a customer for permission to use her lavatory he felt so unwell.

Thursday, 21 September. Lil wrote. I phoned Bay. Tablets cost me 2s for 25 and chemist will make no more without written order from Dr. Russ. To Library. Czech Revolution reported and revelations are alleged of the banking of monies and insuring of lives of Nazi leaders outside Germany. I wish I could believe the war would end speedily but too many people are making money out of it for that. I boil with rage, remembering the Kaiser luxuriating at Doorn, Beck over the border, the Red Spanish leaders well away, Zog running round Europe with a bevy of sisters and Benes safe and sound while always the *people* pay. Last night very poor and cheap wit in broadcast song in variety programme was permitted, Hitler and his Germany being the subject. During the Civil War in Spain, 'peasants and workers' were called atheists, Reds, profane, murderous. *Now* 'peasants and workers' addressed and exhorted from alleged secret broadcasting company in Germany are everything to be admired. PHOO-IE! BUNK!

M-O. Walking in the streets, listening to people's conversations, one continually overhears 'I *saw* in the paper' as though that proved the truth of the statement. Popular education has made us a nation of silly sheep. Most people seem jubilant at the alleged revolt in Czecho-Slovakia. I am surprised at the number of people (mostly over 40) who calmly announce they will not go out after dark till peace is declared. One housewife of 60 said 'I'm really afraid to have a bath because of Hitler. I should hate to be bombed when I was naked.' She had no more realisation than a child apparently that, if bombed, the fragments would be so scattered [that] clothes wouldn't matter. Had to pay 1s 6d for a 9d torch.

No pleasure in going to Free Library now. After trying to turn a blind eye to the hateful gas-masks, and extricating oneself from a Fuel Control queue, pushing through the many who read the few advertisements for situations vacant, one finds applications for books from the Central London Library cannot be accepted, titles of books on shelves cannot be deciphered owing to lighting economies and most of the books are piled high above borrowers' heads, quite out of reach because space has been usurped by various local bodies and their vast accumulation of forms, etc.

Friday, 22 September. Met Wellings last night. Ate at the New Restaurant. The fat waitress left London after the first air-raid warning, she said. She went to an uncle at Bargoed [South Wales] but he worked her so hard she was glad to return. Stepping out into the black night was a queer experience but soon I found it exhilarating, adventurous.

Voices, as of disembodied spirits, floated out to meet us, forms loomed up and faded away, dream fashion, light laughter gladdened one's ear. We walked down to St. James's Park. On the bridge, the loving couples were intertwined like simple studies for Laocoon.[11] Went back to Coventry Street Corner house in the moonlight. Had an ice. Saw Miss Herrick looking very old and subdued at the next table. Was she on sick leave or 'up in town' (?) I wondered.

Ordinarily I am pleased to be seen in company of a presentable man but not on this occasion. Wellings talked and talked of the War. He thinks people's faith will be so shaken in this Government the Labour Party will come romping back into power. *I* shall not vote. He's keeping cuttings from paper contradicting reports about our own and enemy activities. He says he phoned the Admiralty for details of *Athenia*'s passenger list, but couldn't get it.[12] These jack-in-office ARP folks *are* officious. Wellings switched on a torch with the regulation two thicknesses of tissue paper over it. Immediately a voice bellowed 'Keep that light down' as one might yell at a dog. Yet there was no air-raid warning and we were trying to negotiate Piccadilly Circus in the gloom. Saw three 'drunks' in five minutes – what else is there to do? Lot of hooligan type about, jostling one in the dark.

M-O. I have had to borrow a gas-mask because I want to go to a cinema and cannot be admitted without one. The threat of death seems to make the urge to love more pronounced. I saw a couple on Highbury Fields today indulging in a bout of ecstatic love-making in broad daylight, and last night, on the seats in St. James's Park and on the bridge there, lovers' limbs were so intertwined as to suggest skeins of wool. The waiters in Coventry Street Corner-House, solemn-looking as ever, and even more gloomy, doubtless through lack of patrons and consequent lack of tips, look so ridiculous with gas-mask carriers tapping their behinds every time they stoop solicitously over their tables. The street-walkers also carry gas-masks, often in cases to match their suits. Their numbers seem to have increased. The darkness must give the older and uglier ones as good a chance as the more attractive now. As usual, the officious ARP men very hectoring in tone though one is permitted to use a shrouded torch. I saw three 'drunks' in five minutes at Piccadilly Circus last night. Oh, Lady Astor![13] But what else is there to do? There are also a number of the undesirable

---

11. Lacoön was a figure in classical mythology. His gruesome execution by two gigantic, constricting serpents after defying Poseidon (Neptune) was a frequent subject of art; it is famously portrayed in a marble sculpture held by the Vatican.
12. The passenger liner *Athenia* was sunk by a U-boat on the night of 3 September, with the loss of 112 lives, 28 of them American. This was a serious German blunder, especially from the point of view of US public opinion, though one recent authority has discounted its negative impact (Susan Dunn, *1940: FDR, Willkie, Lindbergh, Hitler – the Election amid the Storm* [New Haven and London: Yale University Press, 2013], p. 34).
13. Lady Astor MP was a zealous temperance advocate.

Soho underworld type of young man, jostling folk – pickpockets I presume – but I and my friend were purposely carrying little money. There is a queer feeling of elation in pacing dark streets, glimpsing a wan face, hearing a heavy tread or a light patter behind one, noting a trill of laughter (very rarely heard now). There are noticeably more children in the London streets again. Whereas street-hawkers usually sell button-holes, balloons or flowers that open in water, around the Circus last night dim figures cried for sale torches, gas-mask carriers, white or luminous armlets.

7

September–October 1939

Self and Society

Like Chapter 6, this chapter includes everything that Gladys wrote, this time for the five weeks between 23 September and 28 October 1939. There is one major new aspect of her writing: on most days during these weeks she also wrote a 'Dream Diary', which Mass-Observation had invited its volunteers to produce in September–October, a time, of course, of exceptional stress and uncertainty. Since Gladys wrote daily about her dreams between 23 and 28 September, when she was also writing both her private diary and her regular M-O diary, her experiences on each of these six days are recounted in three different entries. (Her regular M-O diary ended on 30 September.) After a brief lapse in her dream diary (excepting 1 October), she resumed it on 8 October and thereafter recalled, sometimes in considerable detail, her dreams on most (though not all) nights up to 28 October. 'In our dreams we live as we wish or fear to live,' she had declared some weeks before (Directive, July–September 1939). Unsurprisingly, most of her dreams in later 1939 were fear-induced.

Before giving details about these dreams, Gladys had replied to M-O's questions about her longstanding experiences of dreaming (Directive, July–September 1939). 'From babyhood I have suffered from nightmares and dreams so vivid', she reported, 'that they persist pictorially for a moment or two after my waking and frequently haunt me for days.' Various fears fuelled these dreams during her childhood, adolescence, and young womanhood, some of them political. In later years, 'As I approached forty I began to dream about being left behind (a justifiable fear, alas!). Trains moved out of station with increasing speed as I approached the guard's van. Motor-car floors gave way and the vehicle rushed away leaving me biting the dust. I spoke in lecture halls to an audience that filed out. (I hate and dread old age.) Nowadays I dream almost nightly (save for the blessed relief of an occasional highly amorous dream) of war and evacuation schemes ... I dream I have hosts of school children to lead to safety and bombs begin dropping and they break and run like the wretched Chinese I saw in a newsreel when a Japanese aerial attack was being shown. I frequently dream my mother is alive again and I am broken-hearted at losing my long-awaited freedom from irksome restraint. This type of dream persists after waking. She is in the room like a Presence and I am so perturbed because I fear she will sense my disappointment in her return and I know she did not realise she was thwarting me, or intend to make my life drear and barren.[1]

Saturday, 23 September. Phoned Em and wrote to Ginsbury and to Clarrie Freeman. This evening went to Baker Street Classic – an attractive cinema – and saw Danielle Darrieux in *Mademoiselle ma mère*, a slightly unpleasant subject and a highly improbable character for Danielle to play. It is indeed jewelled night now. Marylebone Road looked like a length of black velvet studded with emeralds, rubies and topazes as traffic lights changed colour, but poor London is a blighted city. One almost expects to hear the rumble of a plague cart and the cry 'Bring out your dead'. Even the bus conductors have lost their sprightliness.

M-O. Many grocers do not want to supply sugar or Libby's milk it seems, but at a Jewish grocer's in Holloway Road no question is raised if one buys 2lbs or even 4lbs of sugar, and the milk too is forthcoming. It is Yom Kippur (Black Fast or Day of Atonement) but several Jewish-owned shops are open. I wonder why? Do they – the shopkeepers – not want to emphasise their Hebraic origin? I think I overheard rather less comments on the War this morning, perhaps because shopping difficulties loom large on Saturday mornings.

It is indeed 'Jewelled Night' now. Marylebone Road looked like a length of black velvet sewn with emeralds, rubies and topazes as the traffic lights changed colour. London is like a city under a blight. Black figures flit through the streets. No light gleams from door or window. I could almost hear the plague carts rumble along and hear 'Bring out your dead!' Even the bus conductors have given up their gay conversational efforts of peace-time London. What has happened to all the Peace Union, League of Nations and other enthusiasts for pacifism?

Dream Diary. Last night I thought school had re-opened and the children were assembled. I was seated at one of two pianos which were placed side by side. The headmaster, although he knew I was a very poor performer, had ordered me to play accompaniments for national songs. I tried, but my fingers kept picking out the tune of 'On Wings of Song'. He was infuriated and I was worried lest I should be dismissed. Miss Hammond, my only woman colleague who is many

---

1. On 3 December 1938 she had written in her diary of 'how much I have lost by being tied to my mother's apron-strings when I was young. I am afraid of life, afraid of discomforts, and I'm already half-dead.' Later (on 7 January 1940) she again wrote of how she had been treated by her mother: 'Sometimes I wonder if I would have been a more worthy member of society if I hadn't been so "fussed over" in my babyhood, never allowed to cross a road alone, and urged to call out "Mother" if addressed by a stranger.'

years younger than I am, kept patting me and sympathising with me, to my annoyance. I knew she thought I was incompetent and that angered me as I had never laid claim to talent or even ability as a musician. I awakened saying 'I can play "Oh pure and tender Star of Eve"'. Sleeping again, I dreamed I was in a garden reminiscent of Swinburne's Forsaken Garden. It was very neglected and a patch of willow herb was growing there. I noticed its silvery top and knew it was dying. 'Ah, something at least is lovely in death', I thought.

Sunday, 24 September. I have written several good letters today. I have read a little and 'gloomed' a lot. If only I were free from that awful fear of being evacuated! I keep wondering from whom I can borrow money when my sick pay is exhausted. Tonight I thought the Holy Ghost had descended upon me, but it was a white pigeon that had flown into my sitting room and mistook me for a statue. Bay and Editha on phone. The latter was full of an article she'd read on the woman's page of the *Manchester Guardian* (I think) [23 September 1939, p. 6]. It was entitled 'Old and grey and full of sleep'. It apparently asserted that war work should be left to the young as the women of 50 had 'done their bit' in the last year and were now prepared only to doze, lose their spectacles, walk slowly, think slowly, forget phone numbers and names and be unable to grasp directions quickly [this was indeed the gist of the article]. I really felt *I* didn't come into that category as I move *very* quickly, do *not* doze during the day, have an excellent memory and have never yet mislaid my glasses.

M-O. Comments on doing war-service, directly or indirectly reported. An ex-schoolmistress of 50: 'I'm not doing anything save not letting myself be a nuisance to the rest of the community. I did my share in the "war to end war". I'll leave activities for the younger ones who have allowed further war to come. I think middle-aged women are doubtful assets in "movements" and "services".' A businessman around 40 (reported to have said) 'I'm doing no unpaid work. I didn't want war. There are too many people "doing their bit" instead of getting on with their own jobs.'

Dream Diary. Very confused dreams last night. Vague recollection of being in what I knew were London streets though their appearance was that of Caroline [seventeenth-century] rather than modern times. It was very silent in the cobbled streets. Suddenly my mother (who has been dead 14 years) appeared and my niece (now 37) as a child, and I knew we were all waiting for the plague-carts and the cry of 'Bring out your dead!' Then I bought strawberries – huge ones – as big as bullocks' hearts and very pulpy. I was sharing them with the others although neither seemed very anxious to accept the wet, bloody looking fruit. As some berries dropped to the floor they made a pulpy, oozy blotch like the entrails of a dismembered person I saw on the Midland Railway Arch at Leyton after an air raid in the last war.

After waking, I slept and dreamed again. I thought I was discussing with my friend Wellings the desirability or folly of his taking a large house in Tufnell Park and having his elderly brother and that brother's elderly housekeeper to live with him, together with a young male relative (the last is an imaginary person). As I stood talking to my friend I noticed how badly he was dressed – in a soiled khaki macintosh – and how ugly he had become. His lower lip seemed so moist and so sensual, protruding horribly, making him look like Silenus [a notorious consumer of wine]. Suddenly a motor car drew up at the kerb and a well-groomed, Mephistophelian person with only one eye peered out. He said 'I'm the landlord. I'm the one-eyed motorist who killed a boy and drove away.' I wakened with a start.

Monday, 25 September. Letters from Lil and Stelle. The latter only has one refugee who, she says, is clean but cheeky and disobedient. Some folks in Welshpool have verminous children and those who cannot be persuaded to use a lavatory! Evidently England isn't as civilised as she might be. To Queen's Hall today to get ticket for concert on 8th. 'Siren suits' on show in every draper's shop. Clover seems the popular colour with grey for coats. Little trade doing save in Woolworth's. No drawing pins on sale there even. More uniforms, particularly Air Force blue, in the streets than I have seen before. I am now thoroughly sunk in gloom. National Registration forms arrived. Don't feel too pleased to have to fill in 'D' for divorced. I have never mentioned my marital state here. Despatched Dream Diary to Tom Harrisson. No word from Leonard. I *long* to see him.

M-O. Trade seems stagnant in Oxford Street and Regent Street shops. Only Woolworth's is crowded as ever. Small wonder! Boarded shop-fronts, dark curtains shrouding doorways depress the most light-hearted. How different from 1914–18 with the slogan 'Business as usual'. Hardly anyone giving or getting 'a glad eye' in Regent Street. It seemed there were more uniforms in the streets, particularly Air Force variety.

Dream Diary. Last night I thought I was in London in the earliest 1890s. There were stone setts in the streets, horse-buses, the animals' hoofs striking sparks on the roadway, and naphtha flares made the faces of the stall-keepers half-shadowed and grim. Although I appeared to be in Hackney I knew Newgate Prison was nearby. (It made a great impression on me as a child to be lifted up to see the old prison before it was pulled down and to be told about some of the prisoners there.) A policeman was directing traffic, admitting a few people at a time to a waiting tram, and we had to pass round a barricade of barrels. People were joking about the beer therein but I knew it was gunpowder which would soon cause an explosion. A child (a nephew of mine as he once was) sat astride the first barrel. He wore a lace frock like baby boys used to wear and on his sunny curls he wore what used to be called a 'fisher cap' or 'brewer's cap'. People were laughing and saying 'Look at the little boy in the brewer's cap' but *I* knew it was a revolutionary's red cap, a signal to somebody to rise when the time was ripe.

There was another worrying dream about cats but so vague I cannot recall it. I only knew I was bothered (as I am in my waking hours) about what I was going to do with my cat when I rejoin my school unit. There were lots of cats about, skinny or else injured.

Tuesday, 26 September. Wellings phoned last night and arranged to meet me tomorrow. He's still convinced the War is a hoax! If only it would end! I'm getting thoroughly wretched. I haven't money to 'gallivant'. No one is in town that I know and anyhow 'Black-out' keeps folks at home. Talk of War Budget – increased income tax, sugar, cigarette and other taxes – makes me long to 'pull in my horns'. I want to give up this place but I do not know where to go. I do wish women would not wear trousers when their figures are deplorable. Paunchy matrons in navy 'slacks' look sickening. Marlene Dietrich has a lot to answer for!

M-O. The vogue for trousers as 'women's wear' increases and adds to the other uglinesses. Elderly women look even uglier than paunchy elderly men in navy blue slacks. The streets remind me increasingly of Stuart London at the time of the Plague in their present deserted state.

Dream Diary. Last night I thought I was to meet, unknown to his wife, Leonard, to whom I am very much attached. When we met I dared not give any sign of recognition as he had his four children with him. (Actually he has only three.) We all appeared to be in some sort of railway sleeping car and he was apparently wearing a siren suit. When he had gone I noticed he had left a thick roll of £1 notes in the bed. The temptation to keep them was strong as (a) I am pressed for money (b) he is well-off, but I finally handed them over to his father (actually dead). I then began to see the folly of this for the father was notoriously miserly and would doubtless keep the money. I now found myself on a tram and bus route, presumably Whipps Cross Road where the tram lines are close to one kerb and far from the other. I was inviting my brother-in-law (a painfully moral man whom I suspect of wishing to sin sexually if not actually doing so) to whip me and himself with a bunch of thorny-looking herbs.

There was a further chaotic dream in which the National Registration form and Mass Observation manuscripts were involved. I had apparently given too much or too little information in one or both; anyhow trouble was brewing for me with 'the authorities'. The latter dream was presumably inspired by my discussing War news and regulations with a friend over the telephone at midnight last night.

Wednesday, 27 September. Just as I had washed my hair this afternoon Leonard phoned suggesting I should meet him for tea this afternoon. I had so hoped he would come here but I'm hardly a figure of romance at 49, so grey-haired and wretched-looking. We met in City Road, walked to King's Cross, had tea and then walked on to Euston. He was infuriated with me because I criticised the Government adversely and denied the need for war. Jews are *most* patriotic nowadays. He said I sounded like a street-corner ranter demanding Utopia in this generation. After he had exhausted his diatribes against me, including a gibe at my faint Irish streak which sets me 'always agin the Government', I discussed my personal difficulties with him. He has promised to lend me £10 next month if I need it and *he* advises my giving up teaching and going back into business life. He thinks I could still do well in business and that I should enjoy life more among adults than among children. It's a difficult point as, when the slump comes, jobs may be impossible to attain. At 7 p.m. I met Wellings at the New Restaurant. He is still full of theories to prove this is 'a phoney war'. He keeps writing to various newspapers and addressing various ministries – quite in vain, of course. He still thinks Hitler 'will be bumped off'. Saw Miss Herrick again, alone, in the Corner House. Why isn't *she* evacuated, I wonder? Income tax is raised to 7s 6d in the pound. I shall have to do *something* to reduce my overhead expenses.[2]

M-O. How few of the neighbours seem to remove their black-out arrangements during the day! Dark curtains, black or brown paper seems to be dragged aside or looped up carelessly. It's as though people no longer bothered about the neat state of windows or rooms, or else they do not mind actual gloom as well as social gloom begotten of war! I cannot help noticing how patriotic the Jews are. All that I meet are more certain than the Government itself that it is right in all its doings. I suppose English Gentiles feel towards England as they do towards their own families, as though they may criticise and yet still love. Rather more people about in the West End tonight; quite a lot of uniformed men – they must be having a lot of 'leave'. I hear a great number of refugees who came into the country without permits are getting agitated about filling in registration forms.

Dream Diary. I dreamed last night I was taken by my friend Wellings to see our mutual friend Clowser whose new house I have not yet seen. It was very bare and all his fine furniture was gone. He was very tired and looked hungry and had no money so *I* had to put a penny in the gas meter as the light was dying down. I knew his sore straits were due to his having been dismissed from his post. (He has actually had a month's notice.) Wellings had brought with him a Chinese girl in

2.   In a letter of 7 October 1939 addressed to Tom Harrisson at Mass-Observation (filed with her Dream Diary), Gladys summarised her predicament: 'A prolonged bout of psychasthenia [neurotic anxiety] has made me use up practically all my leave with pay and so my sleeping and waking thoughts circle around pounds, shillings and pence and the possibility of finding paid employment other than teaching. Each night "lights out" means a series of nightmares in which evacuated children and attenuated purses loom ever larger.'

Western dress. She offered to show me over what was either a Chinese homestead or camp – I cannot remember which. It was crowded with women and children, mostly in black but all diseased, hydrocephalic, ophthalmic, leprous and wounded with dirty, bloodstained bandages round them. I was nauseated and my guide said 'Even after years of war, some beauty remains'[3] and she led me behind a gilt, carven screen, reminiscent of the one used in the recent production of *Romeo and Juliet*. I was ushered into a courtyard where pink almond blossom was in flower, gracious Chinese ladies in lovely, colourful gowns were strolling about and green and blue jars and carven dragons abounded.

It is strange that, ordinarily, dream scenes are in steel gray. I never see colour but latterly I see vivid colours in dreams. It is as though the colour I miss so much in London now all day is vouchsafed me at night.

Thursday, 28 September. Wakened feeling very gloomy and suicidal. Letter from Mr. Ginsbury inviting me to have tea with him next Wednesday raised my spirits slightly but 'this money business' worries me a lot. I think I shall have to give up the phone to begin with. Lil sent me lots of apples and some jam yesterday.

M-O. Evidently Mosley is getting busy again. Several walls are decorated (?) with his Fascist sign and bear slogans 'Mosley for Peace', 'Why fight in a Jews' war?', 'Britons in Khaki, Jews in ARP'.

Dream Diary. All last night's dreams are very blurred. I can faintly remember myself as a sort of Charles Dickens, living at Enfield, apparently near where Lamb had lived in retirement, where I was writing novels 'with a purpose'. The purpose seems to have been to illustrate the number of our recently lost liberties. I appeared to be writing in bed but was constantly distracted by spiders which I had to catch and kill without soiling the sheets. There was another dream about a great white phosphorescent eye that kept staring down from heaven but as soon as anything ugly or frightening appeared on the ground, it closed up into a plain, thin line of light!

Friday, 29 September. Mental turmoil all over again. Miss Hammond wrote last night telling of her suffering as an evacuated teacher. I *know* I could not face it.[4] I *feel* I should go mad and even when the news-

---

3. Parts of China had been at war with Japanese invaders throughout the 1930s.
4. The children and their teachers from Gladys's school had been evacuated to Leighton Buzzard, Bedfordshire and billeted in the region. The *Leighton Buzzard Observer*, 19 September 1939, p. 2, reported on the stresses at the school in nearby Wavendon, Buckinghamshire. 'The school is being run under trying conditions for the teachers. The premises are quite inadequate for emergency requirements. Unlike many schools in which classes are working on a shift system, the teachers have decided to run their classes concurrently and keep the normal school hours. In consequence, the six teachers have a hundred or more children in three classrooms. The two Wavendon teachers have their own classes plus the senior

papers moot a movement for starting schools for London children in parks and playgrounds, I still feel that way lies madness. I shall have to resign if I can't get a breakdown pension. I think I'd rather beg than teach. Anyhow I'm writing to the London Teachers' Association for advice. To Em's. She *has* lost weight. Met Bee too. He looks like a pricked balloon. Phoned Bay. She sounds wretched, fearing evacuation.[5] Wrote to Tom Harrisson asking if there be a chance of paid occupation on Mass Observation staff.[6]

M-O. People gathered like flies round the loudspeaker in Ilford Public Library to hear the 12 o'clock news. I have overheard several women say 'Oh, I don't listen any longer. I'm so tired of it all.' The Income Tax seems to bother people more than the War.[7]

children, who formerly attended Bletchley Central School, and the four members of the LCC staff have their own fifty children and several unofficial evacuees. Despite the lack of equipment, the teachers are making the best of a hard task and are adapting their teaching to the new conditions.'

A letter from a Shoreditch teacher published in the *Hackney Gazette*, 18 September 1939, p. 4, was at pains to reassure parents that their children were being well cared for in Bedfordshire – 'as peaceful, safe and pleasant [place] as any in this kingdom.... The people of these villages with whom the Wenlock-road School Group [a half mile west of Hamond Square] is billeted are full of the spirit of kindness, patience, friendliness and helpfulness towards the London children.' There were, however, problems to be anticipated. 'Under the conditions of country life, especially as the weather rediscovers its habit of being wet and cold, it will be absolutely necessary for the children to have good strong water-tight boots or shoes and warm clothing. Many of the children who came with us are very badly off for these things, but I am sure that no parent in Shoreditch will expect, or can expect, the people who are billeting their children to pay for such necessities out of their own pockets. I would suggest that the London parents send boots and clothing when needed by the children, or that they send the money to the people at the billets for purchases that have been made or that have to be made.' Appeals for boots, warm clothes, and other necessary garments for evacuated children were published in the *Islington Gazette*, 27 September 1939, p. 3. Many children had undoubtedly been sent away earlier that month poorly attired. The Greater London Record Office published a useful collection of information in an undated booklet edited by Richard Samways, *We Think You Ought to Go: An Account of the Evacuation of Children from London during the Second World War* (ISBN 0 9518109 1 X).

Much indoubtedly remains to be learned about the experiences of London's schoolchildren and their teachers who were evacuated in September 1939. An example of the sort of detailed study that can be produced is Roy C. Boud, 'The Great Exodus: The Evacuation of Leeds schoolchildren, 1939–1945', *Thoresby Society*, second series, vol. 10 (2000), pp. 41–155.

5. Many departments of the civil service were evacuated to the provinces during the war.

6. With the exception of 1 October 1939, Gladys did not write a Dream Diary for this and the following eight days, and she remarked on this change in her letter of 7 October to Tom Harrisson mentioned above (p. 137n). 'I have neglected to keep a record of further dreams because it seemed to me that I am becoming as abnormal as some of Freud's patients and that therefore my dreams were not really typical of the times.' She added that 'When I have dreams inspired by international rather than personal troubles, I will duly chronicle them.' Gladys received an immediate reply to this letter from Harrisson (see below, 7 October), encouraging her to continue her good literary work, and she resumed her Dream Diary the next day, as the following chapter shows. (Same-day exchange of letters was still possible in London in 1939.)

7. The standard rate of income tax was to be raised from 5s 6d to 7s 6d, and the reduced rate of tax on the first £135 of income from 1s 8d to 2s 4d (*The Times*, 28 September 1939, pp. 4d and 8a). Moderate income earners such as Gladys (around £4 to £6 a week) were to see their annual income taxes rise by at least 50% and those at the top end by around 100%.

Saturday, 30 September. Drew £12 from my salary and sent £4 to Lil. Bought a grey winter coat at 55s 9d. Last week it was 49s 6d but I hadn't money to pay for it. Leo phoned last night, inviting me for Thursday. His wife has returned. He wouldn't say anything about her save that she thought revolution against the existing regime in Germany was highly improbable. *If* she's a Nazi spy she would, of course, say that. Wellings phoned. He read long extracts from the *New Statesman* in a deadly monotone. Mrs. Rosenberg wrote. She is very mopy. To Pyrland Road tonight. Mesdames Chambers and Jones gave me a very warm welcome but I do get bored there. Left about 10 p.m. and walked home in the silent moonlight when one feels nervous as a jungle animal. They advise against throwing up teaching! If only one could see the end! I hear nothing but tales of friction among evacuated teachers.

M-O. Prices mount steadily. The winter coat marked 49s 6d last week cost me 55s 9d this! The big store where I purchased [it] has lost (or dismissed) many of its staff. I also heard of many dismissals in a dyeing and cleaning firm. My friend's German-born wife has recently returned from Germany. He says her comment is: 'There's not much likelihood of a revolution *there* – 80% of the people are as sheep-like as they are in other nations and suffer whatever their leaders impose.' Many flats have fallen empty locally.

Sunday, 1 October. Mr. Wellings phoned last night, full of his reading of world events. This sounds feasible, particularly in the light of some of the *Sunday Times* comments today. He believes Germany and Russia dropped the idea of a truncated Polish state and have now arranged for contiguous frontiers [and] that England and France may propose, nay demand, the making of such a state and then pretend they have actually done something for Poland. He thinks that Hitler will be 'thrown overboard'. If only something could be done to stop the war, I'm selfish enough not to care. I do loathe the idea of this break-up of my home. Wellings urged me not to give up teaching. He offered to lend me £5 to eke out my resources. How utterly absurd to have a Day of Intercession! Why ask God to give peace when we have *made* war ourselves?

Dream Diary [the sole such entry in a nine-day period]. I thought I waited for hours in a food queue and finally obtained a leg of mutton from which a cutlet was sawn and the two portions wrapped up. I carried it away, rode in a tram, got out and found I had dropped my meat rations. I rushed back to the tram-stop. There lay the paper

---

As one authority has observed, arguments supporting a delay in major tax hikes 'were overruled in favour of an early budget which would tell people where they stood. Heavy taxation was going to be necessary very soon, hitting incomes of every size, and the sooner people realised this [the Government concluded] the better.' (R. S. Sayers, *Financial Policy 1939–45* [London: HMSO, 1956], p. 26; and pp. 504–5 for a summary of the budget.)

and the cutlet, both much the worse for handling. Several harpy-like women rushed towards me and helped me retrieve the small portion of meat but their evil smiles and carneying [i.e., wheedling] ways did not deceive me. I knew they had filched the main joint, but I was afraid to say anything, they were such a formidable pack.

Monday, 2 October. Lil wrote. Replied. Met Bay. Gave her a meal at Patisserie Valerie [Dean Street, W1]. Bought black shoes, 24s 9d. Sold Bay my 12s 11d hat for 5s. Outside the Islington Library is a notice, 'Health and Beauty classes discontinued till the end of the War'. I should have thought the present the very time they were needed. Em on phone. Bee and one other man at Achille Serre's [dyers and cleaners, with their head office in Walthamstow] retain their jobs on the executive side. More children are to be evacuated. Poor Nina will fret.

Tuesday, 3 October. Card from Lottie, who is on sick leave, inviting me to tea on Wednesday or Thursday but I am engaged for both days. Had a frightful nightmare. Thought I was arrested by an awful, ugly constable, when I was in bed in flannelette pyjamas, on suspicion of having murdered a Jewish boy named Sobay in billets. I was innocent but while the policeman was cross-questioning me, mother would keep 'chiming in' and her words condemned me. I was carried off to a cell to await hanging while I could hear the gallows being erected outside! I was nearly paralysed with fear when I awoke. Went to Dr. Colin Russ this morning. He gave me a sedative and said he thinks I'm very far from being fit to return to school at the end of this month. Bought a pair of corsets. Cost has leapt from 4s 11d to 5s 11d. Air-raid shelters delivered and dumped in gardens next door and next door but one. Wrote to Mrs. Haughton.

Wednesday, 4 October. Met Wellings last night. He came armed with newspaper cuttings to prove his War theories. I enjoyed my evening though it was so dark after I dropped my torch in St. James's Park and he would go through such gloomy alleys. We went to Lyons for ices and the waiter glared fearsomely. We don't spend much and Wellings doesn't tip well. He says he will take me out to dinner in style when peace comes. Em phoned this morning. Denys is nearly starving, she says. She is going to try to sell my tea set for me and Mrs. Lucas talks of buying my mirror. Met Mr. Ginsbury at 4.30 at Coventry Street Corner House. How I like a Jewish escort! The harem atmosphere lingers among them. He held my hand and patted my arm as though he really were glad to see me, conveyed me upstairs, put me in my seat as though I were a belle whom he was ardently courting, fussed over my food (incidentally over an overcharge on the bill, too), walked back with me to Cambridge Circus and held my hand so long I nearly laughed, and patted my cheek as the Rosenberg boys do their mother's, urging me to let him know how I'm getting on. I wore my new coat and shoes. Ginsbury is superlatively patriotic like all Jews.

Thursday, 5 October. My satchel was appropriated by another borrower at the Library this morning. To Emperor's Gate tonight. Murray cooked his usual delightful evening meal but Mrs. Dunlop's presence caused restraint. Murray never addresses her nor she him. Leo spoke viciously of foreigners who complain about England and the English but are only too pleased to take refuge here. She spoke little but she did say she had a dreadful crossing and was detained four hours at Folkestone where she was searched and re-searched. She says she was carrying a film scenario in MS entitled 'Dynamite' which she had taken out from England to return to its author [in Germany] but she was unable to discover him. She said she had not seen a single pamphlet dropped from a British plane all the time she was in Germany. She speaks as though she were an ardent anti-Nazi, referred to the belief that Goering was supposed to have ordered many assassinations. She said she couldn't think a German revolution was likely to be successful as so many were apathetic, so many more were terrified of the Gestapo and its agents.

Friday, 6 October. Mrs. Haughton wrote, suggesting I should go as a sort of companion housekeeper for my board and lodging. Not _ _ _ _ likely! Underpaid domestic service isn't my aim. Even teaching would be better. I had hoped Wellings' prophecy that Hitler would be assassinated might have been fulfilled when he flew to Warsaw, but he's speaking in the Reich today. My spirits are very low. Bay on the phone. Her spirits are little higher. Em also rang. Bee has a 25% cut in salary.

Saturday, 7 October. Wellings phoned last night, very jubilant he's so sure the peace terms mooted by Hitler will be those accepted in part or in their entirety by the Allies in the very near future. He is still sure Hitler will be assassinated. Did nothing save prowl to find the cheapest market for food. Paid 2d for case for identity card. A kerb hawker was selling various kinds at this price. Many, many more children are back in town. I saw several helping their elders crying and selling fruit and vegetables. Wellings says Shaw had written a letter to the *New Statesman* deploring our lost liberties.[8] Lottie wrote. The billeting of her TB pupils seems to be particularly badly arranged.

---

8. In 'Uncommon Sense about the War', *New Statesman*, 7 October 1939, pp. 483–4, Bernard Shaw complained (among other things) about the expansion of state powers. 'Whatever our work in life may be, we have been ordered to stop doing it and stand by. Wherever our wives and children are they have been transported to somewhere else, with or without their mothers.' Traditional British liberties were to be further restricted a few months later by the Emergency Powers Bill, passed into law on a single day, 22 May 1940, and described by one authority as 'the most drastic Act ever passed by a British Parliament' (Alan Bullock,

They are sleeping three in a bed in some cottages. There is no sanitation nor running water in the village, no extra milk for the children, no tents for open-air work. Lottie seems very enthusiastic about her duties as acting Head. I suppose she is glad not to be overshadowed by a man, her husband or her headmaster or her father. She doesn't so much as mention the first and last. If I were as well-off as she is, I wouldn't teach, much less allow myself to be billeted in an inconvenient cottage with old-age pensioners as hosts. Tom Harrisson wrote asking for further dream material.

Sunday, 8 October. Phoned Bay. She seems rather more cheerful and indeed the news suggests the possibility of Wellings being right. To Queen's Hall this afternoon. Charles Hambourg conducting, very like an ape, and wearing so short a lounge coat his bottom protruded so far one almost expected it to be blue and red like a mandrill's. Myra Hess's playing of Beethoven's 4th pianoforte concerto evoked much applause.

Dream Diary. I thought last night I was billeted in a hotel where, among other guests, was an admiral, on leave, aged about 70 and very like Nelson, save that he had Wellington's hooked nose. I was so wretched at having been evacuated and I hated teaching so much I set out to flirt with the admiral, hoping he would make me his mistress as I had heard him say he could afford four guineas a week for such a purpose. To further my aims I bought a high-waisted, very narrow, clinging, diaphanous white gown such as was fashionable about 1815 I think, and I not only submitted to but invited the admiral's somewhat intimate love-making, seeing in it a way of escape. However, he received an official notice telling him he must immediately sail for MINSK (or MURSK, I'm not sure of this word) on the White Sea as England wished to trade with Russia before the ice prevented ships from sailing.[9] He came to say 'goodbye' and I was so sure my plans had succeeded, but alas, as he stooped to kiss my hand, he said 'I'm sorry, but your first name is not Emma'.

I wakened here and laughed heartily.

Monday, 9 October. Em on phone, fretted by her husband's folly in the matter of changing houses. His purse is so lean and his ambitions so lofty. Phoned Miss H. Brown for details of Balletomanes Club [for ballet enthusiasts]. I'm determined to make new acquaintances and

---

The Life and Times of Ernest Bevin: Volume Two, Minister of Labour 1940–1945 [London: Heinemann, 1967], p. 15).

In October 1939 Shaw was questioning the point of the war, now that Poland was lost, and of continuing resistance to Hitler. 'Our business is now to make peace with him and with all the world instead of making more mischief and ruining our people in the process' ('Uncommon Sense about the War', p. 484).

9. Murmansk may have been the actual port to which her dream was connected.

develop along other lines when and if the War ends. Mr. Gaye wrote. He's very depressed at the effects of this vile War. Lil wrote.

Tuesday, 10 October. Lil wrote. She is suffering from internal trouble again. I do hope it isn't cancer. Sent two more dreams to Harrisson. No word from Editha so far. She thinks *I'll* phone and *she'll* save 4d. Bought knickers and gloves. Placard tonight read 'Amazing German Rumours', 'Strange Rumours from Berlin'. Meanwhile Russia is said to be massing an army ready for attack on Finland if the latter won't grant air bases for Stalin's aerodromes. Met Wellings casually in Highbury. He's still full of war-theories and naval lies.

Dream Diary. I dreamed last night I was on holiday and spent it riding round London on top of the old-fashioned open-topped motor buses. My trips were spoiled by the repeated appearances of aircraft in the sky but no one except myself appeared perturbed. They went on eating at tables on the pavement for suddenly London appeared to be Bruges and every other shop was a café. I was sitting with a man who looked like someone I knew. He was apparently German and reminded me of the ring-master at Hengler's Circus who impressed me as a child; then he appeared very like the riding-master I saw on the screen in a trailer of a German film years ago at the Academy Cinema. I said to him 'People don't seem very nervous at these frequent threats of air-attack, do they?' 'No', he said sourly. 'We'll have to think of something else. Everyone's reaching saturation point in fear!' '*WE?*' I asked. 'Are you German?' 'No, I'm the man in *Bleak House* who keeps the shooting gallery,' he said. I was annoyed at the obvious lie. 'You're all in league together to swindle people,' I declared. 'Aircraft makers and armament makers – and – and – international oppressors of the peoples.' Then I ran off in fright and boarded what was now a lorry-bus such as were used for a while either during or at the end of the 'Great War to end War'! A herd of huge black shaggy cattle charged the bus and the herdsman or drover was a sullen, menacing fellow of gigantic height. He cried out 'The years, like great black oxen, tread the world', and I wakened with a start.

Wednesday, 11 October. Lil wrote, also Tom Harrisson. Enjoyed my evening with Wellings last night. He's still convinced this is no real war and that effects are being engineered. He is also insistent that Hitler has been or will be assassinated. We walked around in the darkness, went back to the Corner House and talked still more. Again he proffered the loan of £5. This morning met Editha at 11 a.m. Took her to coffee at Lyons, then to lunch at the Cock. Here her husband joined us. He was telling of the provision made by Bart's for possible war casualties. They even had collapsible coffins in readiness! Editha *is* unsympathetic. She was quite gleeful because Miss Hammond is so uncomfortable. E. looks as old as I feel! She messed up my afternoon.

I had to come home and prepare tea while she went gallivanting among her old acquaintances. Phoned Em. Bay on wire. She is again threatened with evacuation and feels correspondingly depressed.

Thursday, 12 October. Letters from Lil and Ada. To Em's early. Sold my mirror and coat to her. I'm banking this 16s 6d for emergencies. Another letter from Tom Harrisson.[10] Peace Union are apparently active.[11] Bay and Em on phone.

Dream Diary. I fancied last night I was in a big open square like the one at Norwich and yet it was really High Street, Homerton by St. Barnabus Church. There was a tramping of feet and a heaving motion, caused by wave upon wave of people converging on the main square, and there was a sort of wailing noise that was also a murmuring of hatred and discontent. I thought at first it was the Gordon rioters. (I had been reading about the Massacre of St. Bartholomew, also about the fall in the present-day receipts from pilgrims to Rome before I slept, and anyhow the Gordon rioters often haunt my waking and sleeping thoughts thanks to the impression made by the reading of *Barnaby Rudge* in my adolescence.) When I noticed the people's faces I found they were all dark, vivacious, beady-eyed and rather oily-looking. Most of them wore black but a few wore garish ornaments or coloured sashes. *I* knew foot and mounted police were lurking in alleys and courts round about the square, but no one else was aware of their presence. One little cul-de-sac (we called it Hot Water Street when I was a child because street fights so often occurred there; it was really Tranby Place and no longer exists) was crowded with police and the crowds kept surging towards and then away from this ambush. At last a tiny woman (very like a Mrs. H. who actually kept a greengrocer's in this district years ago) addressed me. She was swaying like an Eastern mourning person and she waved a very gay fan rhythmically. 'You're with us, my dear, I know,' she said. 'You'll take what's coming to us.' 'Why are we all gathered here?' I asked. 'To bury our Gypsy Queen,' she replied. 'But I'm English. Where are all the other English?' I demanded. 'They're on the side of the police,' she said. 'Why am I here?' I asked. 'Because you're friendly with the peoples of all nations and you mourn their sorrows.'

Then quite suddenly I appeared to become a kind of Solomon Eagle and started running wildly about and bawling 'This is all wrong! You're mourning the wrong things and spending your money on the wrong things. This old queen drained dry your resources and she robbed you of your right to live your own lives. Down with the dead past and up

---

10. Gladys replied to Harrisson on 15 October. 'Your flattery or my natural inclination towards mild exhibitionism urges me to continue the dream diary. It is interesting, too, to note how war conditions affect people's deletions in letters and verbal mistakes in conversation.'
11. The Peace Pledge Union was a prominent pacifist organisation.

with the living!' And then the police rushed out with their horses and it was Peterloo [disturbances in 1819] all over again.

This dream was very disjointed but very long. I always seem to be having very long conversations in dreams now, but in peace time in dreams I usually experience things rather than talk so much. Now I waken myself by my talking.

Friday, 13 October. Very uneventful day for I see no one, and the few amusements the Government allows I cannot afford to patronise, so there's nothing to do but read, write (and my eyes are in revolt) and pace the local streets. Bay on phone this evening. She's very depressed lest she [a civil servant] should be sent to Westmorland.[12] Em on phone too. She may buy my tea set. Wellings rang late. He says he should think something definite would have to happen this weekend with regard to the War.

Dream Diary. I dreamed last night I was a young girl and my niece, who was brought up with me, was very young, as she would have been. We were to be billeted with many other children at Brixham where the fishermen's huts appeared to be of the wattle-and-daub type, while a few resembled sentry boxes or coffins standing on end, plastered with mud. (An air-raid shelter was yesterday being erected in the garden next door and I think this influenced the dream.) My niece and I were very wretched. We didn't want to be evacuated. We wanted our own home in London so we separated from the main crowd of evacuees and made our way down to the coast where I paddled and carried her high aloft in my arms, resting myself from time to time by seating her on smooth topped boulder (?) stones, for the coast appeared to be like Amroth, South Wales, as it was thirty years ago.

Suddenly a fisherman appeared as I was pausing to show the child the beauty of the clear, green water and the wonders of the sea-floor. He looked like any old sailor who lets boats for hire but *I* knew he was St. Peter. 'Do you want to celebrate peace?' he asked. I very definitely did. 'Then tell your sister to buy the wonderful Vasari masterpiece I have for sale.' (My sister wrote yesterday to say she'd take me and my niece 'out to a Peace Dinner and you can get drunk on champagne,' to quote her words.) Suddenly she appeared in the dream and she was wearing Edwardian dress. (I was taken to Trafalgar Square to celebrate Peace Night after the Boer War and I celebrated it in the Armistice Night crowds at Piccadilly.) She wasn't at all enthusiastic about purchasing the Vasari, which was shown to us in a second-hand shop in Balls Pond Road, opposite one of Mosley's strongholds which is actually there. It showed the Holy Child in the nude with some bewildered looking cattle gaping at Him as He blew aloft a huge, iridescent

---

12. Various government departments had already been evacuated to regions deemed safer and others were soon to follow.

bubble. She didn't like the subject and she declared she could have drawn better cattle herself. (This is a very typical remark of hers when we succeed in luring her into any Art Gallery.) I kept saying the picture would provide permanent beauty. (My niece had disappeared now.) To please me my sister went back and bought the picture, which was packed in corrugated cardboard and we never saw the actual picture till we got it home, when it proved to be no Holy Child but a very beautiful but obviously evil Lilith [female demon] against a background of peacock's feathers. I was very disappointed and wept bitterly but my sister announced 'Ah, well, it's more suitable for the evil of the times than the Holy Child would have been. I saw a woman like that at the Standard music hall, singing "I don't want to lose you but I think you ought to go".'

I hope this account is not too lengthy, but it was all so vivid, even to the colours in the bed of the sea and the details of the picture.

Saturday, 14 October. The uncertainty continues. I continue to economise – not easy since prices still sky-rocket. Have been nowhere and seen no one. This is death-in-life and I've an appalling headache.

Dream Diary. Last night's dreams were a queer hotchpotch of which little remains clear except that my ex-husband had returned and we were preparing to spend the night together. I was not very enthusiastic at the prospect as (a) he looked commoner than I remembered him, (b) shabbier too, and (c) we apparently had no home of our own but were accommodated in a tiny bedroom of a jerry-built house belonging to my Headmaster's wife. Adjoining the bedroom with its bulging walls and ill-fitting door (through which we could glimpse another bedroom in which a funny old man of the night-watchman type was undressing and donning a grey flannel shirt like those served out to soldiers in 1914) was a very primitive earth closet but it was brilliantly lit by electricity! Many noisy children were playing on the stairs and numbers of unemployed men kept appearing and disappearing and I was trying to persuade myself the reunion would at least solve *my* money difficulties for my returned husband would have to support me.

Sunday, 15 October. Another day of unceasing rain! Before I breakfasted I was plagued by the whining of a small kitten and try as I would, I could not discover whence came the wail. Finally, people in one of the houses at the back came and retrieved the poor mite who was squeaking at their back door. About mid-day Bay phoned. She was hysterical and screamed and raged because she is so afraid of being taken away from her home and above all from Miss Wilshin. I said 'Isn't your religion any comfort to you?' and that set her off. She bawled 'You idiot! What can console me for the loss of my home that I have slaved for and sacrificed for all these years?' I tried to remind her there were other women losing loved sons and losing homes through the unemployment of their husbands, homes they would never recover. She feels it because Miss Wilshin doesn't worry so much about losing her as *she* does at the prospect of losing touch with Miss W. Poor Bay! She has to learn the cruellest lesson Life has to teach – that the ones we love to desperation do not need us. My brother Fred's wife did not want him and Fred's life ran to waste accordingly. My ex-husband George did not want *me* and my pride lay in the dust. Worse still, Leonard wanted a Jewish wife and family and money; although he loved me a little for a long while he would not risk his reputation nor even inconvenience himself to see me at last, and my heart broke. Even Griffiths soon found me tiresome and again my pride was muddied. Clowser dropped me like a hot chestnut – but that time only my self-esteem was injured. *Now* I have nothing left. Faith in God and MAN is gone, but at least I cannot be hurt that way again. Only physical pain can hurt me now!

Dream Diary. More chaotic dreams last night! One dealt with crowds of working people who were gathering together and driving in decorated coal-trolleys to the docks to sail for America in the *Mayflower*. Progress was slow because huge tram-cars – the old chocolate-coloured ones – kept 'jamming' the coal trolleys so they could not move. A puritanical looking man with a spade beard on my right kept muttering 'Ah, they don't want the workers to go! They want to keep an army of unemployed to keep wages down! America for me, lads!' The next time I slept I was again part of a mighty concourse all going to demonstrate about something. Again progress was slow because one stream of people was coming away from the meeting-place while another was making towards it. I wakened struggling to extricate myself from the bed-clothes.

When I dozed again after day-break I was still one of a crowd, all going to hear my friend P. speak against war. His wife was afraid there would be a riot and asked to come home with me and I agreed but was inwardly distressed as I knew my home was bare (I am actually parting with 'bits and pieces' of furniture to eke out my money in hand) and I also knew I could not afford to offer her the food she would like (also painfully true just now). She was very disdainful when she saw my poor home and she was turning over the 'elderly' cakes and stale bread like a dog routing over pieces in the gutter and I wakened crying.

Actually I was moved to tears yesterday by overhearing an old-age pensioner talking when I was shopping in a street-market yesterday. He said 'I look forward to me bit o' meat on Sundays, but there ain't a-goin' to be none this week with these 'ere prices a-goin' up an' up'.

Monday, 16 October. Lil my only correspondent but Em phoned. To Library this morning. To Piccadilly this afternoon and bought two cheap black hats for 10s 10d. Gave 3d to a young 'down-and-out' who was very lame and looked exhausted. His response was 'Gee, mum, but that's a s'prise!' His young face lit up. I wished I'd had cigarettes for him but I don't smoke myself now I'm so hard up and I'd just paid 1s for a ticket for a Beecham concert on October 29th. These people in this house do annoy me. Before 9.30 a.m. Sybil was phoning her grandmother. While I'm at tea Mrs. Lucas comes up –'Can my Syd phone his 'Governor?' Now a phone box is at the corner and Syd is at home with influenza so all his germs go down my mouthpiece. I've washed it with carbolic soap. War news hangs fire! How long a sick leave can I get? I'm not fit for work. I'm 'all on wires' and cry such a lot.

Dream Diary. Last night I thought I was back in early Edwardian days. Mare Street, Hackney was as I then remembered it, with horse-trams driven by bewhiskered old fellows in weather-worn 'bowlers'. A few broughams bowled along. Shop blinds were gaily striped, a green water cart 'drowsed' along and it was summer. I went into a shop of many departments. The assistants were dressed as they would have been then and I was buying curtains from a charming young man with blonde moustachios of prodigious size and spikiness thanks to wax. There were foaming cascades of curtain material, Nottingham lace and Madras muslin and spotted net, all *white*. Suddenly a shop-walker in a frock-coat took me by the arm and led me into a warehouse. He thrust a cup of tea into my hand. 'Drink!' he cried. 'The Boer war is over!' Actually, at 11 a.m. on November 11th, 1918 my then employer called me out from the office into the warehouse and thrust a tumbler of whiskey into my hand, saying 'Drink it up! The war is over!' I did and for the first time in my life was intoxicated and went out to celebrate Peace.

Tuesday, 17 October. Wellings phoned last night. He thinks the reported raid on Scotland was a fake.[13] He still declares the war will end very soon. I hope he's right. Lil wrote. This afternoon I walked for about five miles around Islington and Stoke Newington streets. I had not realised how London has changed in these past few years – apart from present War sluttishness. Roads in Stoke Newington that once housed Nonconformist ministers, upper grade Civil Servants and works managers are now let out in floors and slatternly women and dirty children crowd the streets. Even I begin to hanker after suburbia. It is very frightening to realise how powerful these mobs of unedu-cated, 'unwashed', unthinking people could become! No wonder the Government soddens them with radio and cheap cinemas so they've no time to become politically minded.

Dream Diary. Last night it seemed I was at home again with my mother when my present window cleaner announced Leonard was

---

13. On 14 October the battleship *Royal Oak* was sunk by a U-boat at Scapa Flow.

waiting for me outside. I rushed out and Leonard said he was going to Eastbourne for four days to see his mother who was staying there till peace came again. He added 'Pack your bag. I'll take you down. You can stay at a boarding house and I'll spend the nights with you. I'm leaving my wife behind. The war loosens all morals.' He dashed off but omitted to say where he would meet me with the car. I was bitterly disappointed. I had wanted for so many years to go away with him and now it was being bungled at the last moment. Instead of packing my suitcase (I identify packed suitcases with evacuation schemes, which haunt my waking and sleeping hours), I rushed round the streets hunting for Leonard. When I found him he insisted I should phone his wife so that she should think I was still in town while he was supposedly on his way to Eastbourne. I couldn't find an empty phone box and I knew the precious four days were slipping by. People kept pushing me away from the receiver and putting through enquiries about relatives after air-raid scares. Crowds of aged refugees surged round the phone boxes and when I did get connected the wife said 'Oh, you're not deceiving me! I know you're with Leonard. He's been years deciding to take this trip with you but the wife always wins. His petrol tank is nearly empty and *I've* got his ration book.'

We finally set out. I was chafing inwardly because I knew I looked old and worried and because I was wondering how long the petrol would last. It gave out on what appeared to be the Stanstead Road in Essex. I was pleading with men in tin hats (these recur again and again in my dreams because they offend my waking eye so much: men do look such fools in them!) but they dragged Leonard from the car and said because he was a Jew (he is) he must clean the road of the 'sear and yellow' leaves. As they hauled him out of the driving seat he turned to me and said 'Those who won't sin when they are young *can't* sin when they are old'.

I awakened sobbing bitterly.

Wednesday, 18 October. At the New Restaurant last night I saw Clowser when I arrived but I suppose he didn't want to talk to me so chose a table out of sight. However, he saw Wellings and me on our way out and came over, sat down at our table and began to talk. He then suggested we should join him in visiting Julian and Stella Jackson. We did. They live in a fifth floor flat in Charing Cross Road. On entering we found Stella (looking much younger) lolling in a chair, Julian, dishevelled and unkempt as ever but with his beautiful, sensitive hands well-kept, and a young 'tough guy' cousin of Stella's in the chester-field, displaying ragged slippers and a dirty shirt quite unblushingly. It would have been a delightful room had it been less littered. The cousin was in 'the film game'. Julian played – among other records – the Purcell Golden Sonata – very lovely. The assembled company talked books, war-news and economics. Wellings could get no support for his war-theories although later, when Tom (or was it Don?) Clellorn,[14] a New Zealand cartoonist who works for the *Tribune* and uses Stella and Julian for models, came in, Wellings got an interested if critical listener. The conversation of these intelligent men gave me a wonderful fillip. If only I could get out of this dismal Highbury backwater into a gayer, more alert atmosphere, I should soon be better. If only Wellings' theory were true and the war would end this month! Tom Harrisson sent another appreciative letter of my dream-diary, recently sent.

Dream Diary. Last night's dreams were phantasmagoric. Of all the people who crowded through them there remains a 'Miss Docker', a little, drab schoolmarm, not unlike Charlotte Brontë, who, by her continual demands on my time in what was apparently a school for evacuated children, successfully prevented me from having a *free* bath in the school furnace room, although the burly Mr. Marsh (an actual and very obliging school keeper I once knew) was prepared to connive at my economical bathing.

Thursday, 19 October. Lil and Mrs. Haughton wrote. Em on phone. War news no more consolatory. I have no faith in Wellings' theories now. To Library. Young male librarian commented on my having read Professor Black's book on Queen Elizabeth. He said 'I thought it was for your son'. 'Why?' says I. 'Do I look such a fool you thought it was beyond me?' Got Stendhal's *Rouge et Noir* – in translation – mentioned by Somerset Maugham and shall probably sample Dryden's prose for the same reason. Am reading Joad's *Guide to Modern Wickedness* [1939].[15] If only return to school in a 'safe area' didn't hang over me, I could go on.

Dream Diary. It seemed last night I was determined to escape from teaching in a safe area so I had arranged to re-marry. My bridegroom was to be H., who was a witness at my former marriage.[16] I must admit *he* didn't seem very jubilant at the prospect of marrying me and *I* realised I was only using him as a means of escape from teaching and as a source of economic safety. Anyhow he duly arrived complete with silk hat and white spats and buttonhole together with a completely

---

14. Gladys's writing of this name is unclear, and it may be that this man in fact had a different name.

15. This is a collection of essays on values, social attitudes and beliefs, and modern life. Cyril E. M. Joad (1891–1953) was a prominent populariser of philosophy. His outlook at this time was rationalist, agnostic, and pacifist, and he was much given to provocative pronouncements. During the war he became a regular member of the BBC's hugely popular *Brains Trust*. In one passage in *Guide to Modern Wickedness* [London: The Scientific Book Club, 1939] Joad makes a remark that is relevant to a point made earlier concerning the casual anti-Semitism of the 1930s. After several pages of praise for Jews and their accomplishments (p. 228) that 'on meeting a Jew, my first reaction is one of defensive distrust. This, however, is a fact, a wholly deplorable fact, about me.' Few of his fellow Gentiles were likely to have been any more easy-going in their attitudes to Jews.

16. This man's name was Alfred Hewlett (from her marriage certificate).

unknown bridesmaid in diaphanous Oxford-blue chiffon dress and a huge Merry Widow hat. I very much disapproved of the fact that her gown had two circular pieces cut out so that her breasts were plainly revealed. (Through my dream passed a hazy idea that she had come from Bali but she looked quite English.)

Then the whole party went through hall after hall, filling up form after form – coal supply, milk supply, ration cards, birth certificates, doctors' certificates, death certificates – we kept filling them up and black-coated officials kept snatching them away. (This part was very reminiscent of Priestley's *Johnson over Jordan*.)[17] I seemed so clumsy, dropped pens, dropped forms, crossed out words, could not remember details, and finally I found all the bridal party had disappeared but there were numbers of elderly men, some without noses, some one-eyed, some halt and maimed, and they kept moving along like mannequins in a dress parade. A man like a ring-master in a dress suit that was crumpled and over-large touched my arm. 'Look', he said. 'This is all I've got left in men-folk. Choose your partner quickly. The Dance of Death is just going to begin.' (H. actually was maimed in the last War!)

A second dream dealt with my going into a street-market where I was turning over old clothes and rabbit skins, looking for something I could afford to buy for winter wear. A little beady-eyed woman (I cannot think whom she represents but a similar figure frequently recurs in my dreams lately) kept bustling around me and saying 'Hurry up! Don't be fussy! Don't pick and choose! Take the cheapest! You're a poor relation now.'

Friday, 20 October. Marjorie Rose phoned last night. She says she is 'living in sin' with Alexander Haffner now. She is doing ARP work now at £2 weekly but her brothers are helping her. I am to visit her, she says. Then Wellings phoned to say he'd been entertaining 'P.' Monk-house and his (W's) views on the speedy ending of the War were now strengthened. Suddenly I grew hysterical and began to howl and had to ring off. This morning saw Dr. Russ. He said LCC doctor had been on the phone and they had talked about my leave of absence and he had said I was not yet fit to return. Have started looking for rooms.

Later. Met Bay at 4 p.m. Looked at flat in Doughty Street – £1 for basement kitchen and sink in area. Tea at Patisserie Valerie. Police whistles called us from our meal and we watched a Soho running gang

---

17. This play, which was performed at London's Saville Theatre in early 1939 with Ralph Richardson in the lead role, was itself an enactment of a dream. In Act One, Johnson (the main character) is forced to review his life and fill in endless forms, never to the satisfaction of two other-worldly examiners. For details, see the reading version of the play with Priestley's additional commentary (J. B. Priestley, *Johnson over Jordan: The Play and All about It* [London: Heinemann, 1939]). Gladys had seen the play on 23 February – and was not impressed. 'Thought the play a curious hotch-potch and Britten's music ordinary.' Parts of the plot 'seemed queerly fantastic to me, and I hate fantasy'.

fight. Walked in St. James's Park, then returned to Regent Palace Hotel for tea and ices. At least it was bright there. Another air-raid on Scotland reported.

Dream Diary. In order to get a little peaceful sleep last night I had to take sleeping tablets – just a stupor, no dreams.

Saturday, 21 October. Letter from Lil. Phone call from Wellings last night. He's still convinced the war is a hoax and about to end shortly. I ought not to complain about loneliness or not being loved. I got offended with Latcham's [grocery, 11 Highbury Park] about the supply of sawdust and stopped shopping there. Then today, while I was in the butcher's, Miss L. spoke to me – said how they'd all missed me, said how they and their staff regarded me as a friend rather than as a customer and begged me to call in from time to time as a friend though I was under no obligation to shop with them. As my purchases are negligible, I presume this profession of friendliness was genuine. Walked in Highgate – delightful spot. Man phoned about flats in Mecklenburgh Street. I'm viewing them on Monday, but make up my mind about moving I cannot. It's as though a blight fell on me whenever I thought of leaving this hateful house. I don't know *what* to do – whether to warehouse furniture, keep a home going here in town or what – and I've no idea when I'm likely to return to school. Somehow Hampstead seems a wiser proposition than WC1. Couldn't read Hasek's *Schweik, the Good Soldier*!

Sunday, 22 October. Em phoned. Her husband makes her furious. Bay phoned. Mrs. Lucas came up, Mr. Lucas came up. The Pyrland Road fogies drove me to despair. They are never satisfied. If you go once, they want you 20 more times. Tonight they are inveighing against their rich relative.

Dream Diary. Last night's dreams were vague but worrying. Jewish refugees were billeted in a training college and people were being actively and passively unkind to them. In the intervals of helping them, I appeared to be whirled hither and thither by surging, eddying crowds. There was another dream in which my mother (actually dead) and I were trying to placate a landlord to whom we owed rent. I gave him my engagement ring but tore out the diamond first, its gleam was so delightful. Cats and dogs were mixed up with this dream. People were trying to catch and eat them although the animals were in sore straits. (I was reading *Schweik* just before I went to bed and the repulsive details of his dog-dealing sickened me.)

Monday, 23 October. Renewed custom with Latcham's. Mrs. Lucas gave me fried fish at midday and a fruit tart yesterday. I *do* wish she wouldn't. It puts me under an obligation, and that when I'm thinking of removing. Looked at a flat in Mecklenburgh Street. The last tenants had walked out and would like to let it furnished! Beds were unmade, ash-trays unemptied, glasses unwashed. Their greasy heads had marked the wall above their divans. I never saw such a spectacle. Walked home via Caledonian Road and Barnsbury. In Richmond Road the early Victorian houses have flights of steps leading to the hall door and at the top of each flight is a pair of sphinxes and behind each sphinx is an obelisk about a yard high. Evacuation cards are now on sale in stationers' shops. No more children and expectant mothers are to be evacuated by the authorities.

Dream Diary. Very muddled dreams again last night, hosts of people scurrying about like frightened rabbits, skies full of aircraft. Some aeroplanes had reapers attached to them by ropes and as the aeroplanes flew along the reapers cut down people by the legs and left them, torsos on bleeding stumps. Many ARP workers and special constables were rushing about and some of the latter were indulging in shameless love-making (being a Victorian, I use a euphemism you see), with a huge, blowsy female very like Laura Cowill in *Mourning Becomes Electra* [1931, by Eugene O'Neill].

I wakened crying and struggling to escape from the bed-clothes.

Tuesday, 24 October. Lil sent apples and jam! Editha phoned. No word from LCC. Very dark at 7 p.m. so I had to buy a new torch. To the New Restaurant. Mr. Clowser came in, came to my table and settled down – not, I think, to Mr. Wellings' satisfaction. Eric Hunt was already there and he came over and spoke afterwards. We went on to the Ambassadors'. The officials did not challenge Wellings, who had no gas mask. I wished I had not taken my borrowed one with me. The revue was funny, satirical but often perilously 'near the wind'. I cannot discover how the Censor's mind works. The 'La Palma' item was *very* broad; so was 'Only a medium medium'. 'The brave idea' depended largely on gesture and the idea of a man's doing a strip-tease act for its salacity. The guffaws of the men and the titters of the women showed how successful 'smut' is!

Dream Diary. I thought in the night I had returned to school which had re-assembled in the London area. Conditions were difficult, children troublesome, colleagues antagonistic. Suddenly I was transported to a bus queue and I was carrying a baby's chair which made an awkward accessory for its legs not only got in other people's way but also prevented me from getting a foothold in the vehicle. Buses were few and crowded. I was continually losing my place in the queue like the family in the [1938] film *Bank Holiday* [which starts with a rush of trains to the seaside]. I was very flustered as I knew I should be late for afternoon school. Suddenly I realised I had no money. My mother, who had appeared out of space, suggested my selling my engagement ring as gold had great value nowadays. (Actually it is sold long ago.) I took it off with difficulty but found the gold had worn through and the ring was broken while the diamond was obviously only a piece of glass. 'Everything is a fraud nowadays!' I announced solemnly. I then appeared to be in a cinema but as soon as I was comfortably established in a seat, the screen was removed to the other end of the hall and we all had to move round, facing the other way. I wakened myself by crying angrily 'Isn't *anything* stable nowadays?'

Wednesday, 25 October. Letter from Miss Hammond who is still having a hard time,[18] also note of appreciation from Tom Harrisson regarding 'Dream Diary'. Bay and Em on phone. Electricity up ½d per unit; 3d a unit present price. Spoke to Marjorie Rose on phone. She's going back to the office. I suppose the money tempts her or else there is too much talk about paying out money for ARP work to the moneyed. Alexander Haffner spoke to me. He is more patriotic than the most patriotic Englishman and is very angry at any of us English who deplore our lost liberties. I cannot see that the sufferings of an agricultural population in Romania lessen the enormity of our losing our liberties that have long been ours and which were obtained by [the] suffering of past generations and efforts of particular individuals.

Dream Diary. Last night's dreams remained centred around landlords, flats and money. Either the landlords were browbeating me for money or I had to remove to progressively poorer accommodation. The dream which finally awakened me dealt with an elderly, satyr-like landlord in a silk hat (I appreciate the symbolism of this recurrent hat in recent dreams!) being very angry when he discovered I was approaching fifty and past the age of romance and turning me out neck and crop in the scantiest of attire. The details of this dream are inspired by a previous night's visit to the Gate Revue and the items 'Faun in Manhattan' and 'Madame La Palma', together with the fact that I have a landlord who is prone to pawing. (I trust I am not being libellous!)

Thursday, 26 October. Lil wrote. Only read and wrote letters today – reading Aldous Huxley's *Ends and Means* [1938].

Dream Diary. Last night I appeared to be living in a small house with my mother and we let half of it to G. and his father. (G. is a young, enthusiastic, artistic erstwhile colleague of mine.) Crowds of young men in their early twenties kept visiting G. and they appeared to be of

---

18. On 21 October some London teachers attended a meeting in Leighton Buzzard of the South Bedfordshire Teachers' Association, where its Divisional Secretary spoke about 'evacuation problems and stressed the sterling work the Union is doing in protecting the interests of the teacher who has had to leave house or flat behind him, and in safeguarding his superannuation. After some discussion, it was decided to form, for the benefit of the evacuated teachers in the area, two sub-Associations with centres in Dunstable and Leighton Buzzard, and to entertain all the evacuated teachers to tea. The South Bedfordshire teachers were thanked by their London colleagues for the kindly way in which they have been received' (*Leighton Buzzard Observer*, 24 October 1939, p. 5).

all nationalities as his friends actually are. They were playing, singing, dancing and reading MSS to each other – again as they actually do – when the father (a purely imaginary figure here appeared) insisted on my medically examining these young men as they had to join the Army immediately. They were so healthy and happy and it seemed criminal to send them to be butchered. I turned to the morose, hideous elderly man – like G. F. Watts' *Mammon*[19] – and cried 'Why don't *you* go?' 'Old men never die, they only kill the young,' answered G's father and he hustled all the young men into a Black Maria – not the natty police vans of today but the old horse variety of my childhood.

Friday, 27 October. Rose with an appalling headache after a distressing night of worrying dreams. If only the war would end! Phoned Dr. Russ to enquire what I should do since the LCC send no instructions. He counsels waiting till Monday then 'doing a spot of phoning' if I've heard nothing. Em phoned. Her husband aggravates her so much; he won't *do* anything. I wonder if Em notices that his 'sitting on the fence' dates from her ceasing marital relations with him. It's as though he's been robbed of the urge to do anything. Miss Hammond phoned. She's very sympathetic: I do feel sorry for her. The promised scheme to keep the schools as units has never fructified. If only one knew how long this upheaval would last! Am reading *Lucie Duff Gordon* [*in England, South Africa and Egypt*] by Gordon Waterfield [1937] – very entertaining. How I envy these people who knew all the 'right' people – i.e., the ones who 'did' things. Have been nowhere and save for buying a packet of Players, I haven't spent any money since Tuesday.

Dream Diary. Throughout the night my dreams centred around lost cards. I was helping to catch dogs for food because my ration cards were lost. I was being pushed out of queues for coal permits. I was being turned out of restaurants because I could not produce identity cards and being turned off ships because I had dropped my passport in the sea. I woke in a sweat trying to catch a cheetah (evidently I dream in puns) that looked more like a sphinx with a certain politician's face than the actual animal.

Saturday, 28 October. Letter from LCC at last. I have to see their doctor next Wednesday. Very cold and bleak but I went to the Paris Cinema in Regent Street to see *Les Rois du Sport*. The film moved very slowly and I *do* not like Fernandel. He can only do certain inane things. Raimu is good and so is Jules Berry. The latter looks like a more refined Chevalier. How 'alive' French actors look! To Library, back to read. Miss Hope wrote. Her brother-in-law, who is Vicar of Leeming, had child evacuees and a helper from Gateshead. The children were

---

19. A human image of ugliness and evil painted in 1884–1885 by George Frederick Watts (1817–1904).

so lousy that the Vicar's wife caught vermin in her own hair. Miss H. says that villages near York had to burn bedding because the evacuated children were so lousy and incontinent! Mr. Wellings invited me by phone last night to supper tomorrow. He is still confident the war will end soon! In the newsreel appeared a man saved from the *Royal Oak*. He carefully announced that the *officers* were so brave and gave their lives for their men. What about the 'other ratings'? The *Evening Standard* [p. 3] gives a picture of a bride 'congratulated by a Queen' – in other words a factory girl seen at her bench by the Queen, who doubtless promptly forgot her existence. Ugh! Subtle propaganda! The radio news pronounces à propos of the Scottish mine accident today 'To the *management* it is a terrific grief'. It also goes on to emphasise how docile the wives and families of the injured men were, how they stayed indoors and left everything to the management, who doubtless never want to be overlooked too much. Aldous Huxley's book is teaching me to be hypercritical.

Dream Diary. In the night I thought I had arranged to marry Wellings, my friend of many years' standing. I knew I felt no great affection for him but I thought he would prove the economic solution of my present difficulties. He was *very* demonstrative and as he kissed me cried 'We'll call our first child the Prince of Peace!'

This appears to have been the final instalment of Gladys's reporting of her dreams to Mass-Observation, though she wrote of this dream diary on 29 October 1939 in a note to Tom Harrisson, in reply to one of his appreciative letters to her.

Dear Mr. Harrisson,

I deserve no thanks for the 'Dream Diary' I send you. Writing it offers some scope to my thwarted ambitions as a writer. Together with the keeping of a voluminous diary and much letter-writing it panders to my taste for the ink-bottle.

As long as I can afford postage and paper (which may not be long) and as long as you need it, I will continue to dispatch it from time to time – but give me a hint when you have had enough.

Yours sincerely,
Gladys H. Langford

8

October 1939–July 1940

Life Goes On

For Gladys, October 1939 ended with a stark crisis – not for her, but for her friend Wellings. 'He suffers me in many moods – as I do him,' she once wrote (28 June 1939), and this seems a fair remark.

Sunday, 29 October. Phoned Bay. To Queen's Hall. Beecham conducted a wonderful concert. I particularly like the Mozart symphony (the Haffner). Met Leo who tells me his wife is acting as secretary to Epstein. Set out for Glenmore Road in high spirits, only to get the shock of a lifetime. A strange man (who proved to be the landlord) opened the door. He said I mustn't see Mr. Wellings. I said 'I must. He's expecting me.' Then he took me by the arm and pulled me into the ground-floor room. He kept repeating 'He won't see you tonight'. I thought I must have gone mad since I left home and the signs were visible to this man who was shielding W. from contact. Then he said 'Mr. Wellings has religious mania!' I thought *he* was mad then and refused to believe him, insisting I *would* see W. Finally this man – Mr. Murray – fetched Clowser who was with Wellings. Alas! It was too true. Wellings imagines he's God come to bring peace and light into the world. He thinks his landlady is the Virgin Mary and Clowser is St. James. He didn't appear to connect me with any Biblical character. He has broken up some of his home, torn down his black-out curtains (the landlord has taken out the fuses so we had to sit in the dark). He has invaded his fellow tenant's bedroom in his pyjamas and told her he wanted her, [and] also told her all about the mysterious woman about whom he used to tell me. He sat like a smiling Buddha, talking about breaking down barriers by love and saying the world would know all things through him. He let Mrs. Murray smooth his hands and face and fuss him but he showed no demonstrativeness in return. Clowser was very good. He stayed with him all night but I left about 11 p.m. promising to phone for news during the day.

Monday, 30 October. I had a distracted night despite the sleeping draught. I feel dazed and bewildered. Poor, poor Wellings! I phoned

Editha. Sympathy isn't *her* strong point. She said 'I always knew he was "crackers"'. She proceeded to add that 'Birds of a feather etc.' and if I read as much as I've been doing, I too should have similar mental indigestion. Phoned Em, whose family doctor has died suddenly. *She* was upset. Phoned Mrs. Murray who said Wellings had had a very bad night and she had called a doctor and Wellings was full of 'sex-talk' and wanted 'that'. Then Clowser phoned to ask if I were all right and told me to phone Mrs. Jackson. Went to buy liver for the cat and cried so much that Mr. Godfrey [the butcher] almost carried me upstairs and let me sit by the fire while his wife made coffee for me. She's a sturdily built, self-possessed young female not good enough for him. Phoned Bay tonight and also Stella Jackson. Samuel sent cheque for £10. Mrs. Rosenberg wrote.

Tuesday, 31 October. Em on phone, then I phoned Mrs. Murray. She told me of Wellings' past doings – *News of the World* revelations. As I always suspected, his blonde manageress was his mistress – used to go home and drink and openly make love to him on Thursday nights. There have been other women too. Mrs. Murray said she couldn't quite 'place' me as I didn't 'look' the part. (Small wonder.) I have promised to have tea with her on Friday. Then Mr. Gaye phoned – wanted to take me out tomorrow but I'm booked for the LCC doctor and Bay tomorrow.

Later. At first I thought I never wanted to see Wellings again but I've been turning over in my own mind the business and remember that I'm always complaining criminals can't get back to ordinary life because ordinary citizens won't receive them – then why should I pose as so respectable a woman I can't receive him? Admittedly he's not normal – his illness proves that – but I have always received respect as well as friendship from him. Then too I remember how he spoke of missing his mother's love and I think his devotion to me and to Miss Monkhouse has been born of his longing for a maternal affection. Incidentally, I'm not sure that subconsciously I'm not annoyed because he's never made love to me. This nurse in the house whom he persecutes with his attentions is very like the 'blonde'. I want to laugh when I remember him, stooping, going bald and rather inclined to shamble along, and try to imagine him as a Don Juan. I ought to have known those soft, fleshy hands betokened sensuality. Miss Hardwick wrote. Bay phoned. Clowser did too. He wants me to work in Wellings' shops but I don't care to interfere with other people's money affairs. Saw today rehearsals of rescuing air-attack victims in Holloway Road. Debate in House on need for raising Old Age Pensions.

Wednesday, 1 November. Lil wrote, also Tom Harrisson. To County Hall. Felt ghastly and wept myself into a fit of hysteria. Saw a male doctor who examined me more thoroughly than they usually do. He has given me a further two months' leave. I have now written to enquire how much longer I shall receive salary. Met Bay. Bought dressing gown for 12s 6d. Mine is in holes. Phoned Em.

Thursday, 2 November. Letter from Lil. Sent instalments due to London Teachers' Association and Whirlwind Ltd [manufacturer of carpet sweepers]. Met Mr. Gaye at 5.15 p.m. at Piccadilly. He took me to Appenrodt's for tea and talk. He was very interested in Wellings' case and thinks it will only be a passing phase. He regards his sex activities as a searching for something to salve his uneasy ego. He thinks Wellings is a minor genius and not to be judged by ordinary standards. How different from Editha who, on the phone this morning, declared she and Frank always knew Wellings was mad and that his sense of values had always been all wrong and that his predilection for psychoanalysis had always been unhealthy. Editha ended by saying 'And we all know you're going the same way – another sex maniac'. I'm *very* glad I never got near Maudsley [Hospital]. Mr. Gaye said Seymour Arthurs went there and was so unhappy that the first time they let him out on parole he ran away from his wife and committed suicide. Gaye thinks he would have kept sane outside the walls of the mental hospital. I enjoyed myself with him – but alas, I fear he never regards me as a potential wife. He thinks Wellings' idea about this being an engineered war is quite correct, that diplomats are at work and when they can arrive at a settlement there will be a long truce with America probably acting as negotiator.

Friday, 3 November. Letter from Lil. The first floor ceiling fell with a crash and my kitchen ceiling is declared unsafe. To Mrs. Murray's this afternoon and found that Mr. Wellings had been told I was going and expected me. I was first introduced to his brother, a ruddy-faced pocket edition of Sydney Howard, the comedian. I didn't like him very much – he was too voluble and too jocund. I went up alone to see Wellings who looks like one already in another world. He has eaten nothing since last Friday, won't go out and won't wear his clothes ordinarily, but, apparently in my honour, he was dressed normally and although his hair was tousled he combed and brushed it. At first he seemed to have difficulty in mouthing his words but gradually he spoke more fluently though he was very quiet for long periods. He spoke vaguely of my affection for my father, said I was ill and didn't know it, talked of a heavenly restaurant where Clowser, he and I should be happy together. He sat silent when his brother came into the room. Mrs. Murray doesn't appeal to me. She's bursting with details of her married life and keeps talking of Wellings being more or less in love with her. She says he demanded intercourse on Monday and lay naked for her to wash him. He reminds me of Oswald in [Henrik Ibsen's] *Ghosts*. Anyhow when I left him after sitting in the dark 'listening in' with him, I felt a nerve-wreck for I expected him every minute to leap upon me. He kissed my hand and held it fast. I was so overcome I kissed his cheek and he kissed me gravely, like an archbishop a confirmation pupil. Phoned Bay. No news about Bumpstead.

Saturday, 4 November. Last night at 11 p.m. down came the kitchen ceiling with a bang. This morning and all day, up and down have come the Lucases. Bought liver for a stray dog. Flat-hunting this afternoon. Most of the places are grimy, badly papered and undesirable. One pleased me despite some disadvantages. It was a huge room in an evacuated school – 15s weekly included light and constant hot water. The garden is glorious – almost like looking out on an estate. The owner, a headmistress, was very pleasing, though very bewhiskered.

Sunday, 5 November. To Highgate this afternoon to look regretfully at the room (or rather the outside of the house) I've decided not to take. It's a lovely district. Perhaps one day I'll be able to afford it.

Monday, 6 November. The last day I receive salary till I return to school! The furniture dealer failed to appear. Rain, hail, thunder and lightning banned flat-hunting. Meandering in the streets and reading save by artificial light. Phoned Em last night. Started reading [Michael] Sadleir's *Blessington-D'Orsay*. I don't like the style. The author persists in describing thoughts and actions that could only have been known to the characters concerned.[1] Lil wrote. Quite an agreeable letter from Mr. Pickering who says it's a good job I'm not with the school as he thinks I should not be very happy in the village. I feel like a dead woman, or rather a perambulating ghost. Everyone I knew is out of town, ill, or, like Bay, not anxious for my company. For hours I speak to no one. Sometimes I feel I never shall be able or even want to speak to anyone again. I miss Wellings fearfully. I knew I was leaning on him too heavily for mental support. I feel as though I begin to look vacuous but what can I do and where can I go? I dread the long winter ahead and I dread Leighton Buzzard [Bedfordshire, where her school was evacuated] nearly as much as I did Maudsley Hospital.

Tuesday, 7 November. Em and Editha on the phone. The dealer came and paid 35s for divan and wardrobe. He sent a man with a barrow to collect it. This person had hardly rung and my hand was only just on the door knob when that unwashed hag from downstairs [Mrs. Lucas] bounced up. She thrust her Gampian form in front of me, 'You can't take them things out single 'anded', she bawled. He said 'The man next door will give me a hand'. 'You wait till my 'ubby comes 'ome', she

---

1. This 1933 book was a biography of Marguerite Gardiner, Countess of Blessington, and Count Alfred Guillaume Gabriel d'Orsay.

squawked. 'He can't wait as long as that,' I interpolated, knowing an hour must elapse before Mr. Lucas came. 'I'll get a coalman to help,' said the man. 'No, yer won't. I doan 'ave no coalmen in my 'ouse,' yelled the virago. Finally he went off to get casual help. He returned with a beady-eyed scavenger. Meanwhile I stood white and silent with hatred. Had I spoken I would have sworn at the woman. I longed to kill her but thought she wasn't worth incarceration in Broadmoor. Went flat-hunting in Highgate. Viewed a three-room flat over a shop in the Village. The rooms were on the 3rd floor. The view was delightful, the smell was overpowering.

Wednesday, 8 November. Queen Wilhelmina and King Leopold have suggested acting as mediators but methinks profiteers and armaments-makers will be doing too well to listen to peace overtures. The broadcasts and press reports don't sound very hopeful. Here I was interrupted by the phone. It was Wellings – speaking from the West End! I nearly collapsed. He said he was all right, hadn't seen a doctor, and was in the West End having seen *Thark* [a 1927 farce by Ben Travers] this afternoon. I don't know whether he knows he has been ill. Went flat-hunting around Highgate Road district, quite in vain. It grows difficult to get small-size tinned goods.

Later. Excitement on excitement. Bay phoned. Just as she spoke the door-bell rang. My rabid imagination thought Wellings had come to kill me. I was afraid to open the door. I *never* have casual visitors. I called Mr. Lucas. The visitor proved to be Vera Mannering who wanted to know if I could tell her how to get back to service in London. She stayed a long while then took away the parchment certificate of Father's Masonic membership to see if her friend Tom Aunal could do anything about raising a loan for me. I felt guilty as I've never cared for Vera and have never been very complimentary when referring to her.

* * * * * *

Sunday, 12 November. Wellings on phone last night. I had hoped he would have invited me for tonight but he didn't. He didn't sound very normal, was slow in speech and said something about [how] he'd had a revelation from on high – something about a tail he'd seen in the sky. He said his brother had gone home. Called on Miss Astra Kamberian at 28 Devonshire Place. She has a flat under the eaves approached by a stairway narrow and winding. She was very young, very smart and very pleasant but I've no desire to live in what would be a death trap should fire break out. No one lives in the place except the housekeeper. Several doctors rent reception rooms there and after 6 p.m. the place is deserted. Walked most of the way home.

Monday, 13 November. Em phoned, otherwise unrelieved blankness.

When black-out meant octopus-darkness pulling me down into the pit, I went to the local cinema – Astoria [Seven Sisters Road, Islington] – and paid 1s to be bored inexpressedly and sickened by the stench of oranges, sweat and potato crisps. Claudette Colbert appeared in an idiotic picture. In it a man emerged from the river dripping wet, climbed into a car, drove off, got out and spoke with strangers and no one noticed his condition (not even the camera after he came ashore), nor did he make the car or the woman he kidnapped wet from contact with him. The second picture was all gangster stuff. Then came *'Arf a mo', Hitler*, a paean of praise of present-day Army conditions. The marvellous *obedience* of the marines was commented upon. It isn't obedience we want, it's rebellion.[2] Then came the Queen's speech – rank sentimentalism including twaddle about what she and the King suffered from being separated from their children!! As though they ever had any home life as working people know it! Our politicians appeared. How ugly they are! Bull-necked Churchill, smug Belisha, horse-faced Halifax, and Gort, gorilla-like. The only cheer forthcoming was for the wizened little Duke of Windsor – not unlike wee Georgie Wood. Told Mrs. Lucas I'd stay till after Xmas.

* * * * * *

Saturday, 25 November. Wellings phoned last night. Alas, he did not invite me for tomorrow as I had hoped.[3] To the doctor's this morning, also to the Library where a load of three new books awaited me.[4] Much housewifery today including cake-making which I haven't done for years. Queerly enough I find my improved health is all in response to the stimulus 'Thou shalt not be a nuisance', not to a positive one, but then I have no positive reason for going on. I have to admit I am grievously hurt by the Rosenbergs' indifference. Leonard doesn't even give a phone call, Leslie doesn't offer a loan, Marjorie and Clarrie alike offer no hospitality. The wind is very high again tonight making the house haunted by odd noises. Novelists so often describe 'a beautiful

---

2. 'What hypocrisy to talk of "our glorious dead" when we're bent on hustling another generation of corpses to join them! I could vomit.' These were her sentiments two days before, on Remembrance Day. Gladys did not abandon her pacifist sentiments. On 11 January 1940: 'To Em's and much inclined to weep by the way. A contingent of young Scottish soldiers marching along Eastern Avenue put the finishing touch. I could *smell* death and the thought of the "old men of the tribe" who send these boys into war infuriated me.' At this time in the 'phoney war', many women felt as she did.

3. 'Met Wellings by accident this morning,' she had written four days before, on 21 November, 'by appointment this evening. He looks strangely altered, has a strange, starry-eyed appearance and is very silent for a long time between speeches. Otherwise he seems normal though he is still very irritable.'

4. The previous day she had got from the Library Joseph D. Unwin's *Sex and Culture* (London: Oxford University Press, 1934). This long (over 600 pages), turgid, and wide-ranging academic anthropological study examines the 'connection between sexual opportunity and cultural behaviour' in numerous indigenous societies – in Melanesia, Africa, Polynesia, and the Americas. We doubt that Gladys read it from cover to cover.

character'; I've never met one. The very virtuous and worthy folk I've known have either been hard and unsympathetic to other folks' follies and only capable of enthusiasm for a 'cause' and its victims, or else they have been of such inferior intellects as to be almost morons. Miss Mary Monkhouse typified the former, Mrs. Richardson and the Misses Hardwick the latter.

Sunday, 26 November. Day of loneliness again. Cooking, letter-writing, reading. Phoned Bay and she *did* hurt my feelings. When I commented that she never gave me any news she said sourly 'You're never interested in *my* concerns'. This is a libel. Whether it was the Norse dictionary she said she'd publish or the house she actually achieved, I've tried to further her plans as best I could. I've spent money on her holidays, handed over clothes, and I even try to phone her at such a time as would not interfere with her conversations with Miss Wilshin or her listening in to *Band Waggon* which she so much admires.

Later. Bay phoned this evening to apologise for her words this morning. She has invited me for next Saturday. Am much enjoying Julian Tennyson's *Suffolk Scene*. It is very well written. His grandfather's mantle has presumably fallen upon him.[5] Is there anything more hypocritical than the BBC announcement that men at the Front will be prepared for confirmation and bishops will, if necessary, officiate in the trenches or immediately behind the lines. Chamberlain broadcasting tonight – 'soft-soaping' the Navy, Army and Air Force, talking about other people's discomforts – having none of his own. No evacuees are planted on him; *his* salary isn't cut.

Monday, 27 November. Lil wrote. She keeps moaning about increased cost of living – you'd think she was penniless. She says she can only afford to give 7s 6d for Xmas present *but* she is paying 8s 6d for a 5lb tin of toffees to give to the villages. Of course, it's *her* money ---![6] Vera left a note asking for help in teaching Arithmetic and English as she is an Infants' Teacher ordinarily. I left a detailed account at her house. Some cooking today. Talked to Em. To my great astonishment found last night I was menstruating again after a fortnight's interval.

Tuesday, 28 November. Needless to say Editha did not phone as promised. She can't bear to part with 4d. I find I'm getting very bitter again,

---

5. This 1939 book is subtitled *A book of description and adventure.* Unlike many books she liked, it is non-sociological, impressionistic, and highly subjective.
6. In a more positive vein, on 17 November Gladys recorded that 'Lil sent a big box of apples, pears, jam and sweets'. (Two years before, on 9 October 1937, she had observed that Lil 'has always been wonderful to me,' especially in her generosity.) Gladys did not like being in her sister's debt, or the debt of others, and often was. This sometimes caused her embarrassment. 'I have no right to be in need,' she wrote the next week, on 5 December. 'I shall hope to be more thrifty in future.'

echoing Jaques 'Most friendship is feigning, most loving mere folly'.[7] I can't say anyone except Em among my intimate friends and acquaintances has made any effort to relieve my gloom. Not even a phone call from Leonard. I am worried about myself. I find that, although I fight off the dread melancholia that engulfed Fred and Mother enough to go about, like them I look backwards continually and just wait for the end. The black octopus has its coils gripping me fast today. I went to Leicester Square Theatre to see the much praised English film *The Night of the Fire*. I don't echo the praise. Diana Wynyard is badly made up, badly cast and badly spoken. Why she can't study a working woman's manner of speech before playing such a part I don't know. She was just as poor a representative in *Pygmalion*. Ralph Richardson is no better. He looks wooden; he moves slowly; he *never* suggests passion; and he seems to imagine that an occasional 'ain't', an equally occasional dropped aspirate, suggest the small shopkeeper. Quite a number of small shopkeepers and shop assistants speak correctly. It is their accent and their servility that 'gives them away'. Miss Monkhouse wrote. I wrote to Ada and Lily.

Wednesday, 29 November. Em and Editha on phone. Mr. Kiernan's father is dead. To Glenloch Road to look at a flat and, on the spot, decided I wanted it and no other, but the house is empty save for a schoolmistress evacuated and therefore home only at weekends. It's a nice house, well decorated, and bathroom, stairs and lavatory cleaned by landlady's 'char'. Rent is 23s and the flat is self-contained save bath and lav shared with schoolmistress. I've left it at this – as soon as the other occupants go in I'll take the flat if no one else has taken it meanwhile. Education officer wrote. Further sick pay refused but I shall get money for Xmas holiday when I return. Wrote thanking him for information and asking if I might hope to work in London area when I started work again. Wrote to Bank Manager about overdraft, also to Mr. Pickering and Lil.

Thursday, 30 November. Had a terrible night so 'doped' myself with bromide. LCC sent cheque for £5 2s 7d, salary to November 6th. It will nearly clear, together with my savings, the new Income Tax Assessment. Mr. Kingston, landlord of Glenloch Road flat, wrote. I replied. Russia bombed Helsinki! What devils men are to each other! I'm getting terrified by this all engulfing melancholy. By late evening it has got me throttled. I don't even know if a removal to Glenloch Road would cure me. I *ought* to commit suicide. I'm of no use to anyone. The only people who care for me are fogeys like the Pyrland Road dames.

---

7.   Shakespeare, *As You Like It*, Act II, scene vii; these words were actually spoken by Amiens.

Friday, 1 December. Letter from Miss Hyde, the woman I met in the Corner House just before war broke out. To Bank and interviewed Manager, a toothy person full of fat laughter. He urged me not to go to moneylenders or to reversionary societies whose terms were prohibitive. He advised appealing to the LCC for an advance. Finally he said the Bank would grant me an overdraft if I could find a reputable guarantor. I've written to tell Leslie this to see what happens. As a matter of fact I can borrow from Em and pay her 5%. To Miss Hardwicks this afternoon. There they sit, two desiccated spinsters, calm in a world of chaos. Stopped two small boys in Hackney to enquire if any schools were open. Gayhurst Road and Eleanor Road are so I'm hoping I shall get employment in London and not have to have my beloved cat destroyed. Mr. Gaye wrote inviting me to a dramatic reading of an Anthroposophist writer at Caxton Hall tomorrow but I'm going out with Bay. Feel less melancholy today.

Saturday, 2 December. Hurried to meet Bay at noon. Phoned Mr. Kingston that I would call tomorrow regarding the flat in Glenloch Road. After a mid-day meal at Bay's had cross country walk to Ruislip where we bought cards for Xmas. Back to tea and talk and then Miss Wilshin came in. She ages like I do and her mouth *is* hard. Dreary journey home in the unlit train.[8]

Sunday, 3 December. Cooking this morning. To Belsize Park by 3 p.m. and Mr. Kingston showed me the flat. The two rooms, bedroom and kitchenette, *are* small but the sitting room is very nice and he has had the landing and kitchenette fitted with brown inlaid lino. He's a small, perky man with false teeth, and too warm a manner (shook hands and said 'Goodbye, Gladys'). The wife gave me tea and I sat in for a while talking to her. She's 60, has a tic and an inane smile but apparently isn't as silly as she looks. Her husband is apparently not on too good terms with her. He has a separate bedroom and says he couldn't retire – he'd hate to be at home all day. Twice she made reference (in his absence) to her plans for possible widowhood. He wants six months agreement, a month's rent in advance and there will be a clause against animals, washing and musical instruments. I've said I'll take it. I hope I'm doing right. I actually prayed for guidance – without much hope of it's coming to me.[9]

Each time I passed Wellings' flat [which was nearby] he was standing in front of the window with a small mirror in his hand, combing and re-arranging his hair! He looked mad. I hope he won't call on me and

8. In wartime the lighting in trains at night was severely dimmed or shut off entirely.
9. The deal fell through, partly because the landlord decided to insist on a lease for a year. He also said 'he could not waive the rule about domestic animals in the agreement but he gave me verbal permission to keep a cat' (5 December). This was a time when landlords were struggling to find tenants since many Londoners had fled the metropolis.

kill me if I go to Glenloch Road – half kill me, I mean. I long to die.
I'm very gloomy. I hate Sundays. Bay phoned.

*Wellings made a few more appearances in Gladys's diary. 'Tonight
Wellings phoned,' she wrote on 16 December, 'but alas, how he is
altered. He doesn't appear to grasp what one says and there are long
blanks when he neither speaks nor replies when spoken to.' 'Apparently he wanders off during the black-out and is found in odd places
– brought home once by a taxi-man from the Albert Memorial!' (17
December). From time to time Gladys tried to make some sense of
Wellings' disorder. 'I wonder', she wrote on 31 December, 'if Wellings' recent preoccupation with Swift was due to a feeling of menace
at his own approaching mental disintegration. He is of the same type,
bitter but concise in speech and peculiar in his dealings with women.'
Several weeks later, on 18 February 1940, Gladys 'Phoned Clowser
for news of Wellings. He says W. is still peculiar, no longer religious
but pleasure-loving. Was lost for ten days and found at Regents Palace
Hotel where he'd taken his meals in bed for ten days and his pleasure
where he could.' On 4 March Gladys was told by Mrs. Murray that
'Wellings is no better, refuses to see anyone, lies in bed till midday and
never goes near his shops'; and several weeks later Gladys met her old
companion on Shaftesbury Avenue – 'He looked dirty and unkempt and
most peculiar' (13 April). (This is the last we hear of Wellings for some
time, though he reappears in her diary later in the war.)*

Monday, 4 December. Income Tax authorities wrote. They announce
balance due will be deducted from rest of salary when I begin earning
again. Lil wrote. Mrs. Haughton wrote too. Her monkey is ill. Editha
on phone. She said she would guarantee my overdraft if I liked. She
has points in her favour and probably doesn't realise how often she
speaks harshly. Mrs. Godfrey is unwell so I left 1s worth of yellow
chrysanthemums for her.

Later. To Pyrland Road. Those old ladies *are* kindly. They prepare
an elaborate meal for me and they are doing very badly now I know.
They are very anxious I should go to them and I could have their flat for
17s but there's no bath, [and] the house is dark and silent and I cannot
endure that. All the same I'm not at all sure I want to go to Hampstead.
I wish someone could decide for me. That's how my nervous illness
manifests itself. I can't drive myself into action and for so long I've
identified myself with Highbury I shall feel like a dislodged hermit
crab away from it.[10] It's partly the cat I worry about. Oh, I am tired!

10. 'One reason I cling to Highbury is because so many people know me here' (5 December).
    Gladys, clearly, needed to feel connected, and often did not.

Miss Hammond phoned. She's settling down at Soulbury now.[11] Mr. Fitzpatrick is back in London, teaching.

Gladys continued to search for new housing, and she continued to be hard up for money. She was still worried at the prospect that she might be evacuated with schoolchildren, and she pointed out to an education officer that 'my screaming nightmares make me to be regarded by landladies or hosts as a nuisance or a peculiar person and this fact aggravates my original disability' (6 December). The next day she heard from a friend that 'many of the teachers are very badly accommodated'. However, as children started to return in droves to their urban homes, the threat of evacuation receded, and a doctor Gladys saw was to recommend to the LCC that she not be required to leave London (12 December); perhaps all this accounts in part for the lifting of her depression. 'I feel a little better and slept fairly well' (7 December). 'Feel more cheerful than I've felt for weeks,' she wrote on 12 December. 'If only I could meet fresh people!' On 19 December, 'Everyone says I'm looking so much better', and three days later 'Despite fog and frost I really feel well at last.' Mood swings were central to her personality and she seems to have been rarely free of them; of one acquaintance she remarked, 'she's more unbalanced than I am myself' (10 January 1940).

Tuesday, 2 January 1940. Many soldiers in steel helmets on motorcycles about today. Editha phoned. She says McGuire's son is a conscientious objector and went up before the Tribunal supported only by his mother (Maud Davies). The young man was exempted as a Civil Servant in the Public Trustee's office. Sybil Goddard came up here this morning, squatting *an hour* in my kitchen waiting for a phone message

11.   Soulby is a village in Buckinghamshire, near Leighton Buzzard, Bedfordshire, where the children at Gladys's school had been evacuated and then billeted there and in the surrounding area. On 9 December Miss Hammond phoned Gladys and 'told of Mrs. Beale whose twin children have been evacuated and for whose keep she is charged nothing. The foster parents have mended clothes and boots till they will mend no more and they applied to Miss Hammond for new clothes. She wrote to the mother who declared her husband was in a mental hospital, she only had 15s 6d weekly and she had to pay 5s 6d weekly for a visit to her husband. She wrote to the foster parent (a chauffeur) in quite a different strain, abused him, told him she'd reported him to LCC, billeting officer, and Public Assistance Board. She then wrote to his employer and tried to get the man dismissed.' Two days later Gladys met Miss Hammond at Old Street for coffee. 'She also says the Hoxton children have terrible fights in the village streets and throw stones at whatever is breakable.' Such unflattering stories were commonplace in connection with evacuees; however, one rarely knows how reliable the alleged facts were, and how responsibility might be justly apportioned. There is no doubt that problems with evacuation were perceived by most people in late 1939, wherever they chose to lodge the blame. Such a massive and inevitably disruptive scheme was bound to generate vast numbers of individual complaints, and probably much regrettable behaviour.
      In September and October 1939 the *Leighton Buzzard Observer* was full of reports, many of them unfavourable, concerning the arrival of these Londoners.

from her sweetheart. *Then* it came when I was at lunch and she had gone home! To London Teachers' Association Emergency meeting at Northern Polytechnic at 2 p.m. Only a score of people present. They all knew one another and gaily proceeded to compliment one another publicly before voting one another into position. Of course the fault lies with people like me who rarely, if ever, attend meetings. An elderly woman, a Mrs. Good, attached herself to me and began to carp at the farcical business. Queer tales were told! Schools have been rigged up as mortuaries, some for people unhoused by air-raids. Cups and mugs stand waiting for drinkers – like the collapsible coffins at St. Bartholomew's. ARP wardens give orders to teachers! Schools recently re-modelled by ratepayers' money are defaced and damaged by Auxiliary Fire Service and ARP occupants! One thousand, seven hundred teachers are back in London. Marjorie Rose on phone. Mr. Haffner is staying on with her.[12]

Wednesday, 3 January. Murray sent a delightful letter and a box of Hanover wafers. He is 'called up' in February and is indignant as he disapproves of war but, being a member of no sect, he stands no chance as C.O. [conscientious objector] before a tribunal. He said a woman said 'The King, Chamberlain, Hore-Belisha,[13] etc. go to the Front. Why shouldn't you?' Murray replied 'They go to *look* and then *they* come back. That's the difference!' He says he can't feel moved to kill a German; if he encounters a good-looking one, he'll feel inclined to go closer to admire him, for he'd hate to destroy anything pleasing to the eye! God send us more 'pansies' say I. Oscar Wilde a criminal, and Napoleon a hero! I ask you!

And *how* ugly London is now. Cold weather causes women to wear most hideous garments, hoods round moon-faces, kerchiefs around the hatchet type. Fat females and lean hags in trousers, greasy suede jackets. Oh Eve! Where are thy charms? Em on phone. Says Denys has a job as junior inspector at rubber works at Eastwood. I doubt if he'll hold it a month. Window cleaner says Mrs. Thomas (of 50 Highbury Park) has two rooms to let and wished I would take them. I told him to tell her *I* was prepared to bury the hatchet. Pipes all frozen

12. On 22 December Gladys had been informed that this relationship was over, and that Marjorie Rose complained that Alec Haffner 'is thriftless, spending money as soon as he makes it, giving her only £1 weekly and leaving her to bear the brunt of the expenses.' But Gladys evinced little sympathy for her acquaintance. 'She might have realised a young man in his thirties was only using her (in her forties) because he was pressed for a home. She has to wear a wig. She is a fool and he is a cultured and travelled man.' Gladys usually treated men more tenderly than women (though her brother-in-law Herbert Challis was an exception).
13. Leslie Hore-Belisha, Secretary of State for War, was in fact about to be dismissed from this position.

here.[14] Washing one's self is a major problem. I'd like to know what's behind the Unity Mitford business? I suppose the bled-white ratepayer finances the armed guard on the Quay.[15]

There were three major changes in Gladys's life this month. First, her beloved cat, Lallie, became very ill and either died naturally or had to be put down (she is not clear on this point). Second, she resumed teaching, on 22 January, though hardly enthusiastically, at Hamond Square school – 'How I hate work!' continued to be her sentiment (5 January). Third, she finally moved residence, on 25 January – not into another flat but rather into a boarding house, the Woodstock, Highbury Grange, N5, 'a residential hotel where I'm to pay 32s 6d for bed and breakfast and Sunday luncheon. It accommodates 60 guests, has billiard, card and writing rooms, a dining room like a Soho restaurant and a cocktail bar. I think I may enjoy it there' (17 January). In making this move she had to dispose of much of her furniture.

Saturday, 27 January. So much has been happening I've had no time to write.[16] Letters have poured in including one from Ginsbury and one from Mr. Gaye, who will take me out on Monday. I've made innumerable visits to Pyrland Road and Lucases have been most unpleasant, causing me to damage a lot of my goods. I sold my bed for a pound. I've visited Em in an awful snow storm. Today I saw Cronin's film *Stars Look Down* and enjoyed it immensely. The producer even dared an unhappy ending. I've settled down at Woodstock and like it immensely. It won't be a cheaper way of living but it will be pleasanter. The first night I had dinner here and sat at table with some of the smallest fry of the film world. The two women were pleasant, the young man was adorable, plain, dressed in the queer fustian manner beloved of modern youth, with all its extravagance of speech, irreverence of manner and with a rich vocabulary and a wide range of topics. Still no word of Wellings. LCC sent me a cheque for £6 6s 1d so I promptly sent Leonard £5 and the Income Tax people have been paid £2 7s 0d by the LCC.

Sunday, 28 January. Despite heavy snowfall I went to Bay's.[17] Alas!

---

14. The early weeks of 1940 were exceptionally frigid. 'Shop assistants are wearing outdoor coats behind the counter,' Gladys reported on 20 January. 'Every day becomes *more* arctic. Now *all* the water pipes are frozen!' (21 January).

15. Unity Mitford was notorious as a Nazi-sympathiser and friend of Hitler. She chose to stay in Germany after the outbreak of war, later attempted suicide, and was subsequently sent to Switzerland in poor health, from whence at the beginning of 1940 she was taken by her family back to Britain, where many thought she should be interned. She was allowed to retire to Oxfordshire and avoid imprisonment.

16. Her diary entries earlier this week were brief and, unusually, she did not write at all on Thursday and Friday.

17. Bay probably lived in Acton at 5 Cumberland Park for most of the 1930s; Mary Wilshin was often listed at this residence as well. Sometime in 1939 Bay moved to 15 The Grove in

Trains were stopped later and I could not get back so I had to stay the night.

Monday, 29 January. What a nightmare experience! To Hillingdon Station before 7.30 a.m. to find a lengthy queue awaiting tickets. Those obtained, we crowded onto platform like a veritable shoal of herrings, waiting, waiting, waiting for a train. After 8 a.m. one arrived but no one knew its destination, though we all clambered in. Movement was impossible. Gas masks bruised my breasts, attaché cases assaulted my buttocks. I chatted with a few, grinned understandably at many. A woman fainted but could not fall. Finally we were ejected at Baker Street and a worse scrum began. Almost suffocated, I emerged at Moorgate to travel by bus to Hoxton – at an equally slow rate. So I was late for the second time in 20 years! Mr. Gaye phoned me to meet him at Piccadilly at 6 p.m.

Tuesday, 30 January. I wonder if I do make progress in Gaye's affection? He beamed as much as I did when we met. We decided on a cinema – his choice. He called a taxi and off we skidded, chuckling and chatting. In the cinema, we chuckled more, leaning towards each other like young lovers. Then the programme ended, we went to the Criterion brasserie for supper. Here we sat till 11 o'clock, talking, talking! I suggested his coming here to dinner and he accepted at once – for next Thursday. Joy![18] School *is* wearisome. The age and attainments of children range so widely work is well nigh impossible. The lack of discipline adds to one's trials. Children dash about like maniacs, yell and bawl like Indian braves in battle. By 3.30 p.m. I'm worn out. Now my wireless functions. I gave porter 2s 6d.

Wednesday, 31 January. Weather conditions remain appalling. The roads were like glass this morning and had I not been warned by the wireless I should certainly have fallen from top to bottom of the house steps. Yet tiny children came to school. The dinner-hour arguments were as fierce as ever, mainly political in tone. Leo wrote. His wife has had a bad fall. My spirits are much higher and I'm sleeping well. Went into lounge tonight for an hour but no one said a word to me. Two silly young women talked of their illnesses and the family of three did crosswords. Am reading David Garnett's *Go She Must!* because

---

Hillingdon, where she was still living after the war. For help in tracing her movements, we are indebted to Carolynne Cotton at the Hillingdon Local Studies, Archives and Museum Service and Amanda Knights of the Acton History Group.

18. Earlier this month, when she was wishing she had more friends, she emphasised that she wanted 'normal friends, not like Wellings or even Mr. Gaye with his peculiar religious views', which she did not specify (9 January). Wellings was still in the picture in 1943. After an evening with him on 1 June, she asked herself, 'Why does fate foist on to me a man I like so little?'

Charles bought it for me. The descriptive passages are prose poetry but the story is one of the most shapeless and improbable I've read.[19]

In the following weeks there was not a lot to cheer Gladys up, though she was 'very flattered' by the suggestion of one man that 'I should do play and film reviews for the papers' (1 March). Her moods were, as usual, decidedly variable. At least her new residential arrangements made for some new friends and acquaintances, including a refugee doctor with whom she spent a fair amount of time. On 8 March she went walking with Leonard: 'We have no common tastes now, only common memories.' 'Everybody seems uneasy about the possible course of the war,' she remarked on 6 March, though actual references to the war almost vanish from her writing, at least until mid-April. 'War news disheartening,' she wrote on 18 April. 'I think the whole of Europe will be embroiled. Oh, God, give us peace!' Gladys's 'diary habit', as she called it, was becoming wobbly; indeed, she was threatening to end it. During more than two months after 18 April she wrote on only four days. The following are her last two diary entries for 1940.

Friday, 28 June. Everything in a state of flux! Quite suddenly it was sprung upon us that, as schools are to remain open, teachers' holidays are to be reduced and to begin immediately being staggered. I said I'd have the period no one else wanted and had July 1st onwards. I'm in high favour among Head Teachers. Both Mrs. Spalding at the Whitmore and Miss Hocken at St. John's want me for teaching boys. The former is fat, cheerful and kindly. The latter is lean, toothy and cattish. How I wish someone would set me free from the schoolroom! The latest idea is that invaders should not know their whereabouts, parachutists their points of local attack, so postal numbers, phone exchanges, district names are all being blotted out, but often posters remain or bus timetables should clues be needed. Fields are all trenched and sand heaps are everywhere. There's a rumour that Chamberlain is running a peace party dissension among Conservatives.[20]

Wednesday, 17 July. Queer psychological fact! I have commented favourably on several occasions on James Huxtable, a very tall, good-

---

19. This 1939 Penguin book was originally published by Chatto & Windus in 1927 and may well have spoken to some women readers between the wars. In one passage (p. 89 in 1927 edn.) the author wrote of an unfulfilled young woman, daughter of a clergyman: 'All her experiences had been no more than to pour out tea, and to teach in the Sunday school. Other women of her age she knew were able to be bank clerks, or the secretaries of business men, they worked in Government offices, they did typewriting, indeed there seemed nothing women did not do, but Anne doubted very much if she could become a useful person of that kind.'

20. Neville Chamberlain, who had resigned as Prime Minister on 10 May, was a member of Churchill's five-man War Cabinet and continued to be the leader of the Conservative Party. By November he was dead.

looking laughing lad of 14. I have not slapped a child since I resumed teaching – six months – but, for a piffling misdemeanour, I pounced upon him and spanked him violently. Quite suddenly I felt ashamed for I realised I had wanted to *touch* the boy who looks most like a man.[21] To Tatler tonight. In West End there are illuminated street names and taxis bear an illuminated sign.

At this point Gladys's diary is discontinued – for over a year. Thus we have no evidence as to how she coped with and reacted to the raids on and widespread damage to the city she loved – at least loved when she was in humour. She resumed regular diary-keeping on 21 July 1941, when the attacks on London had virtually ceased, and thereafter she had little to say about the war or its impact, and continued to write mainly about her social life (or the lack of one that satisfied her) and her intellectual and leisure engagements.

21. Two years later she admitted that at her then school 'my annoyance is heightened by the knowledge that I shall not always keep these top class boys but shall have younger lads who do not satisfy my thwarted sex instinct' (7 October 1942). 'I sometimes wonder', she remarked a couple of months later, 'whether my affection for these elder boys is not born of sex-hunger' (12 December 1942).

173

EPILOGUE

Gladys's frustrated ambitions continued to be a theme in her life during the 1940s. 'Reading Howard Spring's book *In the Meantime* [1942] fills me with sick longing for a literary life. If only I had been permitted to take up journalism![1] Now I grow too old for adventure. I suppose I shall teach till I die' (1 September 1942). But then she had moments of buoyancy that take the reader by surprise – diaries as sources are good at disclosing about-turns, ambivalences, and contradictory feelings. 'Reading *Life of Octavia Hill* – very interesting [28 October 1942]. I should enjoy a career like that – understudying God, so to speak.'[2] She even this day spoke well of teaching: 'It is strange how engrossed I am nowadays in my work and how great is my affection for these boys I teach. I think my long dormant maternal interests must at last be aroused. I would willingly give a night a week to running a club in Hoxton if I could get accommodation and be free from political or religious interference.' (Gladys had little taste for politics.) Judgments, as usual, continue to abound, some of them pointed: 'Am reading *A Cornish Childhood* [1942] by [A. L.] Rowse. He *is* unpleasant, self-righteous and colossally conceited. He reminds me of myself' (23 September 1942). Other judgments – plenty of them – were recorded of her fellow residents at the Woodstock Hotel, which became the centrepiece of much of her social life. As one would expect of any residential hotel in the 1940s, people came and went, and friendships, such as they were, tended to be fleeting.

Leonard had not entirely disappeared, and on 2 July 1943 Gladys wrote at length about the state of their relationship. 'I hurried home as we had a half-holiday, changed, and set off to meet Leonard. And what a burden of emotion I have cast off where he is concerned! It is as though I had never loved him for a quarter of a century, never been

---

1. Howard Spring was a Welsh-born (1889) journalist, novelist, and book reviewer who worked for the *Manchester Guardian* and various other papers. After his death, three long essays were pulled together as *The Autobiography of Howard Spring* (London: Collins, 1972). 'In the Meantime', the middle section, covers June through September 1941. The author described his work as follows: 'This book is being what I intended it to be: a bag into which I shall drop a jumble of random thoughts and happenings' (p. 73). On 15 May 1943 Gladys said she would have liked to have been a reporter; and later she spoke of her desire 'to break into a literary circle' (28 December 1944).
2. Octavia Hill, 1838–1912, was a prominent and widely admired social reformer who was active in fighting urban poverty. *Life of Octavia Hill as told in her Letters* (1913) was edited by C. Edmund Maurice. Gladys may, though, have been reading the just-published *Octavia Hill: A Biography*, by E. Moberly Bell.

175

his mistress. Our "love has turned to kindliness"; it may not even be as warm an emotion as that. My heart does not stir, my colour no longer rises at sight of him; his voice no longer sounds in my ear as liquid music. He is just a middle-aged bore, boasting of his prowess as [an] official in various Societies and Associations. He inveighs against the working classes, assures *me* I am well placed – on my meagre salary! We went by bus to Highgate, had tea in the village (he gives no tip), sat in the Waterlow Park a while, and I finally walked with him to the 609 bus route and limped home!' (She had a sore foot.) From time to time she revisited this painful fact of lost love. 'My love for Leonard is as dead as last year's flowers,' she wrote on 21 February 1944. 'I no longer crave his touch nor long to be in his arms.' She saw him rarely and 'when I do my heart no longer stirs at sight of him [11 July 1944]. Something died in me when my love for him died.' She was finding him a bore – 'smug' and 'patronising' were two words she used to describe him (8 December 1944): 'I grieve to realise I shouldn't care if we never met again.'

Gladys continued to keep a diary for most of the rest of her life, and extracts have appeared in several books. There are around seventy-five references to her writing in the three weighty and authoritative volumes on British society between 1945 and 1959 by the distinguished historian of postwar Britain, David Kynaston.[3] She appears never to have moved from Highbury. At the time of her death on 24 July 1972 she was a resident of Highbury Home, 1 Highbury Terrace, having moved there not long before from a flat at Beaver House, 47 Highbury Park (across the road from her home in 1936), where she had been living during at least the previous decade. Gladys died at the age of eight-two, leaving her entire estate of £1374.92 'unto my friends' Albert and Irene Friend, a married couple who lived in Highgate. Albert, it appears, had been entrusted a few months earlier, sometime in 1971, to deposit her thirty-seven diary-notebooks in the Islington Local History Centre, where they have remained since.

---

3. *Austerity Britain, 1945–51* (2007), *Family Britain, 1951–57* (2009), and *Modernity Britain: Opening the Box, 1957–59* (2013), all published in London by Bloomsbury.

APPENDIX A

Gladys's enthusiasm for writing for its own sake, and entertainingly, is nicely revealed in her account of the two days in 1938 immediately after Christmas Day, which she had spent with Em and her family. This writing reads as if it might have appeared in a piece of fiction. And for Gladys it was, in part, a means of venting in style.

Monday, 26 December, 1938. Heavy snowstorm when I left Ilford and journey home a sodden experience. Rather different welcome home from what there once was – no fire, ashes from Saturday in grate and dirty platters still piled high. Mrs. Barber[1] invited me down to her tonight's party (drink by the barrel and bottle much in evidence). I thanked her, accepted a glass of sherry but refused the invitation. I expect I shall suffer their guests' merriment tonight. The birds are so wretched.

Later. I hate aeroplanes and wireless at times. The former makes uproar in the heavens, the latter makes tumult on earth. Down below people talk, dance and sing above the riot of sound from wireless and gramophone. Why must people make a noise in enjoying themselves? Am reading Orioli's *Adventures of a Bookseller* – quite entertaining but *very* gross.[2] I'm getting furious with Barbers. They use my phone as though it were their own. I cannot help noticing how contemptuous I grow of other people's amusements, their choice of wireless programmes and the like.

Tuesday, 27 December. Barbers didn't have a party, they had a Hogarthian orgy. People stamped, screamed, yelled and howled till 2

---

1. Doris Maude Barber and Walter Edward Barber were the other two tenants at 4 Northolme Road.
2. Guiseppi Orioli, *Adventures of a Bookseller* (London: Chatto & Windus, 1938) has a picaresque, earthy quality and is full of low-life encounters. For example, one 'Signora Veronica … had been a singer at one of those third-rate music-halls in the Via Bassi, where they had a kind of carpeted table for a stage, and where, after a song or two, the women went round collecting halfpennies on a tray and having their buttocks pinched by everyone' (p. 148); and on Armistice Day in London in 1918 'a Canadian soldier embraced me in front of the Monico café, swore that we two had won the War, and then, out of sheer joy, gave me a severe bite in the ear. I had to have it disinfected at a chemist's' (p. 167). Some years later, in pursuit of 'my annual liver cure at Montecatini', he spent a few days 'drinking the water furiously among a crowd of over-fat priests and peasants and women who were doing the same and trying to soften their livers. The three or four hundred water-closets at the Tettuccio had not much rest during those mornings' (p. 216).

a.m. Mr. Lucas asked them to be quieter and to have mercy on his ceilings but they merely became abusive. Processions up and down the stairs to the wc were more like streams of ants going to and fro to fetch food or slaves to carry eggs into the sunlight. My bed rocked like a ship in a storm and I couldn't even doze till nearly 3 o'clock. This morning I began to do some laundering when Mrs. Lucas burst in without knocking, screaming, 'For Gawd's sake, don't throw any more water down the sink. You're bringing down Mrs. Barber's ceiling.' I could hear that worthy shrieking down below and I feared a brawl. Result – I've an appalling headache and I'm shaking like a leaf. Mrs. Lucas never brought up any dinner. I suppose in the tumult she forgot I'd paid for it last week.

While Gladys was often bored, she struggled against it, and certainly aspired to sparkle, whether on the page or in society. Her diaries were, in part, opportunities for her to entertain herself. Years later, on 5 June 1946, she visited her doctor and heard words from him that must have reassured her. 'He said he was sorry I was ill but pleased to see me as I always entertained him and he was never sure whether I ought to pay him or he to pay me – an entertainment tax.'

APPENDIX B

BOOKS READ

Gladys clearly read a lot and attended dozens of cultural events in the course of a year. Since our diary selections inevitably disclose only some of this evidence, this Appendix strives to present a more-or-less comprehensive list of what, for her, made up the 'life of the mind' in a period of around twelve months.

Happily, in or around the second week of October 1937 she compiled two book lists for the preceding year, one of fiction, one of non-fiction. It is likely that these are books that she had read during the twelve months since October 1936, when the first workbook of her surviving diaries begins. Here are the titles she named.[1]

Fiction

1. H. Hull, *Morning Shows the Day* (1936)
2. J. Dratler, *Manhattan Side Street* (1936)
3. B. Goolden, *Wise Generations* (1936)
4. J. Metcalfe, *Foster Girl* (1936)
5. A. Calder Marshall, *Dead Centre* (1935)
6. A. S. Turnbull, *The Rolling Years* (1936)
7. Henry Fielding, *Tom Jones* (1749)
8. L. Halward, *To Tea on Sunday* (1936)
9. J. van Drulen, *And then You Wish* (1936)
10. E. Hibbitt, *The Brittlesnaps* (1937)
11. A. Kandel, *City for Conquest* (1936)
12. M. Anand, *The Coolie* (1936)
13. S. Blumenfeld, *Phineas Khan* (1937)
14. M. Deans, *Not With Me* (1937)
15. D. Parker, *After Such Pleasures* (1934)

---

1. All titles and named authors have been checked for accuracy against the catalogue of the British Library. Corrections have been made to her facts where necessary and dates of publication added when known.

16. M. Booth, *Monday's a Long Day* (1937)
17. G. Douglas, *House with the Green Shutters* (1901)
18. W. Y. Darling, *Down but not Out* (1935)
19. P. Mulloy, *Jackets Green* (1936)
20. J. Hilton, *Catherine Herself* (1920)
21. R. Anderson, *Commercial Hotel* (1936)
22. Wynyard Browne, *The Fire and the Fiddle* (1937)
23. D. Runyon, *More than Somewhat* (1937)
24. A. J. Cronin, *The Citadel* (1937)
25. G. Brandon, *Upon this Rock* (1936)
26. M. Roberts, *The Private Life of Henry Maitland* (1912)
27. L. Zugsmith, *A Time to Remember* (1937)
28. J. Curtis, *You're in the Racket, too* (1937)
29. R. Westerby, *Wide Boys Never Work* (1937)

At this point there is an unexplained gap in her listing, for no numbers for fiction appear between 30 and 44. Perhaps the list of these novels failed to get recorded; or perhaps she simply erred in her numbering and no titles are actually missing.

45. S. Goodyear, *Cathedral Close* (1936)
46. J. Hampson, *Saturday Night at the Greyhound* (1937)
47. J. Marston, *The Rocket* (1936)
48. E. D. Hall, *Tambour Terrace* (1936)
49. E. Meredith, *The Wainwrights* (1936)
50. A. Huxley, *Limbo* (1920)
51. M. South, *Apology for a Mercenary* (1933)
52. G. Cornwallis West, *Fortune's Favourites* (1935)
53. P. Stucley, *Private Stars* (1936)

Non-fiction

1. Rom Landau, *Seven: An Essay in Confession* (1936)
2. E. Samson, *Just Imagine! A book of un-natural history* (1933)
3. ——, *Walls Have Tongues*
4. H. Belloc, *New Cautionary Tales* (1930)
5. T. Benson, *Muddling Through, or Britain in a Nutshell* (1936)
6. T. Burke, *The Real East End* (1932)
7. J. Worby, *The Other Half: The Autobiography of a Spiv* (1937)
8. S. A. Clark, *Holland on £10*
9. G. Kaus, *Catherine the Great* (1935)
10. P. Eipper, *Circus: Men, Beasts and Joys of the Road* (1931)
11. E. T. Woodhall, *Secrets of Scotland Yard* (1936)
12. C. Petrie, *The History of Government* (1929)
13. N. Bentley, *Die? I thought I'd laugh* (1936)
14. H. R. Oswald, *Memoirs of a London Coroner* (1936)

15. D. Malone, *The Last Landfall* (1936)
16. H. Kingsmill, *Frank Harris* (1932)
17. H. Pearson, *Tom Paine, Friend of Mankind* (1937)
18. H. Massingham, *I Took off my Tie* (1936)
19. E. V. Lucas, *Only the Other Day: A Volume of Essays* (1936)
20. J. Laver, *'Vulgar Society': The Romantic Career of James Tissot, 1836–1902* (1936)
21. C. Oman, *Henrietta Maria* (1936)
22. A. Maberley, *Commonsense and Psychology* (1936)
23. B. Harvey, *Growing Pains: An Autobiography* (1937)
24. H. Snell, *Men, Movements and Myself* (1936)
25. A. Compton-Rickett, *I Look Back: Memoirs of Fifty Years* (1933)
26. S. McKechnie, *Popular Entertainment through the Ages* (1931)
27. C. E. Vulliamy, *Royal George* (1937)
28. S. Freud, *Inhibitions, Symptoms and Anxiety* (1936)
29. L. Cope Cornford, *William Ernest Henley* (1913)
30. C. Crow, *Four Hundred Million Customers* (1937)
31. S. E. Rasmussen, *London: The Unique City* (1937)
32. M. Eastman, *Enjoyment of Laughter* (1937)
33. F. Swinnerton, *Swinnerton: An Autobiography* (1937)
34. R. Benchley, *The Treasurer's Report, and other aspects of community singing* (1930)
35. S. Kent Wright, *Speaking After Dinner* (1936)
36. R. Bayne Powell, *Eighteenth-Century London Life* (1937)
37. J. L. Hammond, *Growth of Common Enjoyment* (1933)
38. A. Gide, *Back from the U.S.S.R.* (1937)
39. R. B. Utter and G. B. Needham, *Pamela's Daughters* (1937)
40. P. Gosse, *Traveller's Rest* (1937)
41. N. Coward, *Present Indicative* (1937)
42. R. B. Mowat, *The Age of Reason* (1934)
43. M. Lambert, *When Victoria Began to Reign* (1937)
44. L. Randall, *The Famous Cases of Sir Bernard Spilsbury* (1936)
45. E. N. Marais, *The Soul of the White Ant* (1937)
46. H. Kingsmill, *Samuel Johnson* (1933)
47. B. Roberts, *Sir Travers Humphreys* (1936)
48. W. Teeling, *Gods of Tomorrow: The Story of a Journey in Asia and Australasia* (1936)
49. Cumberland Clark, *Shakespeare and Psychology* (1936)
50. M. Hillis, *Live Alone and Like It: A Guide for the Extra Woman* (1937)
51. C. Bax, *Inland Far: A Book of Thoughts and Impressions* (1925)
52. W. S. Berridge, *Marvels of the Animal World* (1921)
53. N. Bentley, *Ballet-Hoo* (1937)
54. M. Burr, *A Fossicker in Angola* (1933)

55. S. Freud, *Civilization and its Discontents* (1930)
56. Fougasse, *You Have Been Warned: A Complete Guide to the Road* (1935)
57. E. Hill, *The Great Australian Loneliness* (1937)
58. J. Agate, *Ego 2* (1936)
59. D. Marlowe, *Coming, Sir! The Autobiography of a Waiter* (1937)
60. V. Heiser, *A Doctor's Odyssey: Adventures in Forty-Five Countries* (1936)
61. M. Grossek, *First Movement* (1937)
62. C. Tomlinson, *Coal-miner* (1937)
63. C. Delius, *Frederick Delius* (1935)
64. V. O'Sullivan, *Aspects of Wilde* (1936)
65. F. Rutter, *Art in My Time* (1933)
66. H. Graham, *Selections* (1934)
67. T. Kromer, *Waiting for Nothing* (1935)
68. L. B. Powell, *Jacob Epstein* (1932)
69. Fougasse, *The Luck of the Draw* (1936)
70. C. Belfrage, *Away from it All: An Escapologist's Notebook* (1936)
71. Anonymous, *1871–1935*
72. M. Benney, *Low Company: Describing the Evolution of a Burglar* (1936)
73. M. von Boehn, *Modes and Manners, vol. 1* (1932)
74. J. Meier-Graefe, *Vincent: A Life of Vincent Van Gogh* (*c.* 1933)
75. D. Gascoyne, *A Short Survey of Surrealism* (1935)
76. G. Gorer, *Bali and Angkor* (1936)
77. H. L. Adam, *Murder Most Mysterious* (1932)
78. M. Muggeridge, *The Earnest Atheist* (1936)
79. W. Sachs, *Psychoanalysis* (1934)

PLAYS AND FILMS SEEN

While Gladys did almost all her reading at home, when she was out and about (and she often was – commonly several times a week), she was probably at the theatre, or the cinema, or a concert, or, occasionally, at an exhibition of some sort. The following lists detail the performances and events that she attended in 1937, along with their venues (when mentioned). In the case of the cinema, she sometimes did not identify the feature film she saw.

Theatre	Cinema
January	
Crooked Cross (Westminster)	*Disney* (Tatler)
	Secret Agent (Academy)

Disney (Tatler)
We Who are Dead (Plaza)
Unspecified (Tatler)
Immortal Swan (Tatler)
Unspecified (Tatler)
Harvest (Academy)

February
Behind Your Back (Strand)   Unspecified (Tatler)
Uncle Vanya (Westminster)   Bergner film (Pavilion)
Suspect (St. Martin's)

March
The Misanthrope (Ambassador's)   Camille (Empire)
Night Alone (Daly's)   Unspecified (Tatler)
George and Margaret (Wyndham's) Three Smart Girls (Gaumont)
Waste (Westminster)   Good Earth (Palace)
Because We Must (Pavilion)
Wise Tomorrow (Lyric)
Road to Rome (Savoy)

April
Climbing (Phoenix)   Elephant Boy (Leicester Square)
Anna Christie (Westminster)   After the Thin Man
                                 Pépé le Moko (Curzon)
                                 Winterset

May
Black Limelight (St. James's)   Unspecified (Tatler)
The Constant Wife (Globe)   Bury Theatre (Academy)
                                 Coronation film, and more
                                    (Tatler)
                                 Der Ammenkoenig & Loyalties
                                    (Studio One)
                                 The Worm Turns

June
To Have and to Hold (Haymarket) We Only Live Once (Pavilion)
Satyr   Mixed (Curzon)
The Great Romance (New)   Mixed (Tatler)
Victoria Regina (Lyric)   'Excellent programme' (Tatler)
                                 Overland Express (Tatler)

July
Women of Property (Queen's)   Unspecified (Tatler)

183

Ravenous Raven & Magician
  Micky (Tatler)
'Two most ridiculous films'
  (Empire)

August
Gertie Maude (St. Martin's)
Old Music (St. James's)
'I never saw so poor a play'
  (Comedy)

Michael Strogoff (Astoria)
Mixed (Tatler)
Easy Living (Tatler)
'Programme poor' (Tatler)

September
Unspecified amateur play
Bonnets over the Windmill (New)
Old Music
Old Winter
Richard II (Queen's)
Pygmalion (Old Vic)

Mixed (Tatler)
Eye of the World (New Gallery)
Victoria the Great (Leicester
  Square)
Le Roman d'un Tricheur
  (Academy)
Unspecified (Tatler)

October
The Last Straw (Comedy)
Youth's the Season (Westminster)
Autumn (St. Martin's)

'Poor programme' (Tatler)
Pearls of the Crown (Curzon)
Unspecified (Tatler)
Emile Zola (Carlton)

November
Yahoo (Westminster)
Yes and No (Ambassadors)
Mourning Becomes Electra
  (Westminster)
Robert's Wife (Globe)

'A terribly poor programme'
  (Tatler)
Double Wedding (Empire)
Paul Rotha film
Dead End (Gaumont)
Mixed (Tatler)

December

Mixed (Tatler)
The Last Gangster (Empire)
Mixed (Tatler)
The Clock Cleaners
Mixed (Studio One)
Garbo film (Empire)
The Underworld (Curzon)

EXHIBITIONS, CONCERTS, AND OTHER PERFORMANCES ATTENDED

January
National Portrait Gallery, new works
Figaro (Sadler's Wells)
Piano Concert, Stanislas Niedzielski (Palladium)
Royal College of Music Concert, Malcolm Sargent conducting
Concert at Covent Garden, Thomas Beecham conducting
Concert at Queen's Hall

February
Royal College of Music Concert
Barber of Seville (Sadler's Wells)
Concert at Covent Garden, Malcolm Sargent conducting
Mozart Concert at Covent Garden, Thomas Beecham conducting

March
Violin Concert, Heifetz (Queen's Hall)
Concert, Malcolm Sargent conducting
Magic Flute (Sadler's Wells)

April
National Gallery, French paintings
Concert (Queen's Hall)
Concert, Malcolm Sargent conducting

May
Concerto, Birmingham Philharmonic Orchestra, pianist Harriet Cohen
    playing (Conway Hall)
Ballet (Sadler's Wells)

June
Ballets Russes (Coliseum)

July
Hindu dancers (Gaiety) (twice)

October
Niedzielski Concert (Palladium)
Concert, Thomas Beecham conducting (Covent Garden)
Concert, Malcolm Sargent and Igor Stravinsky conducting (Queen's
    Hall)
Patrons' Fund Concert, pianist Norman Tucker playing (Wigmore
    Hall)

November
National Gallery, various works
Concert, Malcolm Sargent conducting
Ballet (Sadler's Wells)
Concert, pianist Benno Moiseiwitsch (Palladium)

December
Concert, Thomas Beecham conducting (Queen's Hall)
Concert, violinist Joseph Szigeti (Palladium)
Lecture by W. H. Auden on 'The teaching of English'

INDEX

Names of people and places have, as a rule, only been indexed when something substantive, either descriptive or evaluative, is said about them. Persons unknown publically, notably Gladys Langford's friends and family, have been infrequently indexed, and only when they are connected with topical matters of significance. The letters GL signify Gladys Langford.

LONDON RECORD SOCIETY

The London Record Society was founded in December 1964 to publish transcripts, abstracts and lists of the primary sources for this history of London, and generally to stimulate interest in archives relating to London. Membership is open to any individual or institution; the annual subscription is £18 (US $22) for individuals and £23 (US $35) for institutions. Prospective members should apply to the Hon. Membership Secretary, Dr Penny Tucker, Hewton Farmhouse, Bere Alston, Yelverton, Devon, PL20 7BW (email londonrecordsoc@btinternet.com).

The following volumes have already been published:

11. *Two Calvinistic Methodist Chapels, 1748–1811: the London Tabernacle and Spa Fields Chapel*, edited by Edwin Welch (1975)

12. *The London Eyre of 1276*, edited by Martin Weinbaum (1976)

13. *The Church in London, 1375–1392*, edited by A. K. McHardy (1977)

14. *Committees for the Repeal of the Test and Corporation Acts: Minutes, 1786–90 and 1827–8*, edited by Thomas W. Davis (1978)

15. *Joshua Johnson's Letterbook, 1771–4: Letters from a Merchant in London to his Partners in Maryland*, edited by Jacob M. Price (1979)

16. *London and Middlesex Chantry Certificate, 1548*, edited by C. J. Kitching (1980)

17. *London Politics, 1713–1717: Minutes of a Whig Club, 1714–17*, edited by H. Horwitz; *London Pollbooks, 1713*, edited by W. A. Speck and W. A. Gray (1981)

18. *Parish Fraternity Register: Fraternity of the Holy Trinity and SS. Fabian and Sebastian in the Parish of St. Botolph without Aldersgate*, edited by Patricia Basing (1982)

19. *Trinity House of Deptford: Transactions, 1609–35*, edited by G. G. Harris (1983).

20. *Chamber Accounts of the Sixteenth Century*, edited by Betty R. Masters (1984)

21. *The Letters of John Paige, London Merchant, 1648–58*, edited by George F. Steckley (1984)

22. *A Survey of Documentary Sources for Property Holding in London before the Great Fire*, by Derek Keene and Vanessa Harding (1985)

23. *The Commissions for Building Fifty New Churches*, edited by M. H. Port (1986)

24. *Richard Hutton's Complaints Book*, edited by Timothy V. Hitchcock (1987)

25. *Westminster Abbey Charters, 1066–c.1214*, edited by Emma Mason (1988)

26. *London Viewers and their Certificates, 1508–1558*, edited by Janet S. Loengard (1989)

27. *The Overseas Trade of London: Exchequer Customs Accounts, 1480–1*, edited by H. S. Cobb (1990)

28. *Justice in Eighteenth-Century Hackney: the Justicing Notebook of Henry Norris and the Hackney Petty Sessions Book*, edited by Ruth Paley (1991)

29. *Two Tudor Subsidy Assessment Rolls for the City of London: 1541 and 1582*, edited by R. G. Lang (1993)

30. *London Debating Societies, 1776–1799*, compiled and introduced by Donna T. Andrew (1994)

31. *London Bridge: Selected Accounts and Rentals, 1381–1538*, edited by Vanessa Harding and Laura Wright (1995)

32. *London Consistory Court Depositions, 1586–1611: List and Indexes*, by Loreen L. Giese (1997)
33. *Chelsea Settlement and Bastardy Examinations, 1733–66*, edited by Tim Hitchcock and John Black (1999)
34. *The Church Records of St Andrew Hubbard Eastcheap, c.1450–c.1570*, edited by Clive Burgess (1999)
35. *Calendar of Exchequer Equity Pleadings, 1685–6 and 1784–5*, edited by Henry Horwitz and Jessica Cooke (2000)
36. *The Letters of William Freeman, London Merchant, 1678–1685*, edited by David Hancock (2002)
37. *Unpublished London Diaries: a Checklist of Unpublished Diaries by Londoners and Visitors, with a Select Bibliography of Published Diaries*, compiled by Heather Creaton (2003)
38. *The English Fur Trade in the Later Middle Ages*, by Elspeth M. Veale (2003; reprinted from 1966 edition)
39. *The Bede Roll of the Fraternity of St Nicholas*, edited by N. W. and V. A. James (2 vols., 2004)
40. *The Estate and Household Accounts of William Worsley, Dean of St Paul's Cathedral, 1479–1497*, edited by Hannes Kleineke and Stephanie R. Hovland (2004)
41. *A Woman in Wartime London: the Diary of Kathleen Tipper, 1941–1945*, edited by Patricia and Robert Malcolmson (2006)
42. *Prisoners' Letters to the Bank of England 1783–1827*, edited by Deirdre Palk (2007)
43. *The Apprenticeship of a Mountaineer: Edward Whymper's London Diary, 1855–1859*, edited by Ian Smith (2008)
44. *The Pinners' and Wiresellers' Book, 1462–1511*, edited by Barbara Megson (2009)
45. *London Inhabitants Outside the Walls, 1695*, edited by Patrick Wallis (2010)
46. *The Views of the Hosts of Alien Merchants, 1440–1444*, edited by Helen Bradley (2012)
47. *The Great Wardrobe Accounts of Henry VII and Henry VIII*, edited by Maria Hayward (2012)
48. *Summary Justice in the City: A Selection of Cases Heard at the Guildhall Justice Room, 1752–1781*, edited by Greg T. Smith (2013)
49. *The Diaries of John Wilkes, 1770–1797*, edited by Robin Eagles (2014)

Previously published titles in the series are available from Boydell and Brewer; please contact them for further details, or see their website, www.boydellandbrewer.com